FLATTERING THE PASSIONS

FLATTERING THE PASSIONS

Or,
The Bomb and Britain's Bid for a World Role

HUGH BEACH

AND

NADINE GURR

I.B. Tauris *Publishers*
LONDON • NEW YORK

Published in 1999 by I.B.Tauris & Co Ltd
Victoria House, Bloomsbury Square, London WC1B 4DZ
175 Fifth Avenue, New York NY 10010
website: http://www.ibtauris.com

In the United States and in Canada distributed by St. Martin's Press
175 Fifth Avenue, New York NY 10010

ISBN 1 86064 168 7

A full CIP record for this book is available from the British Library
A full CIP record for this book is available from the Library of
Congress

Library of Congress catalog card: available

Printed and bound in Great Britain by WBC Ltd, Bridgend
from camera-ready copy supplied by the authors

CONTENTS

INTRODUCTION

This book offers a fresh appraisal of nuclear weapons policy in Britain. Ten years after the end of the Cold War is a good time to take stock. It is a period which has seen the early reactions of the British Conservative Government in the review known as 'Options for Change' and the recent, much more mature, reflections of the present New Labour government in their 'Strategic Defence Review'. It might have been thought that the latter would settle matters for the next five years or so, but in fact there is much unfinished business. For one thing, the continuing wrangles between the United Nations Security Council and Iraq about the latter's capability for Weapons of Mass Destruction have kept the issue of nuclear weapons proliferation in the public eye. The recent tests of nuclear weapons by India and Pakistan, while changing little of substance, have brought the issue into even greater prominence, raising the stakes in the dispute between the two countries and threatening to undermine the nuclear arms control regime which has been so painfully built up over the past 40 years. And whereas the future of the British Trident programme may have been settled for the immediate future, this leaves many other issues in the air. Obvious examples are the British government's professed attachment to reducing and eventually abolishing nuclear weapons worldwide, the future nuclear policy of NATO and prospects for the nuclear weapons scientific and engineering Establishment. Hence, there is no shortage of subject matter.

The issue of nuclear weapons has been the subject of an enormous literature. It might well be asked whether there is anything new to say. This book, however, adds to published material through the extensive use of interviews. As an interviewer, one is presented with an experience not otherwise encountered. Interviews combine a lively sense of period with political insight, and touch on the fragile nature of human interaction. They often serve to show that issues are not as simple or as clear cut as might at first appear. Of course, there are weaknesses in this method. It is possible for interviewees to overestimate their own importance and level of input. Some of the events discussed took place over 50 years ago. Memories are imperfect, not always objective, and can indeed be extremely subjective, creating false impressions and misrepresentation.

Important information can be forgotten, while current interests and objectives can also colour recollections. And raw transcripts can jar through the imperfections of the spoken word, most notably in grammar and syntax. In defence of our method, however, the information collected for this book was clear, and those interviewed were generally precise in their recollections. We have checked the interview material against the literature as thoroughly as we could. Furthermore, even through digression, important facts can be found, new evidence unearthed, fresh questions answered and views substantiated.

This book is not a polemic. We try to present the British nuclear weapons programme and the policies that have created it in an impartial way. We give due weight to the various doctrines that have been advanced in support of British policies and balance these by critiques offered from political, ethical and psychological standpoints. We examine the prospects for nuclear disarmament and finish by proposing some courses of action that might be followed in the early years of the 21st century.

Chapter One
In this chapter we trace the involvement of the UK with nuclear physics, the Atomic bomb programme and the British nuclear weapons programme from the early years

of the 20th century to the present day. We try to show why Britain decided to have nuclear weapons, how and why they were created and how nuclear weapons progressively became a part of the British security system. The story is told mainly from a political point of view.

Chapter Two
This chapter looks at the nuclear battlefield - even though the battle never took place. It traces the rise and fall of serious engagement with the idea that nuclear weapons could play a part in the actual conduct of war on land.

Chapter Three
This chapter deals with technology. It examines how different nuclear weapons work and the materials of which they are made. It also discusses the problems of excess fissile material and the state of talks over a fissile material cut-off. It examines the issue of weapons testing and the banning of nuclear tests. Nuclear weapon safety and radiation dangers are touched on. Finally the need for secrecy in the Whitehall establishment is held up for scrutiny. Readers with little appetite for technology can skip this chapter.

Chapter Four
Here, we look into questions of nuclear doctrine and how this is being affected by the new post-Cold War environment.

Chapter Five
Chapter Five traces the history of dissent: the voices of those politicians and scientists who have opposed the acquisition of nuclear weapons and British involvement with the US. It traces the notion of a test ban from its earliest roots in the nuclear mishaps of the 1950s, and the protests arising from the stationing of American Cruise missiles in England. It also covers the history of Pugwash, the Campaign for Nuclear Disarmament and other related movements.

Chapter Six
This chapter investigates the position of the Anglican and Roman Catholic churches on the issue of nuclear weapons. It examines the resolutions of the various

church assemblies and synods; the role of the Church in public debate and the arguments advanced at different levels. It discusses, too, whether the concept of deterrence is still ethically acceptable.

Chapter Seven

The insights of psychologists are brought to bear on the questions: Why did nuclear weapons give rise to illogical and incompatible attitudes and how can saner thinking be encouraged?

Chapter Eight

This chapter examines the prospects for nuclear disarmament, and the part this can play in British policy.

Chapter Nine

Chapter Nine re-examines the case for Britain to retain nuclear weapons, outlines a suitable way forward in the context of disarmament, and discusses some of the difficulties to be overcome.

The Authors

General Sir Hugh Beach passed through the Army Staff College at Camberley in 1953 where, as far as he can recall, students were taught not one single thing about the nuclear battlefield. In 1954/5, he did a policy job at the War Office in a branch called MO1, which was supposed to know a little about everything, so as to brief the Chief of the Imperial General Staff accordingly. General Beach was allowed, under very special handling rules, to see the famous 'Global Strategy' paper written by Slessor and Slim a year or so earlier, together with the Strath report which dealt, quite terrifyingly, with the effects of a thermonuclear explosion over the UK. In 1956-7, he went on to command a BAOR engineer field squadron, which had little truck with nuclear matters at the time. The squadron's job was to deploy in short order to the bridges over the Weser and Leine rivers in Lower Saxony, and the great bridge at Lauenburg over the Elbe at Hamburg, in order to blow them up before the Russians could arrive. This was a task for ordinary high explosives in rather large quantities. After completing the 1958 course at the Joint Services Staff College at Latimer (where the commandant gave a presentation on the tactical nuclear battle, using a huge model) and following interludes in Kenya and Cambridge, General Beach returned to BAOR, as Commander, Royal Engineers of the 2nd Division at Osnabrück, in 1966-7. There, he was compelled to grapple with the quite unreal complexities of letting off an Atomic Demolition Munition (atomic land mine). In 1968, back at Camberley as a Colonel, General Staff, he was sent on a course at the Royal School of Artillery at Larkhill, dealing largely with nuclear fire planning, and was awarded a bottle of Chablis for coming up with the best nuclear fire plan on one of the exercises. Finally, back in Osnabrück as Commander, 12 Infantry Brigade, General Beach found himself responsible for defending the exits from Hannover on the high ground to the south and west. This, however, he planned to achieve without the benefit of nuclear weapons.

Dr. Nadine Gurr graduated from the University of Southampton in 1995 with a doctorate in International Relations (PhD supervisor, Professor John Simpson OBE). She currently works as a freelance writer and independent defence consultant. Dr. Gurr has worked for Dr. Scilla Elworthy, director of the Oxford Research Group, and has written a paper for the International Security Information Service. Formerly, she worked for the Hansard Society for Parliamentary Government, and in the House of Commons for a member of the Defence Select Committee. She has also worked at the Verification Technology Information Centre, and as a researcher at the Council for Arms Control, Centre for Defence Studies, King's College, University of London. She has published extensively on the subject of Weapons of Mass Destruction terrorism. Dr. Gurr is a member of the International Institute for Strategic Studies.

1. THE BRITISH AND THEIR BOMB

Britain has played a unique role in the history of atomic physics, nuclear weapons and nuclear arms control. This chapter traces the history. The story behind the atom bomb's creation was one of the best-kept secrets of the Second World War (1939-1945). However, as contemporary public records have become available and those involved have been able to speak more freely, the story that has come to light is a testimony to remarkable scientific achievement. (1)

Although there was good evidence for the existence of atoms just over a century ago, they were still regarded as the indivisible building blocks of matter and virtually nothing was known about their internal structure. The first clues came at the close of 1895, when the German physicist Wilhelm Röntgen, experimenting with high-vacuum discharge tubes, accidentally discovered a new form of radiation. When 'cathode' rays, i.e. those emitted by the negatively charged plate of a tube, impacted on the glass wall of the tube, they formed a glowing spot. Röntgen found that this gave off what are now known as X-rays. A few months later, early in 1896, the French physicist Antoine-Henri Becquerel found that salts of the element uranium spontaneously emit another form of penetrating radiation. From this point onwards, British science was to play a leading part in what ultimately became a new discipline.

In 1897, the English physicist J.J.Thomson, working at

the Cavendish Laboratory at Cambridge University, showed that the cathode rays were in fact a stream of charged particles broken off from atoms. These soon became known as electrons. Thomson surmised that their mass was very small in relation to the atom and by 1906, he had deduced that the number of electrons in each atom was also small, in the case of hydrogen only one. In 1911, Ernest Rutherford, a former pupil of Thomson's then working at Manchester University, bombarded a thin film of metal with 'alpha' particles (now known to be helium nuclei) given off by uranium. He noticed that occasionally, a particle bounced back off the foil, and concluded that this could only mean that atoms have at their core a very small, dense, reflective centre - the nucleus. Frederick Soddy, a chemist and collaborator of Rutherford's, working at the University of Glasgow in 1913, showed that the element lead comes in different varieties which he christened isotopes. Rutherford followed this in 1919 by transmuting one element into another. He showed that the impact of an alpha particle with a nitrogen nucleus could cause the latter to break up, forming a hydrogen nucleus and an oxygen nucleus. In 1932, his collaborator James Chadwick discovered the neutron. In the same year John Cockcroft and Ernest Walton, also working under Rutherford at Cambridge, used an early form of particle accelerator to bombard lithium with protons, and artificially 'split' the nucleus into two nuclei of helium. In so doing, they showed that the equivalence of mass and energy as described in Einstein's equation ($E=mc^2$) held precisely in an experiment. It was then realised that the time might not be far away when usable quantities of energy might be obtained from the atomic nucleus. (2)

During this bright period in academia however, the political situation was becoming bleak, particularly in Germany. Adolf Hitler took power in 1933 and as the campaign to get rid of non-Aryans began, Jewish scientists were dismissed, retired or forced to resign. Most of them left the country for Copenhagen, Paris, Zürich or Cambridge and a few went to America. In December 1938, Otto Hahn and Fritz Strassman, working in Berlin, investigated the products of bombarding uranium with neutrons and detected the presence of elements of a much lower atomic number. (3) Puzzled by this finding,

Hahn sent word of it to Lise Meitner, an Austrian who had worked for years in Berlin as Hahn's close colleague. She was on Christmas holiday at the time with her nephew Otto Frisch, who was working in Copenhagen. They realised that what was happening was the break-up of the uranium nucleus into two large pieces, a hitherto unrecognised effect. Frisch christened the new reaction 'fission', an analogy with the splitting of bacteria. He was quick to share this discovery with the doyen of quantum physicists Niels Bohr. Bohr set off for America a few days later for a conference with Einstein and other scientists. When Bohr arrived in America, he received more news from Frisch and Meitner; their latest experiment had shown large amounts of energy being released in the fission process. Bohr gave this news to the conference in January 1939. In April 1939, the work of a French group was the first to show that fission released not only energy but also spare neutrons, which could split other atoms, thus releasing more energy and more neutrons. Hence a chain reaction was evidently possible. (4)

Leo Szilard, an exile from Hungary, now working in America, seized upon the possibility of constructing a bomb based on the fission process and urged Hahn and Strassman not to publish their findings. His warning was ignored, and they announced their results in a letter to *Nature*. This became an immediate focus of international academic discourse and led scientists in Britain, America and Germany to alert their governments to the dangers inherent in the discovery. Fortunately, the *Nature* letter did not have the grave consequences Szilard had feared. While Germany still had many brilliant physicists, including Carl von Weizacker and Werner Heisenberg, the German attempt at a uranium fission programme fizzled out. Although by 1942, the scientists, on the basis of their experiments, had little doubt that an atomic bomb could be made to work, they also foresaw that the industrial effort involved might well mean technical bankruptcy for Germany. Hitler had ordered that only those technical projects which could come to fruition within six months should be financed. Albert Speer, Minister of War Production, decided not to invest in the huge programme that would have been needed, and so whatever chance the Germans had of making an atomic bomb slipped by. (5) Some experts have since suggested that

German scientists secretly in opposition to the Nazi regime may have dragged their feet on purpose. (6) Others believe that the scientists did the best they could to create an A-bomb and simply failed. It is certain, however, that Hitler's belief in an early end to the war even in 1942, and the failure of the scientists to recommend to the Supreme Command the huge industrial effort required, ensured that the German bomb project never got off the ground. (7) Nor, to this day, has it ever been revived.

The Frisch-Peierls Memorandum

On 1 September 1939, two days before the outbreak of war, Niels Bohr and John Wheeler (an American student of Bohr's) published a paper on nuclear fission in which they concluded that natural uranium was much less likely to produce a chain reaction than one of its constituent isotopes, uranium 235 (U-235). However this isotope was known to constitute only some 0.72% of natural uranium. A few months later Otto Frisch, by then working in Birmingham University together with a fellow émigré Rudolph Peierls, concluded that a pound or so of pure U-235 might suffice to create an explosion with the power of 1000 tons of dynamite. (8) In describing the background to this discovery, Peierls said in an interview: 'Nobody had thought really hard about how much separated uranium would be required to make an explosion, what was a critical size. Then one day it occurred to us to ask what would happen if you had a large quantity of separated isotope. To our surprise, if you worked this out on the back of an envelope, the amount came out quite small. Then we asked ourselves: if you could make such an explosion, what would happen? Again on the back of another envelope, it came out that while you could not predict the exact power, the effects would be enormous. We were elated but frightened.'(9) Frisch and Peierls wrote a short memorandum on the 'Properties of a Radioactive Superbomb' which showed astonishing foresight on such questions as how such a bomb would work, how it could be constructed, and what its effects would be. They specified the effects of heat - 'a temperature comparable to the interior of the sun' - of blast, which would destroy life over a range which would 'probably cover the area of a big city' - and of radioactive products capable of killing people not only in the immediate area, but also carried as fall-out 'several miles downwind'. They suggested that, because of fall-out 'the bomb could probably not be used without killing large numbers of civilians, and this may make it unsuitable as a weapon for use by this country'. (10)

The Maud Committee

The Frisch-Peierls memorandum was sent through Sir Henry Tizard to the Nobel prize winner Professor George Thomson (11) at Cambridge who took it to the Committee on the Scientific Survey of Air Defence and Air Warfare at the Ministry of Aircraft Production. This committee was wound up in June 1940 and the work was continued by an independent sub-committee which adopted the name Maud. (12) It was chaired by George Thomson and was supervised by British scientists, including three more Nobel prize winners, Chadwick, Cockcroft and Patrick Blackett. Nevertheless, much of the work depended upon foreigners, virtually none of whom had any security clearance. They were allowed to work on atomic fission because at that time it was not officially recognised as important to the war effort. Klaus Fuchs, another brilliant *émigré* German physicist, was recruited by Peierls to discuss theoretical technicalities and was later to play a part at Los Alamos in the design of the first atomic bomb.

The main objective of the Maud Committee was to find a way of separating U-235 from U-238. After examining various methods, it occurred to Peierls and Frisch that a process of separating them in gaseous form by diffusing them through ultra-fine membranes might be successful. The Committee also discussed the possibility of uranium 'boilers' for industrial use. They observed that such boilers would produce, as a necessary consequence of consuming natural uranium fuel, a transuranic element unknown in nature that they called element 94. (The name plutonium was apparently coined independently and simultaneously in Britain and America). This material, they deduced, would be fissile, like U-235. Accordingly, it might be used as an alternative nuclear explosive. This was the first time such use had been suggested. But Maud did not envisage this as feasible during the course of the War and recommended it only as a longer-term possibility.

The Maud Committee produced its report on the 29 July

1941 and this was sent to the Director of Scientific Research at the Ministry of Aircraft Production. The report confirmed the feasibility of an atomic bomb using U-235. It recommended giving the necessary work the highest priority in order to create a weapon which, if it worked, could well affect the outcome of the War. The report said: 'We have now reached the conclusion that it will be possible to make an effective uranium bomb which, containing some 25lb. of active material, would be equivalent as regards destructive effect to 1800 tonnes of TNT and would also release large quantities of radioactive substances, which would make places near to where the bomb exploded dangerous to human life for a long period... As regards the time required, Imperial Chemical Industries after consultation with Metropolitan-Vickers estimate that the material for the first bomb could be ready by the end of 1943.' (13) The delivery of this highly competent and far-sighted report was a turning point. No comparable work had been done by the Americans at this stage, though they had been kept informed as it went on. By August 1941, the report was in the hands of Churchill, and a handful of Cabinet ministers and officials were admitted to the secret. On the basis of the Maud Report, Churchill consulted the Chiefs of Staff. They recommended immediate action on the new bomb as a matter of the highest priority. In September 1941 Churchill gave his go-ahead.

For technical background, it may be useful at this stage to consult the section entitled 'Fission weapons' in Chapter Three of this book. It will be noted that for use in a weapon, the concentration of U-235 has to be raised from its natural level (0.72%) to some 90%. Since the isotopes of uranium are chemically identical, the U-235 has to be separated from the natural uranium metal by a physical process. The chosen method was a molecular one, diffusing a gaseous compound of uranium and fluorine through the pores of a series of synthetic membranes. At each such pass, a small degree of separation of the isotopes is achieved and it takes some thousands of such passes to reach the necessary concentration of U-235. The technology was unfamiliar, and the necessary plant entailed a big capital investment, a large consumption of electricity and a high standard of construction and operation. Another method is to make use of the very small difference in density of the isotopes by passing the uranium, again in gaseous form, through thousands of high-speed centrifuges. This was considered during the War, but rejected as technically beyond the state of the art at that time. Experiments were also conducted with a third method, using electro-magnetic separation, but this was not carried through to success. An obvious alternative to the U-235 bomb, also referred to by the Maud Committee, was to use the plutonium isotope Pu-239 produced as a by-product of the fission of natural uranium in a reactor. A reactor producing one megawatt of heat energy will produce plutonium at the rate of about one gramme every day. Another isotope of plutonium (Pu-240) is formed from Pu-239 in the reactor. Since this isotope is undesirable in the manufacture of weapons, fuel cannot be left beyond a certain time in reactors if it is to be best suited to military use. As a result the extraction rate of military plutonium is only some 5% of what could be obtained from a reactor operated purely for purposes of electrical power generation.

The United States
To begin with, it was only in Britain that the possibility of an atomic weapon was taken seriously. In September 1941, America was not yet at war and there was no comparable government interest in atomic research. (14) On 2 August 1939, prompted by Szilard, Einstein had written to Franklin Delano Roosevelt, the US President, alerting him to the possibility that an atomic bomb could be constructed. As a result, the United States set up the Uranium Committee made up of representatives of the Navy, the Army and the Carnegie Institute. Shortly after this, Vannevar Bush, Director of the Carnegie Institute, persuaded President Roosevelt to set up the National Defence Research Council (NDRC). In the NDRC, Bush together with James B. Conant, the president of Harvard University, spent time demonstrating that an A-bomb was impossible. In fact, the NDRC programme would have ended had it not been for the work carried out in Britain. Nevertheless, a few American scientists did begin to see that a bomb might be feasible. Glen Seaborg, working at Berkeley and using a large particle accelerator (the cyclotron) developed by Ernest Lawrence, showed that under neutron bombardment, U-238 could indeed be

transmuted into a new intensely radioactive element that he named plutonium. He confirmed that the new element was very similar to U-235 in its fissile properties, and could be used for the same explosive purposes. The discovery of this material, which could be cheaper to produce than U-235, encouraged other American scientists to take the possibility of an atomic bomb seriously. In mid-August 1941 copies of the Maud Report were sent to the Americans. On October 9, Bush met with Roosevelt and explained the conclusions of the Report. Roosevelt decided to go ahead with the new weapon, but kept the decision secret, allowing only his Vice-President Henry Wallace, Conant, Bush, Secretary of War Henry L. Stimpson and Chief of Staff of the Army George C. Marshall to know of it. (15)

Roosevelt wanted to progress rapidly with the A-bomb project. He looked to Britain for help because he realised that Britain had expertise in the field of uranium fission that could not be matched in America. Hence, on 11 October 1941, President Roosevelt wrote to Prime Minister Churchill proposing an exchange of views. It seems that the British, believing themselves to be ahead in this field, were reluctant to share information and agreed to help the Americans only within narrow limits. (16).This was a serious error, and the British have had to live with the consequences ever since. British scientists were soon facing intractable difficulties in deciding how to produce enriched uranium and where to locate a production plant. There was every reason for moving the project across the Atlantic. The United States had the resources, Canada would be taking an important part and in Britain, there were the dangers of bombing and possible invasion. There was also the simple desire to avoid duplication. Lord Sherfield (formerly Sir Roger Makins), who was involved in Anglo-American atomic diplomacy for most of the 1940s, has said of Britain's reluctance to work in conjunction with the US: 'I think it was partly perhaps psychological, we thought that we had all the information, and we could get along pretty well on our own. We were willing to exchange information with the Americans, but not really go into a joint project. The result of that was that the Americans were not very impressed with the British attitude, and they decided to go ahead on their own. By the time collaboration was established in 1944, the Americans had gone miles ahead'. (17)

In the summer of 1942, by which time the US had entered the War, control of the American programme was transferred from the scientists to a Military Policy Committee with Vannevar Bush as chairman.(18) Now the American programme to create an A-bomb, code-named the Manhattan Project, began in earnest. It was run by the US army and led by General Leslie Groves. On 2 December 1942, a self-sustaining chain reaction was shown to work by a team at Chicago led by Enrico Fermi. He was an Italian *émigré* with a Jewish wife, one of the pioneers in this field, and had become professor of Physics at Columbia University. Fermi's apparatus con-sisted of a 'pile' of 6 tons of uranium metal, 58 tons of uranium oxide and 400 tons of graphite blocks neatly laid out on a racquets court. (19) This was the final piece of the jigsaw the Manhattan Project scientists had been waiting for. It convinced the Americans that they no longer needed help from the British, as they now had all the main threads in their own hands. The scale of the resulting project was phenomenal. Soon, three com-pletely secret nuclear centres were being built, referred to by the code names W, X and Y. Site W was at Hanford, Washington State, where plutonium would be produced. Site X was at Oak Ridge in the Tennessee Valley, where U-235 would be separated from natural uranium. Site Y was at Los Alamos, New Mexico, where the bombs would be developed and where, within months, many of the most gifted and eminent figures in science began to arrive. (20) By the end of the War in 1945, the project was to consist of 37 installations employing nearly 38,000 employees and costing some $2.2 billion at wartime prices.

The Soviet Union

Owing to the immense secrecy surrounding the whole subject of nuclear fission, American and British scientif-ic communities had been forced into silence. This alerted the Russians to the fact that something was afoot. For example G.N. Flerov, a Soviet physicist who studied nuclear fission, guessed that work on this subject had become clandestine because scientists were trying to build an atom bomb. He sent a memorandum to Stalin accordingly. When in 1940 a group of Soviet physicists led by Igor Kurchatov published a paper in the *Physical Review* on their discovery of spontaneous fission, it was largely ignored by the West and Flerov's suspicions were confirmed. Kurchatov and others alerted their government to the possibility that nuclear fission could be used to make a bomb, adding that work was progressing in Germany under Heisenberg. In 1943 Kurchatov was selected to lead the Russian team in the creation of the A-bomb. (21)

Anglo-American Co-operation
An immediate effect of the Manhattan Project had been to lessen contact between those working on the A-bomb in the United States and Britain. Churchill accordingly pressed for a formal Anglo-American partnership, a proposal that Roosevelt agreed to endorse. In August 1943, the Quebec Agreement was signed, providing full effective collaboration between Britain and America and establishing a Combined Policy Committee. The Quebec Articles of Agreement included the promise never to use the bomb against each other or against a third party without the other's consent. It provided that information would not be passed on to other parties without mutual agreement. Britain undertook not to get involved in a post-War civil nuclear power programme except as might be agreed with the United States. After the Quebec Agreement, when collaboration was resumed with the United States, a small team of British scientists travelled to North America. These were led by Chadwick and included Rudolf Peierls, Otto Frisch, William Penney, and Klaus Fuchs. (22) Twenty of them were to work in the major American weapons laboratory at Los Alamos, New Mexico and thirty-five at Oak Ridge, Tennessee. None had any access to Hanford, although some worked on the electromagnetic isotope separation project at Berkeley, California. (23).

In September 1944, Roosevelt and Churchill again discussed the atomic bomb project at a meeting at Hyde Park, Roosevelt's country home in New York state. The outcome of these discussions was the so-called Hyde Park Aide-Memoire, which provided that full atomic collaboration should be continued after the defeat of Japan. (24) British scientists became involved in all the work at

Los Alamos, so far as their numbers permitted, and there was no artificial segregation within the laboratories. Rudolf Peierls became a group leader in the Theoretical Division. It is now acknowledged on both sides that the work carried out by the British team of scientists significantly shortened the time it took to make the first weapons. The first American A-bomb test, code named Trinity, took place on the 16 July 1945, at roughly 5.30 am Mountain Time, in the desert area known as The Journey of Death, part of the Army Air Force's test range at Alamogordo in New Mexico. It worked perfectly, giving an explosive yield of 18.6 kilotons.

Truman's Decision
When President Harry S. Truman came to office after the sudden death of Roosevelt in April 1945, the War was reaching a climax. (25) The raids on the German town of Dresden in February 1945 probably killed over 100,000 people. In an attack on Tokyo in March 1945, American B-29 bombers set off a firestorm in which nearly sixteen square miles of the city were destroyed, 80,000 people died and 40,000 more were injured. Against this backdrop, the idea of using the A-bomb to end the destruction did not seem disproportionate, although many of the scientists involved in the Manhattan Project had serious misgivings. In May 1945, the same month in which Germany's unconditional surrender left Japan as the last Axis power still combatant, an Interim Committee was set up to make recommendations to the President. (26) The committee discussed how the bomb should be used. They discussed the notion of a harmless demonstration in an uninhabited area, but finally considered this to be impracticable. The committee unanimously decided to recommend the earliest possible use of the bomb on Japan, against a military installation in a built-up area and without prior warning. (27) Throughout these discussions, there was no dissent from British observers and Churchill backed the American Interim Committee. Churchill is quoted in his biography as saying: 'The decision whether or not to use the bomb to compel the surrender of Japan was never even an issue. There was unanimous, automatic, unquestioned, agreement around the table, nor did I ever hear the slightest suggestion that we should do otherwise'. (28) Lord Mountbatten, the

Supreme Allied Commander, who was responsible for planning a possible invasion of Japan said: 'If the bomb kills the Japanese and saves casualties on our side, I am naturally not going to favour the killing of our people unnecessarily. I am responsible for trying to kill as many Japanese as I can with minimum loss on our side. War is crazy. It is a crazy thing that we are fighting at all. But it would be even more crazy if we were to incur more casualties on our side to save Japanese.' (29)

On 6 August 1945, at 15 minutes past eight o'clock in the morning, Japanese time, *Little Boy*, an enriched uranium bomb, was detonated over Hiroshima. It produced an explosive yield of 15 kilotons and killed 140,000 people. On the 9 August *Fat Man*, a plutonium bomb, was dropped on Nagasaki. It yielded 22 kilotons and killed 62,000 people. (30) In an interview Group-Captain Leonard Cheshire recalled: 'I worked on the Manhattan Project and was an observer of the A-bomb attacks on Hiroshima and Nagasaki. I was to be Churchill's personal observer, and my brief was to report back on the implications of the bomb for the future of aerial warfare. There had been a long and bloody war and if it had continued, would have had more war casualties in one week than would have resulted from the bomb dropped on Hiroshima. After Nagasaki, the Emperor said the Japanese should lay their arms down to the world. On 14 August, they accepted this.' (31)

Tony Benn, however, holds a different theory as to why the bomb was dropped. 'We were told at the time that it was dropped to save a quarter of a million US lives. Actually, the Japanese surrendered five days later and the only condition that they made was that the Emperor Hirohito remained on the throne (but the US wanted this anyway, because that was better than a communist power). The bomb was dropped to frighten the Russians, there's no question about this. It was the first blow in the Cold War. When people talk subsequently of the Soviet threat, we have to remember that from 1945 until the Soviets tested their first bomb the monopoly of nuclear weapons was in the West. Very few people questioned the monopoly of nuclear weapons and it was only when the Russians got a bomb that people became anxious. This confirmed my suspicion that the real fear was not that we might have it, but that they might have it and use it against us.' (32)

The Labour Government

In July 1945, a new, Labour, British Prime Minister, Clement Attlee, had taken office. Although he had been Deputy Prime Minister to Churchill during the War, Attlee knew very little about the A-bomb. Throughout the war years, neither he nor his colleagues had been allowed access to Churchill's inner circle of decision-makers. When they came into office, they maintained the same tradition of secrecy and all decisions on the A-bomb were made by a small group of ministers. The Cabinet as a whole was excluded from decisions and Parliamentary Questions during this period about the possibility of an atomic project were always brushed aside. Nor was this seen as a party political issue. Sir John Anderson, who had been the minister responsible for the atomic pro-gramme in the wartime coalition but who now sat on the front bench as a member of the Conservative Opposition, retained his position in the Cabinet Office and continued to advise thc Labour government on nuclear matters.

A crucial strand in British foreign policy in the 1945-1950 period was the need to enmesh the US in European security, avoiding what had happened at the start of both world wars, when the Americans stood back from the hostilities. But any nuclear pretensions on Britain's behalf were unwelcome in the US. The Truman adminis-tration was dismissive of the wartime agreements for co-operation, putting them down to the close personal friendship between Roosevelt and Churchill. The British had to put up with bureaucratic problems and suspicion. Lord Sherfield has said, 'The trouble with the Hyde Park Agreement was that the American copy of the agreement was lost. I had the rather invidious task of taking a copy down to the State Department because they could not find it. What had happened was that the President's sec-retary, or whoever was with him at Hyde Park, had passed it down the line to some official. The code name was 'Tube Alloys', and this official thought 'Tube Alloys' was to do with Naval Engineering, and they sent it over to the Navy Department.'(33) Meanwhile Senator McMahon, Chairman of the Senate Committee on Atomic Energy, was busy pushing legislation through Congress that would prohibit co-operation with any country on nuclear matters. Lord Sherfield adds 'We made the most of it, but in fact Hyde Park was a very weak document, it had no legislative backing and was not capable of being ratified or even produced to Congress. However, we did in fact make a draft and submit it to the combined policy committee in April. The Americans just dismissed it out of hand, the McMahon legislation was in process, and they said that they could not sign.' (34) It was not until 1948 that Lord Sherfield was able to negotiate a *modus viven - di* with the US administration under which America gave up its right to veto Britain's civil nuclear power programme and the British were allowed access to American intelligence on progress made by the Russians. Lord Sherfield has said of this agreement: 'My own view is that a great power cannot allow another country to prevent it doing whatever it needs for national security, and that therefore that provision [of the Quebec agreement providing for a mutual veto on use against third parties] was not in fact enforceable. The other provision, about the President controlling our civil programme, was totally unacceptable to our side. Therefore, by cancelling those two provisions nothing was lost...' (35)

But despite Britain's efforts, the US refused to restore the previous collaboration. In August 1946, the US adopted the Atomic Energy Act, which prohibited the communication of atomic information to any other country. The British took this badly. They saw themselves as a great industrial nation whose most eminent scientists had been involved in the Manhattan Project. Nor were they prepared to give up the idea of a nuclear project, simply because the Atomic Energy Act froze them out. They had no certainty that the United States would not return to isolationism. There was the prospect of a resurgent Germany in perhaps 15 or 20 years' time and there was the looming problem of the Soviet Union. Hence, Britain set out on a course of action the full implications of which she had yet to discern.

The closing down of collaboration with the US had in fact been a stimulus to British independent atomic research. Responsibility for this research was transferred to the Ministry of Supply in December 1945, when the Directorate of Atomic Energy, as it was then called, passed to that department. The Tube Alloys Consultative Committee was led by Lord Cherwell, Sir Edward Appleton and Sir Wallace Akers, a member of the board of ICI. The Tube Alloys Technical Committee included Rudolf Peierls. The main problems the British were to encounter in lacking American aid were not technical, because Britain did indeed have excellent scientists. The major problems concerned the large industrial infrastructure needed to produce fissile material for the warheads. A British bomb would have been a far easier proposition if collaboration had continued, particularly on the industrial side. Even so, by 1946, it had become clear that Britain would have to go it alone.

In December 1945, Attlee set up a small secret cabinet committee known as *Gen 75* to consider a British nuclear programme. The committee authorised the construction of a small atomic pile at Windscale in Cumbria to produce plutonium. In October 1946, ministers were asked for money to build a gaseous diffusion plant, in addition to the plutonium pile, to improve the supply of fissile material. Opposition arose from two cabinet ministers, Hugh Dalton and Stafford Cripps. Sir Michael Perrin, assistant to Lord Portal (wartime Chief of the Air Staff) who was now leading the bomb project, recalled in a BBC 2 *Timewatch* interview: 'When the meeting started, the Foreign Secretary Bevin had not yet turned up. Two other ministers, Dalton, Chancellor of the Exchequer and Stafford Cripps were very much against the proposal. They said we did not have the money to do it, nor did we possess the materials. We want building materials for the present crisis in the country...The Minister of Supply said to me, 'Look, I think we had better withdraw this paper'. At that stage Mr Bevin came in and apologised for being late. The Prime Minister summarised, very much along the lines of what Dalton and Cripps had been saying, that the country could not afford the money or the materials. Mr Bevin said 'No, Prime Minister that will not do at all, we have got to have this'. One of the reasons that he gave was a very striking one, quite bluntly, 'I don't mind for myself, but I don't want any other Foreign Secretary of this country to be talked to by the Secretary of State in the United States as I have just been in my discussions with Mr Byrnes. We have got to have this thing over here, whatever it costs, with a bloody Union Jack flying on top of it. This turned the meeting right round.' (36)

The final decision to make the A-bomb was taken in an *ad hoc* committee set up especially for the purpose called *Gen 163*. Attlee removed Dalton and Cripps and the full cabinet was not involved in the decision. *Gen 163* included Lord Portal and Dr William Penney, who had accompanied the flight over Nagasaki and was now Chief Superintendent of Armaments Research in the Ministry of Supply. These two played a crucial part in bringing the government to the point of decision. At a meeting on 8 January 1947, they asked for the go-ahead and got it. (37) Work started at once in the Armaments Research Establishment at Fort Halstead in Kent. It was led by Penney, the only British scientist from Los Alamos who went into the British atomic bomb project. Once the decision was taken to go ahead, the work was marked as of the highest urgency.

On 12 May 1949, the decision that Britain was to make its own atomic bomb was announced to the House of Commons by the Minister of Defence, A.V.Alexander. The Cabinet as a whole played no part in the process nor was the cost of the programme announced. The government spent £100 million unknown to the House of Commons by submerging this figure in other estimates. (38) Yet despite the implications, not one voice was raised in praise or blame of the decision, the reason being that no one was in the least surprised. Sir Frank Cooper (serving in the Air Ministry at that time) said of Britain's A-bomb decision: 'I don't think it ever occurred to anybody that we should not have it. We were a great power, we were a great scientific nation, we were a great industrial nation, quite natural that we should have a nuclear weapon. It did not seem terribly expensive at the time. It wasn't some great analytical, heavily thought out decision which you read about in text books. As with most things it was taken out of one's guts rather than out of one's head.' (39) Mr Tony Benn, however, argues that Britain's decision to have an atomic weapon was undemocratic. 'The mere possession of nuclear weapons destroys democracy, because, if we are not told by the government of the day that we are building them, this is because they are considered so dangerous and so important that they don't even seek the consent of the British Parliament for having them'. (40)

Roots of British Policy

The British historian Margaret Gowing says of the 1947 decision to manufacture an A-bomb that it was not a response to military threat but a fundamental and instinctive feeling that Britain should possess this climactic weapon. (41) She points out that the War had a thoroughly detrimental effect upon Britain's power and influence in the world, especially *vis-à-vis* the US and the Soviet Union. Britain did not want to face up to this reality, and disguised it by stressing that Britain was the only victorious European power, a permanent member of the Security Council, and one of the Big Three in the councils of war and at ministerial conferences. The reality was that Britain's nuclear role had diminished to that of uranium supplier. She needed American collaboration to support her political and strategic aims. The A-bomb was symbolic of American power and Britain believed that to possess such a weapon would put her on a similar level, halting her decline into a second-class nation, and re-forge a special relationship with the Americans.

According to Margaret Gowing, the theory of nuclear deterrence originated in Britain around 1945. The idea grew from the work of a committee of scientists who believed that bombarding cities was decisive in modern war. They argued that the UK would be vulnerable to aerial warfare because of its concentration of military and industrial targets and that an enemy who possessed atomic weapons could destroy the country quickly. The population had to be protected in some way and the only solution was for Britain to be prepared to use the same kind of weapons in retaliation. (42) The Chiefs of Staff put forward a parallel argument: that it was unacceptable for a first-class nation not to have atomic weapons since atomic weapons were the only effective backing for foreign policy. The Chiefs were unwilling to surrender control in so vital a matter to the United Nations, nor would they accept permanent reliance on supplies of weapons from the United States - an offer the Americans made from time to time if Britain, in exchange, would give up its own atomic programme. At this stage, atomic weapons were regarded simply as an extension of strategic bombing, which Britain saw as one of its strengths, but no doctrine for their use was put forward. The Chiefs believed that for the purpose of facing down an external threat, the first priority was just possessing the bomb rather than the means of delivering it. As early as July 1946, the Cabinet Defence Committee had given high priority to the development of long-range bombers and the Air Staff put out a requirement on 1 January 1947 for aircraft two or three times more effective than contemporary bombers in altitude, speed and range. Three such aircraft were eventually developed - *Valiant, Victor* and *Vulcan* - known collectively as the V-Bombers. But it was not until September 1949 that the V-Bombers were given equal priority with the weapons programme. This resulted in such delays that these bombers, which were far superior in concept to anything possessed by the Superpowers at that time, did not start to become operational until 1955, nor reach their full strength of 180 aircraft until 1961. (43)

There was dissent on the part of some scientists who cast doubts on Britain's decision to go nuclear. The British scientist P.M.S. Blackett presented a notable memorandum to the Chiefs of Staff in which he argued that if Britain were to become a nuclear power, this would decrease rather than increase her long-term security. He believed that since atomic weapons were designed to attack cities rather than armies, this would greatly provoke the Soviet Union, who in turn would become more aggressive towards Europe. The Chief Scientific Adviser to the Ministry of Defence Henry Tizard also came to the conclusion that Britain should not be making its own bomb but should rely on the Americans for atomic protection. His argument was that Britain was no longer a great power, and was only harming herself economically in pursuit of an atomic weapon: 'We are a great nation, but if we continue to behave like a great power, we shall soon cease to be a great nation.' He believed that high priority should be given to conventional weapons. These arguments were disregarded by the government in 1949, as they have been by successive governments ever since, but they have never gone away. (44)

Fear of the Soviet Union
Initially, Britain's primary concern after the War had been a resurgent Germany, but within a year or so, attention had shifted to the Soviet Union, the grip that the Russians had taken on Eastern Europe and the threat of

communist subversion elsewhere. This soon became a very serious worry to the West. The communist coup in Czechoslovakia in 1948 turned that country into a satellite of the Soviet Union. In March 1948, the Soviet Union began to restrict the movement of supplies overland to Berlin and three months later imposed a complete blockade. For a year the city had to be supplied entirely by airlift - a massive and costly operation led by the Americans. In the face of this Soviet threat, various steps were taken to restore confidence in Europe and to resist Soviet intimidation. Of these the most notable was the creation of the North Atlantic Treaty Organisation (NATO) in 1949.

It has recently been suggested by Michael Herman that at the heart of Cold War thinking, there was a tendency for threat assessments to focus on the worst case rather than most likely Soviet behaviour. Basing his work on intelligence assessments of Soviet capabilities Herman argues that over-estimation led to wrong judgments. The experience of the war years affected foreign policy formulation and mental attitudes. The wartime mind-set was carried over into post-War thinking. (45) But by this time, the Americans had their own interests to pursue and had developed global ambitions. They had reversed their pre-War attitude of isolation and replaced it with the idea that America needed to project her forces world-wide. Containment of Soviet communism became the main objective. This required regional military alliances and bases all round the world within striking distance of the Soviet Union. Britain thus became crucial in implementing both short- and long-term war plans for the American Strategic Air Command (SAC). Although during this period SAC possessed few atomic bombs it had detailed plans for strikes against Soviet targets should hostilities break out in Europe.

In 1946 and 1947, conversations were held between Air Chief Marshal Tedder for Britain and General Spaatz of the United States Strategic Air Command (SAC) about the preparation of bases in Britain to take B-29 nuclear bombers. In March 1949, the National Security Council of the US proposed the development of four airfields in the Oxford area and put pressure on the British government to agree. A small committee of the Cabinet approved this request and the bombers duly arrived. Historians argue that during this period the British took the American presence to be a temporary measure prompted by the Berlin crisis. The Americans, however, saw it as a permanent arrangement. On 19 September 1949, President Truman announced the detection of the first Soviet nuclear weapon test. This caused enormous concern to the Americans and led directly to their decision, made public in January 1950, to develop a hydrogen bomb. But the Soviet Union's attempts to develop long-range bombers were not successful and the prospect of intercontinental missiles lay a decade away. The Americans were determined to capitalise on the advantage this gave them and to maintain unchallenged nuclear superiority. There was no doubt that the Americans could 'win' a nuclear war at this stage and they proceeded to put forces in place to realise this capability. By the end of 1949, the SAC had worked out that at least seventeen air bases and facilities in Britain were the minimum needed to carry out American emergency war plans. In March 1950, Air Chief Marshal Slessor advised the Cabinet to arrange negotiations to meet these requirements. The result was an 'Ambassadors' Agreement' in April 1950. The British government welcomed the agreement, but not without misgivings. Bevin obtained an informal understanding that Britain had the right to terminate the arrangement, so helping to allay British fears. (46) In July 1950, President Truman approved the stockpiling of non-nuclear components of nuclear weapons at forward bases in the UK.

A major problem bedevilling Anglo-American relations at this time was that of the atomic spies. As early as March 1946, a reader in physics at King's College London called Alan Nunn May was arrested on charges of spying for the Russians. He had been a member of the 'Tube Alloys' project since 1942 and from 1943 to 1945 had worked on the Anglo-Canadian atomic project as group leader in the Montreal laboratory. He was convicted, and went to prison for six and a half years. Far more serious, however was the case of Klaus Fuchs. He was a German who had fled to England in the early 1930s as a result of pro-communist sympathies, and he was, indeed, a member of the Communist Party. He trained as a research physicist at Bristol and Edinburgh, and in 1941 joined Peierls at Birmingham. Norman Moss takes up the story: 'Fuchs was in the atom bomb project almost from the beginning. He worked with Peierls in Britain and then on uranium diffusion in New York and then went with him to Los Alamos New Mexico where the bomb was to be assembled. He acted as the liaison between the group who were testing explosive effects using high explosives, and the group who were working on fission reactions. When he came back to England, he was taken on as group leader at Harwell and again was brought into British the atom bomb project right at the beginning and knew about it before some ministers.' In February 1950, Fuchs was arrested on charges of passing information to Russian agents and admitted that he had been doing so since 1942. (47) The US authorities believed that the information provided by Fuchs might have advanced the Soviet nuclear project by as much as a year. The first bomb exploded by the Soviet Union, 'Joe-1', was a direct copy of *Fat Man;* Fuchs served nine years of a 14-year sentence and departed to East Germany. Matters were not helped when in October 1950, Bruno Pontecorvo defected to the Soviet Union. He was an Italian Jew who had worked with Fermi in Rome. He left Italy in 1936 and worked on the British Atomic Energy project in Canada during the War. After the War, he had worked at Harwell and then accepted a chair at Liverpool University. Whether he was in fact a spy remains an open question. But the cumulative effect of these episodes did the British no good in American eyes. General Leslie Groves left no doubt that he believed rank incompetence to be at the root of all these woes.

The success of the first Soviet nuclear test had brought with it the certainty that Britain would eventually be in the front line of any attack by the Soviets. But the Americans refused to discuss use of the bomb in their meetings with the British Chiefs of Staff. Hence, when, in 1950, the Chiefs of Staff reviewed Western strategy, they argued that Britain should maintain a small stock of atomic bombs independently of the Americans. They also said that a high priority should be given to developing defensive weapons against atomic attack, i.e. guided missiles. The review took a conservative stance on the significance of nuclear weapons, stating that they should not be seen as an easy short cut to victory. But the Ministry of Supply and the Controller of Atomic Energy, Lord Portal, took the opposite view. They argued that priority should be given to nuclear weapons on the grounds that it would be dangerous to run the project down. They believed that if the teams working on the bomb thought the project was of diminishing importance, they would lose incentive and the whole project would fade away. The Americans would see how little Britain had to offer, leaving Britain extremely vulnerable.

A further intensification of the apparent threat of communist aggression resulted from outbreak of the Korean War in June 1950. This caused the deterrent qualities of the bomb to be strongly emphasised in Parliament and led politicians to start speaking of ideological deterrence. The government embarked on a rearmament programme, costed at £4,700m. over a three year period, and announced it in September 1950. Meanwhile, the British were relying ever more heavily upon American support and believed that only the United States was successfully deterring the Soviet army from overrunning Europe. Keeping American forces physically present in Europe became a major preoccupation. By 1952, Britain had allowed the Americans seven main bomber bases. Despite security advantages, this made the British increasingly subservient to American strategic interests. (48)

The Labour Party had lost office October 1951, by which time the nuclear project was well advanced. When the Conservatives returned to power, with Winston Churchill as Prime Minister once more, they inherited three major legacies from Attlee's Labour Government: a strategic bomber programme, a highly secret nuclear weapons programme and British participation in NATO. The basic dilemma the Conservatives faced was how to maintain a world-wide role despite Britain's economic weakness. Britain was the head of a declining empire, and yet it was still loth to face the fact that its influence was waning.

Strategic ideas
In the early 1950s came a realisation that there were not only ethical problems associated with Britain's bomb but also problems of strategic rationality. It was accepted that a global war would lead to the use of nuclear weapons, but how such weapons would affect the course of war was uncertain. The RAF propounded a 'short war'

concept whereby conventional hostilities would be followed by a brief period of nuclear strikes that would end
the conflict. The Army and Navy favoured a 'long war'
scenario in which a period of 'broken backed war' would
follow the initial intense period of nuclear exchanges. The
short war scenario required resources to be focused on
those forces required for the opening phases, above all
the primary deterrent. The long war scenario also
required conventional forces, not least naval power to
secure sea lines of communication.

By 1952, the factors on which the 1950 review was
based were changing. The Soviet nuclear capability was
growing and the Air Defence Committee had concluded
that there was no prospect of an effective defence against
atomic attack from the air. As a consequence, the Prime
Minister felt that defence policy needed revision. This
would take account of deterioration in Britain's and
Europe's economic position, which meant that the 1950
force targets were unlikely to be met, particularly if the
need was accepted to sustain the continuing costs over
many years. Churchill also believed that not enough
account was being taken of the effectiveness of nuclear
weapons. The Chiefs of Staff were accordingly invited to
undertake a review. The resulting report achieved some
fame as the Global Strategy Paper of 1952. (49)

This report argued that a future war would begin with
an initial phase of unparalleled intensity, possibly lasting
only a few weeks, followed perhaps by a long-drawn-out
period of chaos. A guiding principle of the rearmament
programme should be to ensure survival in the short
opening phase. Hence the report pointed to an effective
deterrent as the first essential of western policy. The key
to deterrence lay in the knowledge on the part of the
Kremlin that any aggression on their part would involve
immediate and crushing retaliation by the long-range air
striking force with the atomic weapon. The effectiveness
of the deterrent would not be reduced by the growth of
the Soviet arsenal as long as the Soviets believed that it
would be used. The world was entering a period of mutual vulnerability and nuclear strategy could exploit this.
The paper identified two key factors: that the West must
keep ahead in the field of deterrent systems and that
delivery technology needed to be given greater priority.
This meant the development of the right types of aircraft,

all the necessary radio, radar and other scientific aids to accuracy, radio and radar counter-measures. Unfortunately, the 1952 report did not provide a long term affordable strategy for Britain and NATO and was quickly superseded by further studies. Within six months, the government undertook another radical review of strategy designed to bring defence spending under control. The main merits of the 1952 report were that it fully addressed NATO strategy and emphasised the value of nuclear weapons while remaining clear that adequate conventional forces were also needed. One historian has said of the 1952 report that it 'eventually led Britain to become the first nation to base its security planning almost entirely upon a declaratory policy of nuclear deterrence'. (50)

The Conservative Administration

Three men known as the 'Atomic Knights' - Cockcroft, Penney and Hinton - created what Churchill termed 'the art and article of the British bomb'. In Lord Plowden's words: 'Cockcroft was the scientist, the research man par excellence, who was always extending his researches at Harwell further and further. Bill Penney was an extremely nice man, with great ability and a great knowledge of nuclear weapons, because he spent a large part of the War at Los Alamos in America. He was very good at leading his team, yet keeping them disciplined. Hinton was an extremely able engineer, a great driving force, determined to have his own way...'.(51) By the late summer of 1952, Hinton had produced enough plutonium for a test. When America had refused British participation in its nuclear programme, this had meant the end of access to their nuclear testing facilities. In the early autumn, Penney took a device to the Monte Bello Islands off the northwest coast of Australia. There on, 3 October 1952, the first British A-bomb test (code named *Hurricane)* was carried out successfully. A month later, on 1 November 1952, the US exploded its first thermonuclear device at Eniwetok in the Pacific, showing that a hydrogen bomb was indeed possible. Less than a year later, on 12 August, 1953 the Soviet Union followed suit.

On 23 October 1952, Churchill made a statement to the House of Commons arguing that the British A-bomb would lead to a closer interchange of information between the Americans and the British. (52) Lord Plowden says: 'At the end of 1953, Churchill asked me to be chairman of the Atomic Energy Authority. He said that my chief task was to get an amendment to the McMahon Act, thus allowing us to share information with the Americans. They had to be persuaded that our security was tight and worthwhile before exchanging information of a technical kind with us. My opposite number was Lewis Strauss - he was very security minded and was not particularly close to this country. But we persuaded the Atomic Energy Commission in the US and we also persuaded Congress. After the repeal of the McMahon Act, the US had to give information to us. But even then we could only exchange information when we had demonstrated that we had the technology'. Lord Plowden says of Britain's decision to develop the H-bomb: 'I got a minute from Prime Minister Churchill asking me to let him know what it would cost and what effort would be necessary to develop and manufacture hydrogen bombs. When I explained he said... 'We must do it, it is the price we pay to sit at the top table'. (53) Victor Macklen, a scientist who was at the centre of efforts to restore Anglo-American co-operation adds: ' The British government wished to re-establish the close co-operation with the Americans which had existed until 1946...the only way that this could be done was for the British to demonstrate that they were capable of producing these very large explosions.' (54)

From October 1952 until the banning of this type of test 11 years later, there were only some 21 British atmospheric tests all told in Australia and the Pacific. After *Hurricane*, the programme continued with two tests in 1953 (*Totem*), four in 1956 (*Buffalo*) and three in 1957 (*Antler*), all at Maralinga in Australia. The first two tests of boosted fission weapons were code named *Mosaic* and took place in 1956 in the Monte Bello Islands. The *Grapple* series was conducted in 1957 and 1958 at Christmas Island: there were nine tests in all, six of which were thermonuclear. If one compares the number of tests conducted by Britain compared with the USA, the USSR and France, the figures are strikingly low. In the half-century from 1946 to 1996 Britain carried out 44 tests. The comparable figure for France was 198; for USSR/Russia, 936; for the USA, 954. (55) Why did the British conduct so few? The main reason was that they had to develop their bombs on a shoestring. Tests are very costly exercises and the British were short of resources - money, manpower, ships, aircraft and weapon materials. Every test explosion reduced the already small amount available for the stockpile. So Britain used painstaking laboratory methods in an effort not to test, and tended to use testing only as final proof. When the British did test, every single shot had to be rigorously justified. This they did very effectively. Another reason for economy in testing was that the British were always very conscious of the need to minimise the world total of fallout and their contribution to it. It has also been suggested that Britain acquired a great deal of information from the US, but this point should not be over-emphasised. The development programme was completed with the last British test series in September/October 1958 before information began to flow across the Atlantic in consequence of the bilateral agreement reached in that year.

Churchill was the one prime minister who involved the Cabinet in key discussions about nuclear weapons. He took the issues to full Cabinet in the summer of 1954, informing them that the cost of the H-bomb programme should not exceed £10 millions (56) and approval was given in the following month. (57) In the following years, despite some protest about the spiralling arms race and the dangers of radiation from nuclear testing, the British government remained determined to carry on with its programme. In February 1955 the Statement on Defence announced development of the British H-bomb but the consequences for defence policy were not spelled out until the Defence White Paper of 1957.

Massive Retaliation
The military policy of the United States at this time was based on the notion of massive retaliation, as enunciated by Secretary of State John Foster Dulles. The strategy was simple and seemingly watertight. It was based on the premise that the full nuclear armoury would be used against any type of aggression so that the fear of this would suffice to deter any potential aggressor. Where major powers were involved, limited war was inconceivable, any conflict would result immediately in a global

nuclear war. As we have seen, Britain's strategy at this time reflected the American doctrine. It was accepted that the US was the leading partner in the alliance, the only stipulation being that Britain might have different ideas as to what targets should be engaged first. These would be targets most necessary to the defence of Britain *e.g.* the bases of enemy long-range bombers and U-boats.

Almost the only member of the British military establishment to offer a different view was Rear Admiral Sir Anthony Buzzard. (58) He believed that the moral implications of the use of nuclear weapons should be taken into account and suggested that the principle of minimum force could be applied equally in the nuclear context. Buzzard argued that the concept of massive retaliation was flawed. As matters stood it greatly increased the potential destructiveness of war, yet decreased the certainty that nuclear weapons would ever be used. He feared that Allied strategy for any contingency short of all-out war was increasingly based on bluff and that this would increase the opportunities for misunderstanding. He proposed a policy of graduated deterrence by which war aims, the geographical area of a conflict, the targets, the size of weapons and the resulting fall-out would all be limited. His strategy involved a counter-force plan using tactical nuclear forces to deny the Soviet Union victory on the battlefield. Escalation would be deterred by means of threats to Soviet cities. This would exploit the inclination of both sides to limit the conflict. By constraining the use of nuclear weapons he hoped to mitigate the effects of crisis instability created by mutual first strike postures. The difficulty lay in establishing distinctions that would hold up in wartime, but he considered that there was little for the Allies to lose in attempting it. This theory was opposed by Sir John Slessor, Chief of the Air Staff, who believed that graduated deterrence within a European context would be seen as weakness by the Soviet Union and cast doubt on the willingness of the West to implement its own doctrine in a show-down. (59)

The Macmillan Administration
After the Suez débacle in 1956, which had cruelly exposed Britain's military and economic weakness, Prime Minister Harold Macmillan was preoccupied with the need for political recovery. Duncan Sandys, then Minister

of Defence, promulgated a new policy in the Defence White Paper of 1957. This reiterated clearly that Britain as a whole could not be protected from nuclear attack and again stressed the importance to Britain of possessing an appreciable element of nuclear deterrent power of her own. Its aim was to restructure the armed forces for greater dependence upon nuclear weapons and achieve economies of manpower and resources. Sir Richard Powell, then permanent secretary at the Ministry of Defence, who was involved in drafting the 1957 White Paper, says of the policy: 'It was thought of as something cheaper than having to provide the enormous conventional forces that would have been required to constitute an adequate defence of Western Europe. In fact it was impossible for the alliance to produce forces of that size, so in that sense it was the only way of achieving the objective.' (60) The White Paper also emphasised that British policy was to prevent and not to prepare for a nuclear war and proposed a number of new options:

(1) Britain was to halve the size of the armed forces by 1962, to reduce the manpower of BAOR and to make up for it with the firepower of atomic artillery.

(2) Britain would reduce the number of aircraft in Germany and would offset this by providing some of the squadrons with atomic bombs.

(3) Sandys also cancelled the operational requirement for a supersonic bomber to succeed the V-bombers, although he retained the projects to retrofit Mark 2 versions of the Vulcan and Victor with improved engines because these were well advanced. Britain would finally rely on ballistic missiles bought from America or developed with American help.

The Defence Committee began planning for 100 H-bombs to equip the V-bombers that were now on the production line. Lord Plowden told ministers this could be done without building a new plant if further tests were successful or technical information was available from the United States. Macmillan was very determined to restore the full Anglo-American co-operation, which had eluded every other prime minister since 1946. He wanted to demonstrate British capability, and so prove that Britain was worthy of collaboration. As Lord Plowden said, 'We were quite convinced that it was right to do everything we could do to persuade the Americans to restore the collaboration. Their nuclear effort was enormously greater than our own, and they had covered a lot of ground that would have taken us a tremendous effort to do. Therefore there were potentially tremendous economies as a result of the restoration of collaboration.' (61) It was decided to develop a British Intermediate Range Ballistic Missile (IRBM), in close co-operation with the Americans. This was to be a liquid-fuelled missile designed to carry the British H-bomb and was code-named *Blue Streak*.

On 15 May 1957, the British tested what were believed to be their first H-Bombs in the Pacific. Eric Grove says: 'It is now known that these tests were not a complete success. Although some fusion reaction was obtained from the H-bomb prototypes the only bomb to give anywhere near a megaton yield was a large fission device. This was the concept chosen for initial production.'(62) But these and subsequent tests did succeed in providing a basis for negotiating with the Americans on collaboration. Victor Macklen, who was present at scientific discussions in August 1958, says: 'The Americans were obviously very friendly, but the first day's meetings were just barely satisfactory and it did not look as though any progress would be made. That night Sir Frederick Brundrett, the leader on the British side, had a discussion with Bill Penney and the Aldermaston scientists and decided that they would offer to present to the Americans one of our designs. This was in fact the best design that we had, but we were not going to tell the Americans that. The Aldermaston staff presented the design as one that they were working on and had tested. After the presentation the Americans asked for a recess and came back ten minutes later. It was at that point that Edward Teller said, 'After twelve years of separation, it was obvious that the laws of physics operated on both sides of the Atlantic, and in scientific terms, the British knew as much about the matter as their American colleagues'. From that time on, the negotiations for the exchange took place quite quickly.' (63)

The launch of Sputnik on 4 October 1957 demonstrated the dramatic progress of Soviet rocket science and led to fears that the Soviets could deliver nuclear weapons anywhere in the world with no chance of putting up a credible defence against them. Spurred on by this, the Macmillan and Eisenhower governments embarked on a series of meetings which resulted in a Declaration of the Common Purpose. Further changes were made to the American Atomic Energy Act and in 1958, a fresh 'Agreement for Co-operation on the Uses of Atomic Energy for Mutual Defence Purposes' was drawn up. This led to exchanges of bomb designs and the decision to adopt an American design for the first production H-bomb. This came into service in 1961. In a parallel move, Joint Targeting was arranged with the American Strategic Air Command.

By 1960, it had become clear that *Blue Streak* was too vulnerable to pre-emptive strike by Soviet ballistic missiles and would have to be cancelled before it swallowed up too much money. Macmillan records another reason for cancelling *Blue Streak*, namely that installing fixed-site rockets near the large centres of populations would cause public anxiety. Britain's difficulties in trying to stay at the forefront of development for strategic delivery systems were thus becoming acute. People began to question whether Britain was wealthy enough to remain a nuclear weapon power on these terms. Closer co-operation with the United States increasingly came to be seen as the most reliable route to maintaining a reliable deterrent for the next generation.

Professor Peter Nailor, who spent some of his career in the branch of the Ministry of Defence concerned with these matters recalls: 'They attempted to provide for a transition, which in the first place was based upon the maintenance and development of an indigenous missile industry. This was the plan to develop the *Blue Streak* missile, which technically was a very good vehicle, but in political and military terms was very quickly overtaken by technology. It was liquid-fuelled, and the advent of solid fuel motors meant that you could get an enormously enhanced state of readiness, which would in fact make the *Blue Streak* missiles on pads or silos in East Anglia very vulnerable to attack.' (64) He goes on to summarise the worries of British policy makers in the late 1950s: 'A change occurred with the successful test and deployment of thermonuclear weapons. This took place in the 1952-1955 period, and immediately afterwards, you got quite unexpectedly fast technical breakthroughs in reliable solid fuel rocket motors and the development of miniaturised components for warheads and for guidance and instrumental systems. The pace of change was accelerating to an extent where a country like Britain was being forced to make technical choices with bewildering rapidity...' (65)

The first move after the cancellation of *Blue Streak* was the decision in 1960 to buy *Skybolt*, an air-launched Ballistic Missile, from the Americans. This was to be fitted to the V-bombers and would greatly increase their reach and survivability because the missile could be launched hundreds of miles from the rapidly improving Soviet air defences. Sir Philip de Zulueta was the private secretary who accompanied Macmillan to Camp David to ask US President Eisenhower for *Skybolt*. He says: 'Macmillan fortunately managed to succeed. Curiously enough when we were asking for *Skybolt* at that Camp David meeting, the Americans in the background were talking about Polaris. This was the new American submarine-launched missile system. Eisenhower's naval aide represented the Navy lobby, trying to persuade us to go ahead with Polaris. I discussed it with Sir Norman Brook, the Cabinet Secretary, and he said 'For goodness sake don't raise that question. We must have an airborne missile because we want to use our bombers.' (66) At that time the Vulcan bombers were due to come off the production line for another three years, so the idea of putting the deterrent on submarines was not an attractive prospect. The *Skybolt* technical agreement was finally signed on the 23 September 1960 and in exchange the British offered the Americans a base in Holy Loch for the Atlantic Polaris submarine force.

In December 1962, however, in the aftermath of the Cuban Missile Crisis, (22-28 October 1962) the *Skybolt* project was cancelled by President John F. Kennedy without consultation, leaving Britain without a plan for its future strategic delivery system. Lord Home, who was Macmillan's Foreign Secretary at the time, remembers, 'It was a pretty big shock. We had set a lot of store by its success, and the success had been advertised and was widely known.' (67) Macmillan and his team were left feeling very vulnerable and had to salvage what they could from this disaster.

On the 18-21 December 1962, a meeting was held between Kennedy and Macmillan at Nassau in the Bahamas. Macmillan, who was shrewd diplomat, played upon Kennedy's feelings. Sir Philip de Zulueta remembers: 'He made a most moving and emotional speech, about the great losses and the great struggles for freedom, about how Britain was resolute and determined ally and was going to stand firm, and that it was very unreasonable for the United States not to assist her to do so...it was very well done indeed and very effective. There was not a dry eye in the house!' (68) Lord Home recalls: 'I didn't think we would be successful when we set out. Jack Kennedy, and indeed the State Department and the Pentagon, were not at all keen on this deal clearly, and from their point of view there was a lot to be said for keeping all the nuclear power in American hands, of course... If it had not succeeded we would have been in a very nasty position politically.' (69) Lord Home also thinks there was a deeper psychological reason for Kennedy's sympathy with the British case: 'Jack Kennedy, I always think, felt fairly lonely in carrying this responsibility as the only man who could put his finger on the button. He and Macmillan hit up an extraordinary friendship, this much older man with the younger man. Kennedy trusted Macmillan absolutely and, feeling as I think he did, he was relieved to know that somebody else was in on the act.' (70)

So by skilful bargaining, Macmillan obtained agreement to buy into the Polaris project. This, of course, entailed transferring Britain's strategic deterrent role in due course away from the Royal Air Force to the Royal Navy. The arrangement was that while the British would buy the US missiles and fire control systems they would still manufacture their own warheads. The missiles would be fitted into British-manufactured submarines and US would help in the propulsion-reactor design. But the hard men of the Pentagon did not care for additional nuclear deterrents in Europe cluttering the field between the superpowers and distrusted small independent forces on principle. So Kennedy insisted that British Polaris would be assigned as part of a NATO nuclear force and targeted in accordance with NATO plans, being used for the purposes of international defence of the western alliance in all circumstances. Macmillan, however, was able to insert the crucial rider, 'except where HM Government may decide that supreme national interests are at stake'. (71) Macmillan used the newly established Defence and Overseas Policy Committee of the Cabinet to review the options and they readily agreed that the US Polaris system was the only suitable system. Indeed, the Polaris agreement solved many problems for the Conservative government, not least the question of expense. It allayed fears about the uncertainty of American support in a crisis. But for Macmillan, possession of Polaris was also a powerful symbol of independence. A nuclear strategic force in British ownership was a valid way of showing that Britain was not just a satellite of America. It was also important for Britain's standing in Europe since France would not be left as the only European nuclear power. In the event, however, Britain increasingly became a minor player as the United States and Soviet Union forged ahead with their nuclear programmes. The Soviet Union was claiming to have tested bombs yielding over 100 megatons. And despite Macmillan's success in winning over doubters in the Pentagon and the State Department, a new problem was to arise closer to home. This time it was in the shape of the new Labour party leader Harold Wilson, who while in opposition never missed an opportunity to criticise Polaris.

During the early 1960s, Macmillan and his government worked hard, not only to ensure that Britain was equipped with a wide range of nuclear weapons, tactical as well as strategic, but also to persuade the US and the Soviet Union to halt the arms race which in his view was creating enormous dangers. Britain took the initiative in pressing for a test ban agreement and played a very important role in the negotiations with the United States and the Soviet Union which resulted in the 1963 Partial Test Ban Treaty (PTBT). This banned nuclear weapon tests in the atmosphere, outer space and under water. Lord Hailsham, who was the British representative at the negotiations and signed the treaty in Moscow on behalf of Britain says: '...I think our role was crucial and I don't think that we would have got it without the support of the Prime Minister. Kennedy certainly wanted a treaty and so did we...moreover atmospheric nuclear tests were undoubtedly an international danger and the fact that we were able to put an end to them was extremely valuable in the interests of safety.' (72)

Wilson's Government
In the run-up to the general election of 1964, the nuclear deterrent was a main focus of debate. By this time, £270 million had been committed to Polaris, with £40 million spent, and work had already begun on the submarines. The Conservatives emphasised that possessing nuclear weapons entitled Britain to a seat at the top table and this was a key element in their manifesto. It had long been an unspoken but deeply rooted opinion that past history had made France Britain's traditional rival and Britain was determined to have an equal role as a middle power with France. Sir Alec Douglas Home (as he was by then), succeeded Macmillan in 1963 and reverted to the patriotic theme of the independent deterrent as a symbol of British political and military power. 'I don't believe the Russians could bank on a British prime minister not pressing the button.' (73) But the Labour Party manifesto promised a re-negotiation of the Nassau Agreement. Harold Wilson had said of the Polaris system: 'It will not be British, it will not be independent and it will not deter.' (74) There was the clear implication that the independent deterrent could be abandoned altogether and substituted by greater conventional force. But Home disagreed. 'I had always found, when dealing with Harold Wilson on security matters, that he was reliable in terms of the national interest. So I did not think, in spite of the manifesto, in spite of what he had said during the election campaign, I did not think that he would bring himself to cancel it when he understood the facts. When he got into government I thought he would carry on the programme so it not worry me unduly.' (75)

The Labour Party won the election narrowly, and Harold Wilson became Prime Minister. His first approach was to propose a collective Atlantic Nuclear Force. It soon became clear that this was a non-starter. After a month in office, he and the Defence Secretary Denis Healey looked again at the idea of re-negotiating the Nassau Agreement, but clearly this, too, was not practical. It was decided that the Polaris project was too far advanced to be cancelled and the idea was dropped. Denis Healey recounts why the Polaris programme continued: 'The basic reason was that the deal which Macmillan had got out of Kennedy was a very good one, it was a very cheap system for the capability it offered. We already had one boat nearly complete and another was on the stocks, so the saving from cancellation would have been minimal. This was only a year or two after the Cuban Missile Crisis and the memory of Hungary (the failed Hungarian Revolution of 1956) was still in our minds. Khrushchev had been deposed the day before the British general election and the Chinese had exploded their bomb the same day. We felt on the whole it was wise to continue with Polaris. (76) No doubt there had been strong pressure from the MOD, service chiefs and nuclear weapons teams not to abandon the project. Another point put to ministers will have been along the lines: 'Would you prefer a world where the American president is going to take the decisions of whether nuclear weapons are going to be used, or a situation where we can have a say in these decisions, i.e. do you trust the Americans?' The answer was clearly No.' (77)

The interesting suggestion has been made by John Simpson that much of Labour Party opposition to Polaris had been a coded way of displaying opposition to British dependence on the US. He believes that there was a strong feeling of anti-Americanism. He cites a speech by Harold Wilson in which he criticised the previous Conservative governments of Harold Macmillan and Alec Douglas Home for reducing the independence of the British nuclear deterrent. Simpson argues that Wilson was complaining about exchange agreements on fissile materials and the fact that the UK was dependent upon the US for tritium (radioactive isotope of hydrogen). Implicitly, he even appeared to complain about being dependent on the Americans for nuclear testing and supply of the Polaris missiles. 'One of the underlying elements of this whole thing, was not so much that the Labour Party was against British nuclear weapons *per se*, but it was against British nuclear weapons that were linked to America. The question really was one of no nuclear weapons or independent nuclear weapons.' (78). The only change the Labour government made was in trimming the fleet, by reducing the number of Polaris submarines from five to four, on grounds of cost. The Chancellor of the Exchequer James Callaghan tried to cut the force back even further at a special meeting of the Cabinet at Chequers. Denis Healey recalls: 'Jim wanted it down to three, just to save money of course. George Brown wanted it down to three on the grounds that with three boats we could not be sure of always having one on patrol and therefore it could not be regarded as being capable of being used independently!' (79) The upshot was that they sacrificed the fifth submarine as the price for keeping the system as a whole. They also agreed not to develop a new generation of warheads, but then there was not necessarily any need to do so. In terms of sheer numbers, they went on to produce more nuclear warheads than the previous Conservative administration. (80) Each submarine was to carry sixteen missiles and each missile three warheads, but it was generally believed that only just enough operational strategic warheads were produced for three deployed submarines.

Polaris lived up to its expectations; it came in on time and was cheaper than anticipated. The first Polaris patrol took place in 1967 and in 1969 nuclear strike responsibilities were formally transferred from the RAF to the Royal Navy. By way of justification, a new theory was developed at the Ministry of Defence. The thesis was that the overall security of the Alliance and of Britain would be greatly enhanced if another country apart from the United States had the ability to respond to Soviet aggression with nuclear weapons. Once the US had itself become vulnerable to nuclear attack, doubts naturally arose as to whether the United States would use its weapons in defence of Europe. And whether or not they would do so in practice, such doubts would certainly exist in the minds of Soviet decision-makers: they might underrate America's resolve and so deterrence would be weakened. (81) The existence of a second centre of decision would ensure that even if United States did not use nuclear weapons in response to Soviet aggression in Europe, Britain, being much more directly affected, certainly would, and the Soviet leaders would know this. There was also a fear that the United States might suffer a radical political change and become isolationist, withdrawing all its co-operation and support from Britain on nuclear matters. Obviously, this would require an independent British nuclear capability. This argument conveniently overlooked the fact that Britain would continue to rely on US support in keeping the Polaris missiles serviceable. Harold Wilson, reflecting later on the Polaris deal, acknowledged this point but turned the argument on its head: 'I never believed we had a really independent deterrent. On the other hand I did not want to be in a position of having to subordinate ourselves to the Americans if they, at a certain point, said they were going to use it or something of that kind. In fact I doubt if anyone ever expected it to be used. We might need to restrain the Americans if we learned about new developments of a devastating character where otherwise, we would feel dragged along by the American coat tails. Otherwise we would have been just regarded as their stooges.' (82)

Tony Benn, however, puts a very different gloss on the position: 'What happened was that the US did agree to resume links with us despite the McMahon Act, so long as we provided them with bases where they could deploy their nuclear weapons in Britain. Secondly, they said: 'We can agree to let you have access to our technology provided that we supervise your security arrangements'. All the security arrangements at Aldermaston and all the policy decisions affecting security would be supervised and checked by the US. They supervised our vetting system and they wanted to know if the people that we employed were reliable. According to them, this was legitimate spying by them on us and checking our operations. That is what was called the 'special relationship'. On one occasion I had to go to the US and get permission to use their technology in the form of a centrifuge. The price we had to pay for the independent nuclear weapon was to accept US supervision over the whole operation. We had an alleged seat at the top table (it never really did give us a seat) and it bankrupted us. It gave us an illusion of being powerful. It was very expensive and very stupid'. (83)

Super Antelope
Even before the first Polaris submarine had put to sea in the British government was contemplating an enhancement for the missile to cope with improvements in Soviet anti-ballistic missile (ABM) technology. Aldermaston sci-

entists and the nuclear community at Whitehall had begun to think that Soviet advances in defence could make Polaris obsolete. Harold Wilson accordingly set up a committee in 1967 consisting of George Brown, the Foreign Secretary, James Callaghan, the Chancellor and Denis Healey, the Defence Secretary. Their first decision was not to seek an American solution in the shape of the new missile system *Poseidon*. (This system had more sophisticated multiple warheads, capable of hitting a number of separate targets and thus diluting Soviet air defences. The Polaris A3 missile carried only three warheads and could not be manoeuvred in space so as to engage separate targets.) Instead it was decided to start research into a British proposal for an improved Polaris warhead system. This would equip the missile with a new front end containing advanced penetration aids, including decoys, and the ability to manoeuvre the payload in space. The number of warheads was reduced to two, giving more room for decoys, but these could be dispersed more widely over the target area, affording a wider destructive footprint and greater resistance to interception. (84)

The British programme was code named *Super Antelope*. It was a study of future needs and was known only to a handful of Labour ministers. David Owen recalls: 'I think there are some things that are wholly legitimate to keep private and secret. I think that what is on the front end of a British nuclear missile is an entirely legitimate confidential secret, and I do not think you should go to the whole Cabinet.' (85) Victor Macklen, who was involved in this work from the outset, adds: 'They put very severe restrictions on us in the period 1968-1970. We were not allowed to place contracts with industrial firms for this work. We were not even allowed to discuss the research work with the Navy. By 1970, a good deal of research had taken place and there were the beginnings of a design of a new re-entry system. But we hadn't really gone beyond the very first development stage; the warhead side was much more advanced than the decoy side.' (86)

Flexible Response

Early in 1968, following a financial crisis and enforced devaluation of the pound, it was announced that British forces would be withdrawn from the Far East and the Persian Gulf, concentrating defence efforts in future on Europe and the Mediterranean. (87) At the same time, a new strategic doctrine was being conceived within NATO. This doctrine was based upon ideas first generated in 1962 by Robert McNamara when he became Kennedy's Secretary for Defence. His idea was to give an American president military options in Europe other than immediately ordering the use of nuclear weapons. This doctrine assumed that any attack by the Warsaw Pact would be carried out by conventional forces in the first place. If so, then the initial responses by NATO should be made in kind. Implicit in this proposal was the belief that NATO both could and should improve its conventional forces to the point where it would be able to halt a conventional attack by the Warsaw Pact without resort to nuclear weapons. The onus of escalation would then lie on the Soviet side. McNamara described this policy as one of controlled flexible response. It did not altogether please European members of NATO because it seemed to signal a lessening of American resolve to put America at risk in defence of Europe.

The argument continued until 1967, when a compromise was adopted by the NATO Council. This provided that NATO policy should be to deter aggression by maintaining forces adequate to counter an attack at whatever level the aggressor chose to fight. A conventional attack would be met in the first instance by direct defence (i.e. with conventional forces only). If this direct defence did not suffice, then NATO would move up to the next level, using tactical nuclear weapons against the Warsaw Pact forces taking part in the assault. If this, too, failed a general nuclear response would follow, consisting of massive nuclear strikes against the full range of strategic targets in the Warsaw Pact countries, including the Soviet Union. The British account of flexible response was presented in the Defence White Papers of 1968 and 1969. In this version, the important thing for NATO was to have an appropriate response at all levels and not to make things infinitely worse by resorting prematurely to nuclear weapons if a conflict arose in Europe. Means were accordingly proposed for strengthening conventional forces. (88)

Chevaline

The Conservatives returned to office in 1970 under Prime Minister Edward Heath. The first thing they did was to look at the existing Polaris fleet. They thought about adding one more submarine to make the number up to five but decided against this on cost grounds. Instead they re-opened the Polaris improvement programme and changed the code name from *Super Antelope* to *Chevaline*. Sir Herman Bondi, who joined the Ministry of Defence as Chief Scientific Advisor in 1971, says: 'Question one was - how long would Polaris serve us? The then existing soft Polaris was distinctly vulnerable to *Galosh*, the latest Soviet anti-ballistic missile system, as we imagined it to be. Was it or was it not sufficient? How long could we maintain an American missile if the Americans themselves retired it? What if anything should be done about either hardening *Polaris* or replacing it? Those were the key topics.' (89)

Once again *Poseidon* was considered. Sir Frank Cooper comments: 'I think some people would have liked to have gone for *Poseidon*, but there was never any serious prospect that in the middle 1970s, the Americans would have supplied it. They were still suffering from euphoria because their technology was so much in advance of the Soviet Union's. They regarded Multiple Independently-targeted Re-entry Vehicles (MIRVs), for example, as something nobody else was ever going to invent, so you were in an 'it was invented here' syndrome, rather then a 'not invented here' syndrome. Some of the senior Americans were also not sure what kind of relationship there should be with Britain in the nuclear field. We were getting more and more into discussions about arms control etc.' (90)

Lord Zuckerman, who was then Chief Scientific Adviser in the Cabinet Office, argued against upgrading Polaris, even if the Russians put a protective anti-missile screen around Moscow. He was sceptical of the need to destroy the heart of government - the so-called Moscow Criterion. He said: 'At that time, I did not believe that if an Anti-Ballistic Missile (ABM) Treaty was to be concluded, we needed to do anything about our warheads. Even if you assumed that the Moscow defence system worked - and our intelligence did not say that it did - there were other targets because the whole of the USSR was still open.

Whatever else we should wait to discover what the conclusions of the negotiations for the ABM Treaty were. Instead of which Aldermaston and the nuclear enthusiasts wanted to go on. I can understand their wanting to, it was their job, but it was merely copying what had been done by everybody else.' (91) In May 1972 the Soviets and the Americans did conclude the ABM treaty. This ended any prospects of an effective ballistic missile defence of the whole country, although the *Galosh* system was installed to protect Moscow.

The *Chevaline* project was kept going, on a drip-feed of monthly funding, by a small group of Conservative ministers in the Heath government. But the crucial decision to authorise full scale development fell to the Labour government re-elected in March 1974. In commenting on this period, John Simpson has pointed out that there was increasing concern lest the Americans, (now led by President Jimmy Carter) might foreclose on the British nuclear deterrent and cut down their collaboration with the UK on nuclear matters. To cover this possibility, the Labour government built a tritium plant designed specifically to free themselves from dependence upon the United States for this material. Simpson points out that while publicly, the Labour party has at times appeared anti-nuclear, in government the party has always moved towards strengthening the independence of the British nuclear force. (92)

Discussions were undertaken by a small group of five ministers, Wilson (Prime Minister), Healey (Chancellor), Callaghan (Foreign Secretary), Mason (Defence Secretary) and Jenkins (Home Secretary), meeting informally and not as a Cabinet committee. This group apparently decided to go ahead with the *Chevaline* project in April 1974 but it was not discussed in Cabinet until 20 November. Tony Benn writing about this meeting says, 'Harold (Wilson) said that in fact we were not interested in developing *Poseidon*. He said that all that was being proposed was, in fact, a very minor addition to the present weapons system. He thought that there were a number of reasons for this. First of all, the European position. We didn't want the French to be the only ones with nuclear weapons with the risk that the Germans might come in, too. Secondly, our influence in the US. Apparently Harold thought the links between Jim (Callaghan) and Henry

Kissinger (US Secretary of State) were very important. Thirdly it brought us onto the Hot Line (the direct communication link established between the US president and the Soviet leader set up in the aftermath of the Cuban missile crisis) and we were consulted. Fourthly, the Soviet Union had never objected and had valued our independent judgment. On those grounds we thought we should continue'. (93) There was token opposition from two committed anti-nuclear members, Michael Foot and Barbara Castle, but there was very little questioning of the project and no attempt to ask for more details. In 1978 a small group of ministers again decided not to cancel *Chevaline* despite the mounting cost overruns, although David Owen and Denis Healey thought it was unnecessary. That was the last that was heard of *Chevaline* until the Labour Party left office in 1979.

The project has since raised a number of concerns. The first is that such a large project, with an estimated cost of £240m. over ten years, was agreed with so little debate. Secondly, there is a perception that the project developed its own unstoppable momentum with a lack of adequate management. In the event, it overran its (secret) budget by some £750 million and the contrast with Polaris was stark. Lord Callaghan said in extenuation: 'I do not recall *Chevaline* being put to us formally. My impression is that the decision to go ahead with *Chevaline* was made by the previous government. This was never put to us formally, it was an ongoing decision, and it only came up when they wanted more money or when the project needed more funds. It was not a cut-and-dried decision.' (94) Lord Healey says, 'The *Chevaline* which hardened the Polaris missiles was not a new generation and as we don't announce new weapons until they are ready, we have not said much about it. The Tories actually started the project and we carried on with it and you don't announce it until you have done it.' (95). But he adds that when the Labour Party won the election in March 1974, he became Chancellor of the Exchequer and had to draw up a budget in three weeks. The physical effort of getting that done wiped everything else from his mind. 'I regard myself as having failed in my duty as Chancellor, especially with the knowledge I gained as Defence Secretary, in not subjecting the whole *Chevaline* programme to severe scrutiny right from the word go.' (96)

Whatever the facts were - and public records of this period are still closed - a further eight years were needed to bring *Chevaline* into service. Hence, the Labour Party were spared the embarrassment of merging rhetoric with practice. In 1981, the Chevaline project was investigated by the Public Accounts Committee of the House of Commons. Its report was critical of costs and project management. Sir Ronald Mason, who succeeded Sir Herman Bondi as Chief Scientific Adviser to the Ministry of Defence, was new to the nuclear world. He says of *Chevaline*: 'It left an indelible message in my own mind, and that is the tremendous resources you have to call into play if you develop a major strategic programme unilaterally. That lesson, probably consciously rather than subconsciously, played a very considerable part when the time came to look at strategic successor systems to Polaris. My feeling is that all opportunities for commonality, particularly of course with the United States, ought to be seen through before one really faces up again to an independent national programme'. (97) *Chevaline* became operational in the autumn of 1982.

The successor to Polaris.
When James Callaghan succeeded Harold Wilson as Prime Minister in 1976, his government was faced with deciding on a successor for Polaris. With a predicted service life of approximately 25 years, the first submarine was approaching middle age; moreover the submarines were becoming noisier both in absolute terms as they aged, and relative to new designs. Despite the Labour party manifesto (for the second of the two general elections in 1974), which contained a promise not to proceed with a new generation of nuclear weapons, senior ministers made it clear that they were prepared to start discussions about the replacement for Polaris. Lord Callaghan says: 'I never considered allowing Polaris simply to waste out, that would have been ducking our responsibilities. I considered that we ought to have all the options in front of us and take a decision on them. The options might have been, of course, not to go ahead with it. But that would not have been a case of letting it die out, but a case of taking a positive decision.' In January 1978, Callaghan accordingly commissioned studies for the options for replacing Polaris. A general election was coming up and

this was a politically sensitive time. He says: 'It was believed on expert advice that the date by which the submarines would start to become obsolescent would be 1990-1992. It was also said that it would take about ten years to build replacements. In 1978, I decided that we had better start examining this, knowing that we would not have to take a decision in the lifetime of the government of which I was head, but expecting to have take a decision one way or another after a general election.' (98) It was decided not to involve the Defence and Overseas Policy Committee of the Cabinet because a number of confirmed anti-nuclear ministers sat on that committee, including Michael Foot. Once again, a small informal group of ministers was set up and its very existence was kept from the rest of the Cabinet. This group consisted of Callaghan, David Owen (Foreign Secretary), Dennis Healey (Chancellor of the Exchequer) and Fred Mulley (Defence Secretary). The group quickly determined that a new submarine-based system should be acquired although it was not decided whether this would be Trident, the new American system or Cruise missiles launched from ordinary nuclear-powered submarines. At the official level, the work was split into two studies. One was led by Sir Anthony Duff at the Foreign and Commonwealth Office, covering political and military aspects of a deterrent for the 1990s and beyond. This was to consider the basic concepts of deterrence, what constituted it and what criteria needed to be met to sustain it for the future. The second study, led by Sir Ronald Mason, was to examine the technical choices. David Owen, however, believed that ministers should make the running and he resented the deployment of his own diplomats on the official committees to which the work was devolved. He regarded the 'Moscow criterion' as misguided Whitehall orthodoxy, and was determined to find a cheaper alternative to Trident. He says that he tasked his personal Foreign Office policy unit to promote the Cruise missile alternative, with the help of Lord Zuckerman, who had excellent contacts in the US, and claims that there was a lot of misinformation during this period. The Ministry of Defence was arguing that Cruise missiles were comparatively inaccurate, slow (sub-sonic) and too vulnerable. In this they were supported by the Americans, who were running both the Trident programme and a Cruise missile programme. The US Navy was concerned that if it admitted how accurate the Cruise missiles had become, it would jeopardise their own case for the Trident system. They needed Trident to penetrate Soviet ABM defences and to deliver reliable strikes on Moscow. It was only in the 1980s, when the Trident Programme was beyond recall, that the US Navy began to sing the praises of Cruise missiles. Until then, it was very difficult, even for ministers, to get accurate information about them. (99)

David Owen prepared his own paper on nuclear weapons policy, with information from the British Embassy in Washington, and sent it to the Prime Minister. He criticised the Duff-Mason Report for concentrating too narrowly on strategic nuclear weapons rather than nuclear weapons in general, and took issue with the use of the term strategic, which was a source of confusion and inconsistency. Duff and Mason had stated that if Britain did not proceed with a further strategic force she would eventually cease to be a nuclear weapon power. Owen argued that everything hinged on what was meant by 'strategic'. He distinguished between nuclear systems that could inflict serious damage on the Soviet homeland and systems that could not. He proposed that there were alternatives to the so-called Moscow Criterion and claimed that the judgments made by the Superpowers were no guide to British requirements. Furthermore, there could be no universal answers to what would constitute unacceptable damage to the Soviet Union in relation to their limited gain in eliminating the United Kingdom. Owen believed that it was the Soviets' assessment of our political resolve to use nuclear weapons that would deter them rather than the precise degree of structural damage that they judged us capable of inflicting. Lord Owen argued that for British planning purposes we needed to have a minimum level of assured capability, but it was enough to express this in terms of a certain number of Soviet casualties. For this purpose, a force consisting of submarine-based cruise missiles would suffice. (100)

Owen believed that Polaris submarines could be made to last long after their stated end-of-life in 1993. Running them on would ensure that full value was obtained for the money the government had agreed to spend on *Cheva-*

line, which, in 1978, was still four years away from entering service. He also argued that, by making Britain less
vulnerable, international arms control agreements would
help the longer-term viability of Polaris. He criticised the
Duff-Mason conclusions for forcing the issue unnecessarily soon. (101) But the Prime Minister was keeping an
open mind and was postponing all decisions until after
the election. Callaghan got the agreement of colleagues to
raise the question with the US President Carter at the
Guadeloupe Summit in January 1979. He was to ask if,
after the election, he were to come back and say that he
wanted to buy Poseidon or Trident, would Carter have
any objection to selling a system to us? Moreover, would
such a purchase be available under the 1962 Nassau
Agreement? It seems that Carter readily agreed on both
counts. (102) In his memoirs, Lord Callaghan says that
he wrote a memorandum to Margaret Thatcher in the
Cabinet Room telling her what took place between himself and Carter. (103) He adds that one of his last acts as
prime minister after the Labour defeat on 3 May 1979
was to break with tradition by allowing the new government to see the papers of the previous government on
this subject.

The Thatcher Years
When the Conservatives came into office under the leadership of Margaret Thatcher, they inherited an ageing
fleet of submarines in need of replacement. The question
for the Conservative government was not whether the
deterrent should be maintained but if the resources
existed to do so. Practical arguments that the country
could no longer afford a nuclear deterrent and that
Britain should concentrate on expanding its conventional force, allowing America to uphold the nuclear elements
of NATO's defence, fell on deaf ears. It was clear that in
any event, the Conservative government would continue
with a nuclear programme. In their eyes, they had
already won the political argument during the election
and the focus should be on practical issues. They were
concerned about what type of force they were going to
deploy, and with which of two possible partners to col-
laborate: the French with their M4 Submarine Launched
Ballistic Missiles (SLBM) or Cruise Missiles; or the
Americans with either Polaris housed in new submarines,

Cruise missiles or Trident. The first option was ruled out at an early stage for both political and strategic reasons. The Conservatives regarded French technology as inferior to American, and this was not surprising given that the French were making do with a fraction of American funding.

The British had been working with the Americans for over 20 years and had built up close ties within the scientific communities. Admittedly, the early 1970s had seen the traditional 'special relationship' coming under increasing strain. President Nixon had singled out West Germany as a key ally in Europe, while Edward Heath had been one Britain's most anti-American Prime Ministers. But Mrs Thatcher wanted to nurture this relationship. She saw the role of bridge between Europe and America as uniquely suitable for Britain, and believed that this would complement rather than detract from British interests in Europe. With the Cold War reaching a new intensity, close nuclear co-operation between London and Washington was seen as a political necessity in both capitals. For Britain, it would reaffirm the country's close ties with America, and for the US, would provide a staunch partner to share the burden of providing Europe's nuclear defence.

Some analysts argued that there was no need to replace Polaris missiles as long as new submarines were built to house them. They suggested that Britain could buy the missile production line from the Americans and therefore become independent again. If Britain had taken this path it could in theory have saved a lot of expense. But many problems were foreseen. Britain would no longer be at the leading edge of nuclear weapon development. The Polaris missiles had a shelf life of approximately 15 years, and after this time their usefulness would be in serious doubt. The maintenance of an ageing weapon system would entail higher life-cycle costs. With production in America ended, Britain would have to deal with any problems that arose. And it was unlikely that the American government would have been as accommodating with its testing facilities once the information collated was no longer of mutual interest. Britain also had recent experience of making solitary nuclear decisions. The *Chevaline* project had cost over £1 billion and had demonstrated the difficulties posed by operating with unfamiliar technology. There was little enthusiasm for following that route again: to have done so would have served no political or strategic end.

Cruise missiles were an attractive alternative. These weapons have a range of around 2000 miles and can be launched from a variety of platforms such as trucks, aircraft or submarines. Using terrain-following radar, they can fly at low level to penetrate an enemy's air defences. But ground-launched missiles would be limited by lack of range in the targets they could attack, and would also be vulnerable to a first strike by the Soviets. Air-launched missiles were vulnerable not only to surprise attack on their bases but also *en route* to the point of launch. Therefore, submarines were still the most promising platform. However, the cost of building boats equipped for Cruise missiles was not much less than for those intended to carry ballistic missiles, even if special strategic submarines were designed and built for this purpose. The Americans were already investing a great deal of money in Cruise missiles, and as a result the Soviets were building defences against them. These defences were designed to counter the large number of missiles the Americans were expected to deploy, and there were fears that these would all but overwhelm the much smaller numbers the British could hope to possess. The British would also be dependent upon the Americans for the accurate targeting (provided by satellites) that the missiles needed to be effective. These were all sound strategic reasons for not purchasing Cruise missiles and there was also an unspoken political one. If they bought Trident the Conservative government could say that they were acquiring a system at the highest level of technical accomplishment.

Trident
Trident was to be the top-line American strategic submarine missile system from the late 1980s onwards, and was a generation ahead of any rival. It became from the outset the preferred option of Mrs Thatcher's government and for herself was an 'of course' decision. There were a number of solid advantages that supported this preference:

(1) As a launch platform, the Trident submarine would be essentially invulnerable. While Anti - Submarine War-

fare (ASW) techniques were improving all the time the advent of a 'transparent ocean' was not taken seriously. There was no serious challenge in prospect to a submarine which patrolled sensibly and quietly. The missiles range of over 4000 miles, coupled with the ability of a submarine to roam the seas unmolested, made possible a much wider target coverage for Trident.

(2) The number of Trident missiles needed to provide a realistic deterrent was much smaller than the number of Cruise missiles which could have a comparable effect, and this made the system cost-effective if one adopted the 'Moscow Criterion'. Existing submarine facilities in Scotland could be used, albeit with some alterations to house the new submarines, and the expertise of existing submarine crews would not be wasted. Trident was a proven system that enjoyed the full support of the American government and the military. Co-operation between the American and British nuclear establishments would be maintained and full commonality would be enjoyed.

There may be some truth in the suggestion that once the decision to maintain a nuclear force was taken, Trident was chosen simply as the most impressive status symbol. But the choice of Trident could equally be defended on the grounds that it was the most effective and economic way to fulfil its role. The government was particularly keen to stress the advantages of buying this system as opposed to opting for an all-British system. As John Baylis has pointed out, Trident was to provide 'a continued assurance of weapon system reliability without the large investment programme which would be required to provide an equivalent degree of assurance with a weapons system unique to Britain. We would also benefit from significantly reduced operating costs compared with those of a UK-unique system.' (104)

The Duff-Mason studies formed the basis on which the Thatcher government worked. Once again a small group of ministers was chosen to carry the project forward. They formed official Cabinet Committee MISC 7, made up of the Prime Minister, William Whitelaw (Home Secretary), Lord Carrington (Foreign Secretary), Geoffrey Howe (Chancellor) and Francis Pym (Defence Secretary). According to Lord Pym, '...because of the immense expansion of nuclear weapons on the Soviet side, it was necessary for the West to have a deterrent that was going to be adequate to the task...in January 1980 [I] persuaded my cabinet colleagues to allow a debate on nuclear weapons policy to be heard in the House of Commons. It was well received on both sides of the House'. (105)

In the same month, an agreement was signed to allow American Ground Launched Cruise Missiles (GLCMs) to be based in Britain. This was followed on 13 June by the agreement to purchase the Trident I system. The missiles (designated C-4). together with equipment and supporting services. would be supplied on a similar basis to *Polaris*. This meant that Britain had to pay five per cent of the research and development costs and was also expected to provide the air defence for American bases in Britain. The outlay was estimated at £4.5-5 billion. This deal was seen as reaffirming the 'special relationship' and it demonstrated the importance America attached to Britain's independent nuclear capability. In July 1980, the decision to procure Trident was made public. The full Cabinet was not consulted until the morning of the announcement although there was never any doubt that it would endorse Trident. Mrs Thatcher was determined to win public support for the decision and letters of agreement were published by the government accompanied by a document that argued the case for Trident at some length. (106) Having won an election just over a year before, and with solid party support Mrs Thatcher felt that it was safe to bring the issue into the open. Hence by 1980, the government had successfully stage-managed the provision of a successor system for *Polaris*. In 1981, the programme was commended in Defence Secretary John Nott's *Defence Review* as providing a deterrent that was both economical and unique. While various arms of the military were to suffer reductions under the Review, Trident was preserved intact. Lord Pym comments: '...People complained about the cost of Trident. However, the actual thinking about it was not criticised...I made speeches in the House of Commons and in the provinces on the whole theory and practice of the nuclear deterrent because I wished the electorate to be fully aware of all the arguments and the rationale of the case. Of course there are always dissidents and nuclear protesters, but I believe that we persuaded people of the intellectual argument and justified the reasons why we pursued the policies that we did.' (107)

The need for a nuclear deterrent was indeed accepted by a large majority in the country. The Soviet Union had invaded Afghanistan on Christmas Day 1979 and was introducing new conventional weapons systems at a pace that many Western analysts feared would threaten NATO's ability to withstand a full-scale assault. There was always the unspoken fear that the American government would desert Europe if a deal were struck between them and the Soviets. Possession of its own nuclear weapons meant that Britain could indeed act as a second decision-making centre. Politics and strategy thus linked hands, and by fulfilling the strategic role of protecting Europe against the Soviets, Britain could help to hedge against any future vagaries of American foreign policy. Trident could be seen as supporting Britain's abiding quest for influence in Europe out of all proportion to her economic strength.

By October 1981, however, a new problem arose. US President Ronald Reagan had come to office at the start of the year on a platform that included a rapid increase in American military power. An important element of this was to be the early replacement of the Trident I, C-4 missile with a new version called Trident II, D-5. This meant that if Britain wanted to continue with C-4, it would do so alone. The D-5 missile was a generation ahead of the C-4 and two generations ahead of *Polaris*. Whilst *Polaris* was a relatively inaccurate system with a warhead designed to land within a mile of its target, Trident was essentially a precision system intended to attack military facilities rather than populations. Both types of Trident missile were to be fitted with Multiple Independently Targeted Re-Entry Vehicles (MIRVs), which allowed each warhead to be guided onto a separate target as it re-entered the atmosphere. The C-4 missile, although a counter-force weapon intended to attack Soviet missile bases and hardened command and control centres, had only a 100kt. warhead and its hard-target potential was limited. Britain had agreed to buy this missile because it was the only design that came close to fitting its needs. But it was also clear that even the C-4 provided a level of capability that conflicted with the government's claim not to be interested in fighting (as opposed to deterring) a nuclear war. Could the move to a further generation ahead of this be justified? If D-5 missiles were deployed with their maximum load of warheads, Britain would possess a strategic arsenal four times its existing size. This would clearly be a significant escalation.

In reality, the Thatcher government had little choice but to agree. The new system was certainly more sophisticated than was necessary for Britain's needs, but this had already been the case with the original Trident project. The dangers of continuing alone with a superseded system that had told against retaining *Polaris* still applied, and the need for commonality was seen as overriding. To carry on with the original Trident programme would have incurred logistic, operational and financial penalties, and the new contract Britain negotiated was more favourable than the old one. So, a fixed price of $116 million was agreed as a fair share of American research and development costs and a new contract was signed in March 1981. While the revised overall cost of the Trident system rose to £7.5 billion, most of the increase was due to the effects of inflation. British firms were given the opportunity to bid for sub-contacts within the Trident system. Britain was able to secure such a comparatively favourable deal because President Reagan was keen to help out what he saw as America's oldest ally, and he believed that Britain remained a key contributor to the defence of the West. This time, the full cabinet was involved in the decision to buy Trident II. As Sir Frank Cooper, who was Permanent Secretary at the Ministry of Defence at this time, says: 'I don't think the full cabinet is brought into a lot of things until just before various announcements are made. I think people worry increasingly about leaks. If they are taking some kind if decision which is likely to cause political problems, they tend to plot a path where a great deal of work is done in a small group or a cabinet committee. They move ahead through the various stages quite quickly to avoid some burglarised account coming out of some unknown source.' (108)

The Strategic Defence Initiative
In 1983, a further problem arose when President Reagan announced funding for the Strategic Defence Initiative (SDI), popularly known as the 'Star Wars' programme.

The intention behind this was to produce a variety of space-based weapons that would be able to intercept and destroy enemy ballistic missiles before they could enter the atmosphere over America, thus rendering such missiles 'impotent and obsolete'. The British amongst others were concerned that America was moving away from a policy of deterrence to one of defence, and in particular a defence that did not seem to include Europe. Fears began to arise that with this system in place, the Americans would be inclined to disengage from Europe and retreat behind their anti-ballistic missile shield. Mrs Thatcher put pressure on President Reagan to make it clear that the SDI was regarded as an addition to traditional deterrence and not as an alternative to it. On the strength of this assurance, Mrs Thatcher entered into the programme with enthusiasm and a number of British scientists contributed to the research. The fears the system had generated at its inception receded through the 1980s as it became clear how large a gap there was between intention and reality. SDI absorbed large amounts of money without producing any credible results. It was all but scrapped by President George Bush's administration after his election in 1988 and continues today as a research programme with much more limited aims.

A White Elephant?
The contract for the first British Trident submarine *Vanguard* was signed in April 1986. In October of the following year it was announced that the missiles were to be serviced in the American King's Bay facility in Georgia rather than the *Polaris* facility at Coulport, Scotland. Whilst the decision was made on the sensible grounds of saving cost and wasteful duplication of facilities, it represented a further degree of dependence upon the United States. On 21 May 1989, the first test launch of a D5 missile ended with a spectacular explosion due to a failure in the first stage rocket. But the problem was corrected and successful firings soon followed. 1989/90 was the peak year of spending on Trident, and it was clear that the system was on course to enter service. (109)

Then, in 1989, the Soviet Union began its rapid collapse and the primary reason for possessing Trident vanished. The programme had survived domestic criticism over its cost, its perceived reliance on America and a mix ture of international and domestic pressures from those who wanted it sacrificed in the name of disarmament. Had it then become a White Elephant at the final stage? It can be argued that Trident provides (rather ironically) exactly the right capability for a post-Cold War deterrent: accuracy, range and flexibility. On this basis. the D-5 missile makes more sense now than it did when it was ordered. But this begs the question whether Britain in particular needs or can afford this kind of capability at all in the new circumstances? This discussion lies outside the scope of history and forms a principal underlying theme for the remainder of the book

Conclusion

In reflecting on this story it is well to bear in mind some salient features of Britain's position after the end of the Second World War in 1945. At that time, the country was still the world's third-ranked power, the only one between the two superpowers with important residual responsibilities world-wide. Britain felt herself highly exposed geopolitically, especially after the US air bases made her a prime target of possible Soviet air attack. Until 1949, NATO did not exist. Britain's economic difficulties and energy shortage in the early post-War years made the promise of unlimited nuclear energy irresistible. And by the late 1950s, Britain was determined to find an effective but much cheaper system of defence which would serve to reduce conventional forces and end National Service. All these were good objective reasons for seeking a modest nuclear weapons capability. A point of particular interest is the degree to which US policy has in fact dominated decision-making in Whitehall. Britain has been determined to keep its nuclear weapons as a restraining influence on the US as well as on Russia and to balance the other nuclear weapons powers. Likewise, once the British nuclear weapons establishment had been set up to design, create and nurture the bomb, as well as to deliver it in anger if need arose, this created a powerful vested interest concerned to perpetuate and if possible extend its influence. Trident is now at sea, with the Union Jack flying above it, almost fifty years on from Bevin's famous comment, and it will endure until well into the 2020's. Nevertheless since 1969, when Polaris came on station, Britain has had to rely increasingly on

American technology and this is not exactly what Ernest Bevin had in mind.

References

(1) For details of the competition between the nuclear physicists, see Alwyn McKay, *The Making of the Atomic Age*, Open University Press, 1984, pp. 28-19 and 35.

(2) J Newhouse, *The Nuclear Age, From Hiroshima to Star Wars*, Michael Joseph, London 1989, p.1-53.

(3) It is an odd fact that the bombardment of uranium with neutrons had been investigated by Enrico Fermi's group in Rome as early as 1934, and in the Cavendish Laboratory soon after, without either realising that the result was to break up the uranium nucleus into two large fragments (barium and rare earths). The Cavendish had even detected strong pulses but put these down to faulty detectors! Hahn and Strassman were chemists and identified the products correctly.

(4) Newhouse: *The Nuclear Age*, p.1-53.

(5) Robert W.Reid, *Tongues of Conscience: War and the Scientists' Dilemma*. Constable, London 1969, p. 101.

(6) An American mission led by the scientist Samuel Goudsmit discovered files in the University of Strasbourg that had been newly liberated by the Allies. These files showed that the German project, while of high scientific quality, never got beyond the laboratory stage. There is still much speculation about what the Germans were actually doing throughout this period and the story arose that Heisenberg deliberately stalled the project. Nevertheless clandestine recordings of German scientists conversations after hearing the news of Hiroshima, made during their internment in Britain in 1945, showed that this was not the case. Roger Ruston, *A Say in the End of The World, Morals and British Nuclear Weapons Policy*, Oxford University Press, 1989, p.85.

(7) For more information see, Rudolf Peierls, 'The Uncertain Scientist', *New York Review of Books*, 23 April 1992, p.43-45 and *The Farm Hall Papers, Operation Epsilon*, 1993. Also Reid: *Tongues of Conscience*, pp. 117-122 and Michael Frayn, *Copenhagen*, Methuen 1998.

(8) Rudolf Peierls, 'The Uncertain Scientist', p. 45.

(9) Rudolf Peierls, BBC Radio 4 Interview (Presented by Peter Hennessy, Produced by Caroline Anstey) Bloody Union Jack on Top Of It, An 'Of Course Decision', 5 May

1988. The text of the Peierls-Frisch Memorandum is given in Margaret Gowing, and Lorna Arnold, *The Atomic Bomb*, Butterworth, 1979.

(10) Margaret Gowing, *Britain and Atomic Energy 1939-1945*, Macmillan, London, 1964, p.43.

(11) George Thomson was the son of J. J. Thomson who discovered the electron in 1897.

(12) For years, it was believed that the acronym M.A.U.D stood for Military Applications of Uranium Disintegration. This was not the case, however, and the story behind the name is as follows. On behalf of Niels Bohr, Lise Meitner, who lived in Stockholm, sent a telegram to her nephew Frisch, assuring him that Bohr and his family, who were Jewish, had come to no harm when the Germans took over Denmark. In the telegram she requested Frisch to tell John Cockroft and Maud Ray Kent. The latter was governess to Bohr's children. For years, it was thought that Maud Ray Kent was a code for the discoveries and work on the atomic bomb. Interview with Sir Rudolf Peierls 1991. See Nadine Gurr 'Arms Control and Middle Powers, The Role of the UK in the Partial Test Ban Treaty Negotiations 1952-1963', (unpublished PhD thesis) Southampton University, 1995.

(13) Report of the MAUD Committee on the Use of Uranium for a Bomb, Ministry of Aircraft Production, July 1941. Quoted in J.B.Poole, *Independence and Interdependence: A Reader on British Nuclear Weapons Policy*, Brassey's, London, 1990. It is reproduced in full in Gowing: *Britain and Atomic Energy 1939-1945*, St. Martin's Press, New York,1964.

(14) An important influence was that the British information converted the Americans to giving priority to U-235 whereas they had been thinking more about the element 94, i.e. plutonium. In the event, of course, the Manhattan Project did both, but U-235 was the better bet for them. Correspondence with Lorna Arnold 12 July 1997.

(15) Newhouse: *The Nuclear Age*, pp.20-53.

(16) Newhouse: *The Nuclear Age*, pp. 20-53.

(17) Lord Sherfield, Radio 4 Interview, see Note 8 above.

(18) The Military Policy Committee was chaired by Vannevar Bush, with Conant as his alternate. Three military members were appointed: General Wilhelm D. Styer for the Army, Admiral William Purnell for the Navy and

General Leslie Groves, who was to be project manager and vice-president of operations. Newhouse: *The Nuclear Age*, p. 55.

(19) If a chain reaction is to take place in natural uranium it is necessary to slow down or 'moderate' the neutrons. Graphite acts as a 'moderator' for this purpose, controlling the energy of the neutrons. Heavy water is an alternative material.

(20) The Los Alamos site was like a small city and it had schools and hospitals for the families of all the scientists. Living conditions, however, were bad and most of the housing took the form of temporary shelters, prefabrication, trailers, caravans and mobile units. There was only one telephone for all the personnel. But most of the chemists, physicists, engineers and technicians were young and able to endure such conditions.

(21) Interview with Norman Moss 23 December 1996.

(22) Newhouse: *The Nuclear Age*, pp. 33-35.

(23) Gowing: *Britain and Atomic Energy*, p.258.

(24) Patricia Lewis in Eric Arnett, *Nuclear Weapons After the Comprehensive Test Ban: Implications for Modernisation and Proliferation*, SIPRI, Oxford University Press, 1996, pp. 99-103.

(25) President Truman, then Vice-President, had visited Manhattan Project sites in his capacity as a member of a senate committee. He was not told of the work of the Project and was as much in the dark as many of the participants.

(26) The members of Interim Committee were Stimson, George L Harrison, Bush, Conant, Karl Compton, Ralph A. Bard, William L. Clayton and James F. Byrnes.

(27) Members of the Interim Committee discussed other ideas, such as a demonstration of the power of the bomb. They rejected this in case the bomb proved to be a dud and America would lose credibility. They also considered warning the Japanese government but again this was vetoed because it was believed that to do so would lessen the bomb's impact and reinforce the Japanese will not to surrender. Members of the committee also managed to convince Truman that using the bomb would save half a million American lives; and moral, philosophical and religious scruples were put to one side in the light of atrocities being carried out by the Japanese. Perhaps the real reasons for using the bomb will never be known. What is

known however, is that America was keen to demonstrate both the U-235 and the plutonium bombs before the war ended.

(28) Martin Gilbert, *Churchill, A Life*, Heinemann, London, 1991, p.1019.

(29) Peter Cole the *Guardian* 6 August 1985.

(30) J Hershey, *Hiroshima*, Penguin, London, 1985.

(31) Interview with Sir Leonard Cheshire 1991. See Nadine Gurr: 'Arms control'.

(32) Interview with Tony Benn 1991. See Nadine Gurr: 'Arms Control'.

(33) Lord Sherfield, Radio 4 Interview, See note 8 above.

(34) Lord Sherfield, Radio 4 Interview, See note 8 above.

(35) Lord Sherfield, Radio 4 Interview, See Note 8 above.

(36) Interview with Sir Michael Perrin, BBC 2 "Timewatch", cited in Radio 4 Programme, see Note 8 above.

(37) Ruston: *A Say in the End of the World*, p.90.

(38) E.Barker, *Britain in a Divided Europe*, Macmillan, London, 1986. p.39.

(39) Interview with Sir Frank Cooper, Radio 4, See Note 8 above.

(40) Interview with Tony Benn 1991. See Nadine Gurr: 'Arms Control'.

(41) Margaret Gowing, 'The Special Relationship', Louis and Bull, *Anglo American Relations*, Clarendon Press, Oxford 1986, p.97.

(42) Gowing: 'The special relationship', p.150.

(43) Ruston: *A Say in the End of the World*, pp.96-97.

(44) Henry Tizard, Minute to Cabinet Colleagues, cited in Radio 4 Programme, Note 8 above

(45) Interview with Professor Michael Herman, 7 March 1998.

(46) Ruston: *A Say in the End of the World*, pp.99-106.

(47) Fuchs passed research materials to Soviet intelligence which were later distributed to Soviet physicists. He had provided descriptions of the American A-bomb which were to help the Soviets enormously. Yuli Khariton, a Soviet nuclear physicist and one-time scientific director of Arzamas-16, the first Soviet nuclear weapons laboratory, said in 1993, 'The information was very helpful but also very difficult. We had sketches but we did not have all the calculations. The experiments done at Los Alamos had to be repeated to make sure that

the Fuchs material was genuine'. After fierce arguments, the team abandoned its own design and copied the American one, a decision Khariton supported. Khariton believed that the material from Fuchs had brought forward the explosion by two or three years. Two years later, a bomb made to the original Soviet design was exploded, equally successfully: it was only half as big, but had twice the yield. Yuli Khariton, *The Times* 20 December 1996. See also Yuli Khariton, Victor Adamskii and Yuri Smirnov, 'The Way It Was', *The Bulletin of the Atomic Scientists*, November/December 1996, pp.53-59, Norman Moss, *Klaus Fuchs, the Man who Stole the Atom Bomb*, St. Martin's Press US, Grafton Press UK, 1897. Also papers by G. Goncharov in *Physics Today* November 1996. Interview with Mr Norman Moss, 23 December 1996.

(48) Ruston: *A Say in the End of the World*, pp.99-106.

(49) Alan Macmillan and John Baylis. *A Reassessment of the British Global Strategy Paper of 1952*. Department of International Politics University of Wales, Aberystwyth in association with the Nuclear History Program, International Politics Research Papers, Number 13, 1993.

(50) Andrew Pierre, *Nuclear Politics*, Oxford University Press, London and New York, 1972 pp. 1,87.

(51) Interview with Lord Plowden 1991. See Nadine Gurr: 'Arms Control'.

(52) Lorna Arnold, *A Very Special Relationship, British Atomic Weapon Trials in Australia*, HMSO Publications, 1987, p.2.

(53) Interview with Lord Plowden, Radio 4, Note 8.

(54) Interview with Victor Macklen, Radio 4, Note 8.

(55) Patricia Lewis, 'The United Kingdom', in Eric Arnett (Editor), *Nuclear Weapons after the Comprehensive Test Ban: Implications for Modernisation and Proliferation*, Swedish International Peace Research Institute, Oxford University Press, 1996, p 101. 'The Comprehensive Test Ban: Not Quite a Treaty'. *Strategic Comments*, IISS, Vol.2, No.6, July 1996.

(56) The cabinet papers about the H-bomb decision are cited in Jan Melissen, *The Struggle for Nuclear Partnership*, Styx, 1993, p.31.

(57) Gowing, *The Special Relationship*, p.194.

(58) Public Record Office Documents: PRO, CAB, 131/12, D(52)26 'Defence policy and Global Strategy', 17 June

1952 and PRO, ADM 205/89, DNI (8529), 6 July 1953.
(59) Ruston: *A Say in the End of the World*, pp.122-126.
(60) Interview with Sir Richard Powell, Radio 4, Note 8.
(61) Interview with Lord Plowden, Radio 4, Note 8.
(62) Interview with Dr Eric Grove 14 November 1996.
(63) Interview with Victor Macklen, Radio 4, Note 8.
(64) Interview with Professor Peter Nailor, Radio 4, Note 8.
(65) Interview with Professor Peter Nailor, Radio 4, Note 8.
(66) Interview with Sir Philip de Zulueta, Radio 4, Note 8.
(67) Interview with Lord Home, Radio 4, Note 8.
(68) Interview with Sir Philip de Zulueta, Radio 4, Note 8.
(69) Interview with Sir Philip de Zulueta, Radio 4, Note 8.
(70) Interview with Lord Home. Radio 4 Interview, Note 8.
(71) The text of the Nassau Agreement was given in the White Paper Cmnd. 1915 and published in *The Times* 22 December 1962. See also *Statement on Defence 1964*, HMSO, Cmnd. 2270, February 1964, pp. 6,7.
(72) Interview with Lord Hailsham 17 February 1997.
(73) Interview with Lord Home. See Gurr: 'Arms control.'
(74) H. Wilson, *Let's go with Labour for the New Britain*, September 1964, cited in M.McIntosh, *Managing Britain's Defence*, Macmillan, London, 1990, p.16.
(75) Interview with Lord Home. Radio 4 Interview, Note 8
(76) Interview with Denis Healey, Radio 4 Interview Note 8.
(77) Andrew Pierre, *Nuclear Politics*, Open University Press, London, 1972, p167.
(78) Interview with Professor John Simpson 21 February 1997.
(79) Interview with Denis Healey, Radio 4, Note 8.
(80) Interview with Professor John Simpson 21 February 1997.
(81) This doctrine was first sketched out in the *Statement on Defence 1964*, Cmnd. 2270, p.6 , but was not given complete expression until *Statement on the Defence Estimates 1980*, Volume 1 Cmnd.. 7826-I, HMSO April 1980, p. 12, para. 203, generally understood to be from Sir Michael Quinlan's pen.
(82) Interview with Lord Wilson, Radio 4, Note 8.
(83) Interview with Tony Benn. See Gurr: 'Arms Control'.
(84) The Ministry of Defence is now refurbishing five *Chevaline* re-entry vehicles for display in museums.

Examination of one of these currently held at RAF Kemble shows that the *Chevaline* had only two warheads. This has now been officially confirmed, see *The Strategic Defence Review*, Cm. 3999, The Stationery Office, July 1998, Supporting Essay Five, page-2 para 10: "32 *Chevaline* warheads were eventually deployed on each *Polaris* submarine".

(85) Interview with Lord Owen, Radio 4, Note 8.

(86) Interview with Victor Macklen, Radio 4, Note 8.

(87) *Public Expenditure in 1968-9 and 1969-70* Cmnd. 3515, HMSO, January 1968, p.5.

(88) *Statement on the Defence Estimates 1968*, Cmnd.. 3540, HMSO, February 1968, pp. 3-5. *Supplementary Statement on Defence Policy 1968*, Cmnd.. 3701, HMSO July 1968. p.8. *Statement on the Defence Estimates 1969*, Cmnd.. 3927, HMSO February 1969, pp. 3,4.

(89) Interview with Sir Herman Bondi, Radio 4, Note 8.

(90) Interview with Sir Frank Cooper, Radio 4, Note 8.

(91) Interview with Lord Zuckerman, Radio 4, Note 8.

(92) Interview with Professor John Simpson 21 February 1997.

(93) *'Tony Benn's Diaries'*, 20 November 1974. This extract of Mr Benn's diary was made on the 25 February 1997, and is reproduced in accordance with the wishes of his office.

(94) Interview with Lord Callaghan 13 February 1997.

(95) Lord Healey, cited in *'Tony Benn's Diaries'*, 30 January 1980. This extract of Mr Benn's diary was made on 25 February 1997, and is reproduced in accordance with the wishes of his office.

(96) Interview with Lord Healey, Radio 4, Note 8.

(97) Interview with Sir Ronald Mason, Radio 4, Note 8.

(98) Interview with Lord Callaghan, Radio 4, Note 8.

(99) Interview with Lord Owen, 29 March 1997.

(100) Interview with Lord Owen, 29 March 1997.

(101) Interview with Lord Owen, 29 March 1997.

(102) Interview with Lord Callaghan, Radio 4, Note 8.

(103) Interview with Lord Callaghan 13 February 1997.

(104) J.Baylis, *Anglo-American Defence Relations 1939-1984*, Macmillan, London, 1984, p.184.

(105) Interview with Lord Pym, 11 March 1997.

(106) *Memorandum on the Future United Kingdom Strategic Nuclear Deterrent Force*, Defence Open Government Document 80/23, July 1980. This explained

not only the strategic background and the main consid-erations affecting the choice of system but also which options had been examined and why Trident had been chosen.

(107) Interview with Lord Pym, 11 March 1997.

(108) Interview with Sir Frank Cooper, Radio 4, Note 8.

(109) *The United Kingdom Trident Programme*, Defence Open Government Document 82/1, March 1982.

Sources

There is an important literature which covers the subject of this chapter. Among the most noteworthy are Margaret Gowing's two works on the early history of the British nuclear project: *Britain and Atomic Energy 1939-1945* St. Martin's Press, New York, 1964 and *Independence and Deterrence: Britain and Atomic Energy 1945-52*, (two vol-umes), (with Lorna Arnold), St. Martin's Press, New York, 1974. For the following period see Lawrence Freedman, *Britain and Nuclear Weapons*, Macmillan, London, 1981; Peter Malone *The British Nuclear Deterrent*, Croom Helm, Beckenham, Kent, 1984 and John Baylis (ed.) *British Defence policy in a Changing World*, Croom Helm, 1978.

Other useful sources include:

Norman Moss, *Men Who Play God, The Story of the Hydrogen Bomb*, Penguin Books, London, 1970.

Norman Moss, *Klaus Fuchs, The Man Who Stole the Atom Bomb*, Grafton Books, London, 1989.

John Edmonds, 'A Complete Nuclear Test Ban', *Security Dialogue*, Volume 25, Number 4, December 1994.

Atomic Energy, HMSO, London, 1945.

Jozef Goldblat and C.Cox, *Nuclear Weapon Tests, Prohibition or Limitation*, Swedish International Peace Research Institute, Oxford University Press , 1988, pp. 8-10.

David Omand, 'Nuclear Deterrence in a Changing world, The View from a British perspective', *Defence and International Security*, Royal United Service Institute Journal, June, 1996.

2. THE NUCLEAR BATTLEFIELD

Fortunately, there has never been such a thing as a nuclear battlefield. Nevertheless, the British Army of the Rhine spent much time and effort in trying to imagine what such a battlefield might look like and in preparing to cope with it. During the 1950s and 1960s, these efforts were taken very seriously. This would be an incomplete account of Britain and nuclear weapons if we did not pay some attention to it. We start, therefore, with two vignettes that give the views of military men, both American, as it happens, on nuclear war as it could have affected them

The first comes from William F. Burns, a retired American gunner general, who became a US representative to the Intermediate Nuclear Force negotiations, and then head of the US Arms Control and Disarmament Agency. A big gun, therefore. He is speaking of the mid-1950s when the US Army was first coming to terms with tactical nuclear weapons, in this case the 8-inch howitzer shell. He writes:

> The first nuclear weapon I saw was a training round. It contained only Uranium 238, not Uranium 235 and was not capable of nuclear detonation. It was in the back of an M 109 [howitzer] van tied down with a frayed piece of hemp, and a corporal in the van was going to tell us how to put five components together

and make a 8-inch projectile. After about three hours and many false starts on his part, we were able more or less to put the projectile together with the help of the manual. After this we were certified as being able to build 'a nuclear round', and two weeks later, we deployed to the United States Army, Europe.

In Europe we suddenly found ourselves proud owners not only of a training round but several of those olive green nuclear rounds. It was an interesting situation, because there was very little guidance compared to the guidance in later years. This was before the days of Permissive Action Links or very elaborate release systems. Release was basically tied to the command chain. *'I had no doubt in my military mind that if my battalion com - mander said 'Shoot', we would shoot, and if my battalion commander said 'Don't shoot', we would not shoot. It was as simple as that.* (1)

We move forward 20 years and hear from another important American, Admiral Stansfield Turner, who eventually rose to become head of the Central Intelligence Agency. In 1975 he had been appointed NATO's Commander of the Allied Forces in Southern Europe, with his HQ at Naples. Being a naval man he sought expert army advice on how best to stop a Warsaw Pact advance through the Brenner Pass

I decided to start by talking with Colonel John B. Keely of the U.S. Army, a good friend whom I knew to have an imaginative approach to such problems. Just before coming to the staff of the southern flank, John had commanded the 2nd brigade of the US Army's 3rd Armoured Division. This division was positioned astride Fulda Gap, the principal invasion route from Eastern Europe into West Germany. Although the terrain at the gap was different from that at Brenner Pass, I wanted to talk to John about defence of passes and gaps.

John described the tactics he and his superiors had envisioned for plugging the Fulda. He mentioned that they included atomic demolition munitions (ADMs) to blow up a hillside and send debris cascading onto a key highway. With a wry smile, John said that he had an interesting story about these demolition munitions. During his tour in command, the brigade had been relocated from one position to another just a few miles away. That made it necessary for John to adapt his plans to the differences in terrain. He discovered there was no sensible way to employ ADMs in the new location. He sent his plan for defending his portion of the gap without the use of ADMs up the chain of command. It quickly came back disapproved. His superiors said that the ADMs simply had to be included. Argue as he might, John found there was no way he could turn them in or just hold them in reserve. He had to find the least worst way to incorporate them into his plan. That left him the dilemma of what he would actually do in the event of war. *It was clear that the purpose of these weapons was more for deter - rence than for fighting.* (2)

This conversation led Admiral Turner to ask about plans for using ADMs on the Brenner. He discovered that the plan was to use them to blow up the slender concrete piers supporting the highway. When he asked whether conventional munitions would not do the job just as well, he was greeted by stunned silence.

The fact that we had nuclear weapons that would do the job more assuredly than any other option was enough. There were no calculations to compare not only the effectiveness of the two kinds of explosives, but also their ancillary effects, like radioactive fallout, fires, and electromagnetic interference. Getting the road closed and making use of these weapons, not the total consequences, were what mattered.

I did not tak these ADMs out of the war plans.
It was not worth the probable arguments. *I
just assumed I would not use them if war
came.*' (2)

In these three extracts, the sentences in italics sum
up fairly accurately where the tactical nuclear project
stood in military thinking: the first in the mid-1950s,
the second two in the mid-1970s. The change over that
period is very striking.

We will now try to sketch out how the technology of
tactical nuclear weapons developed, what policies
emerged to justify their use, how they became incorporated into orders of battle and into war plans, the doctrine that sought to make sense of these plans and the
exercises and training that followed from the doctrine.

Technology

The total nuclear stockpile of the United States, at its
highest point, had an estimated explosive yield of some
nine billion tons of high explosive, and the Soviet stockpile must have been much the same. In the 20 years
from 1945 to 1965, nuclear warheads evolved to fill
every possible ecological niche on the battlefield and in
numbers far greater than any rational person could
possibly have considered useful. Why this occurred is
an interesting topic for historians. In our opinion, a
large part of the explanation must lie in 'technology
push' rather than 'demand pull'.

The effects of a nuclear explosion are not pleasant to
write about, but they are necessary. First comes the
heat flash carrying about one third of the total energy.
X-rays from the explosion are absorbed by the surrounding air and progressively re-radiated on longer
wavelengths. This leads to the formation of a luminous
mass of air called the fireball that grows and rises. The
resulting heat can sear the flesh off people in the open
and dry-roast or asphyxiate those in shelters. If it
touches the ground, the fireball gouges out a crater and
vaporises everything in it. Over a town, the effect of heat
flash can cause a fire-storm. Against troops dispersed,
protected and under the cover of armour or dug in, it is
much less of a hazard.

Blast comes next, carrying about half the weapon's

total energy. Its effects depend on the height of burst. In an airburst at medium height, the blast front extends out in two spheres, from the point of detonation and in an echo from the ground, merging into a single so-called *mach* front with roughly double the intensity of each. Behind this come winds of up to several hundred miles an hour. The human body stands up well to blast and can take up to twice normal atmospheric pressure. Much more dangerous, normally, are the shards of masonry, glass etc, propelled around with all the deadly effects of a cluster bomb.

The rest of the energy emerges in the form of radiation: neutrons, X-rays, gamma rays, alpha and beta particles. Dose for dose, neutrons are more dangerous to the human body, but do not travel as far as gamma rays. The effects of radiation fall off faster than blast or heat and of course work more slowly. But it is possible to engineer a weapon so as to increase the amount of neutron flux relative to the other effects. This is the principle of the so-called neutron bomb. Clever propaganda characterised this as a 'capitalist' weapon because it killed people without destroying property - which was absurd. The point was that, within a radius of, say, one kilometre, it could kill troops even in tanks or slit trenches with overhead cover (relatively immune to blast or heat) while causing the least possible 'collateral damage' to the whole area because the total yield could be much smaller.

In addition to the prompt radiation, a nuclear explosion releases some 300 different radioactive products, with half-lives ranging from a fraction of a second to millions of years. These condense on the pulverised fragments of the bomb itself and later on any dust and ash thrown up if the fireball touches the ground. As the mushroom cloud cools these materials fall back to earth in a plume, whose footprint is shaped by local climatic conditions. When in contact with the human body, these materials irradiate the tissues and affect the cell nuclei, chromosomes and genes. The tissues most sensitive are lymphoid tissue, bone marrow, spleen, testicles and the gastro-intestinal tract. Victims get sick, perhaps quite quickly and sooner or later, they may die. Finally, in speaking of the effects of nuclear weapons on the battlefield, one must not overlook the psychological impact. Armies know from experience how soldiers stand up to the hazards of being bayoneted, hit by rifle- or machine gun-fire, or by shrapnel from mortars, guns, howitzers, and rockets. They know how people cope with being brewed up in tanks or APCs, rocketed or bombed from the air, attacked with Napalm or even gas; how they tackle booby traps and anti-personnel minefields. These are all horrible things in their different ways but have some familiarity. But what about nuclear weapons? The first British military publication to tackle this point offered the following thoughts: (3)

> Wide dispersion and isolation, lack of information and fear of the unknown will in future greatly increase the tension of all ranks in battle; and these will be in addition to the awe-inspiring effects of enemy nuclear explosions which will occur throughout the battle area. Furthermore, the impact of high nuclear casualties occurring in a moment of time, rather than being built up over a period, must inevitably tend to affect morale. Indeed, morale will depend on a frame of mind induced by a mixture of anger, hope and confidence, and based upon strict discipline. Morale has always been a prime factor in the conventional battle; in the nuclear battle it will be the supreme factor.

Others, no less wise perhaps, have suggested that after one nuclear weapon had gone off on the battlefield, that would be the end of it; armies would simply refuse to fight. It is impossible to know which view is right, though our own view is closer to the official one than to the radical doubters'. Let us hope that humankind never finds out.

Battlefield weapons
On 17 August 1945, there were no more nuclear weapons left, all three having been expended. The Americans promptly set about making more, and in the next ten years were to amass an inventory of 20,000. In 1946, the US Strategic Air Command (SAC) was formed and nuclear tests carried out at Bikini Atoll. By 1948,

the first large Boeing bombers, B-50 and B-36, became operational. In the summer of 1949, 32 B-29 SAC bombers arrived in Britain. And surprisingly soon, the huge and cumbersome weapons of 1945 had been miniaturised and streamlined down to tactical proportions. First came free-fall bombs, shortly followed in the 1950s by artillery shells, both 8-Inch and, later, 155mm. By 1958, these had been followed by the *Honest John* free-flight rocket with a range of some 15-20 miles, the *Corporal* missile with a range of 70 miles (to be replaced in the 1960s by *Sergeant* with solid fuel propellant and an inertial guidance system); and the *Redstone* missile, derived from the German V-2 rocket of the Second World War (to be replaced by *Pershing*, a two-stage solid- fuelled version with a range of 300 miles). At much the same time (early 1960s) it was decided to equip *Nike Hercules* surface-to-air defence missiles (SAM) with nuclear warheads and produce nuclear landmines (the ADMs already referred to) as well as nuclear depth charges for anti-submarine warfare. Finally, and most absurdly among tactical nuclear weapons, came *Davy Crockett*, described as a two-man weapon carried by hand or mounted on a small truck, usable by any infantry battalion (or even company) in place of an ordinary mortar. This went into service in the early 1960s. It had a range of 2000 meters and a sub-kiloton yield. (4) It was soon realised that in most tactical settings the Army's own forward troops would be within the danger radius for blast, and after about five years *Davy Crockett* was quietly withdrawn. But it took a further 20 years, till the mid-80s, before NATO recognised, for very similar reasons, just how dangerous the nuclear air-defence missile and the nuclear landmine were and to make plans for their removal.

Here is an unoffical inventory of NATOs tactical nuclear stockpile in Europe in the 1970s: (5)

  2250 artillery shells
  1850 free fall bombs
   700 NIKE Hercules SAMs
   300 Atomic Demolition Munitions
   400 Anti-submarine Warfare weapons
   180 Pershing 1a
    90 Honest John
    97 Lance surface to surface missile

There are two important points to note. First, all the warheads for these weapons were in American ownership and custody. One third were for use by American forces. The rest were for use by other nations under 'dual key' control. This meant that bilateral agreements had been reached with the governments of Britain, the Netherlands, Germany, Italy and Greece whereby the aircraft, missile or gun belonged to the 'host nation' while the warhead, shell or bomb remained the property of the US, even after launching. When the moment came to fire, this needed the concurrence of both the American and the 'host nation' officers at the firing point, each having been properly authorised *via* his own national chain of command by his respective national release authority. All this could take a long time, even days. A second very important point is that, with a few years' time lag perhaps, the Soviet Union matched the Americans in nearly all this weaponry. But they did not make their weapons available to allies under a 'dual key' system, no doubt because they did not trust them. Nor, as far as is known, did they have anything to match the *Davy Crockett*. For many years. their inventory of tactical nuclear weapons was assessed as being about half that of NATO, but this imbalance had little operational significance. For all practical purposes, where tactical nuclear weapons were concerned, the situation between NATO and the Warsaw Pact was symmetrical.

Strategic concepts
For some 12 years after 1945, the United States enjoyed a period of unchallenged nuclear superiority, in spite of the explosion of a Soviet atomic bomb in 1949 and the development of thermonuclear weapons in the 1950s. Lacking intercontinental missiles, and with their long-range bomber programme proving a fiasco, the Soviet Union could not get anywhere near the continental United States. In the Eisenhower era, there was no doubt who would 'win' a nuclear war. The strategic policy of 'punishing aggression' by what was called 'massive retaliation' at 'times and places of our own choosing' against Soviet centres of power - often described as the 'Dulles doctrine' - was typically arrogant but credible. A complementary strategy was evolved for NATO. The conventional forces being mustered on the conti-

nent would need to be sufficient only to identify aggression and delay advancing forces until the forces of SAC could be brought to bear. It was not a policy that anyone much liked but it was unavoidable until such time as NATO's forces could be built up to constitute a deterrent their own right. Until then their task was to act as 'tripwire' or even more disparagingly as a 'plate glass window'.

Nor did the process of force development go at all smoothly. At Lisbon in 1952 NATO ministers had adopted the goal of building up defensive forces to a level of 96 divisions, ready within thirty days. 25 of these divisions were to be stationed in peace time on the Central front. Two years later, this goal was abandoned as unrealistic and a new target adopted of 30 divisions on the central sector, including the twelve divisions to be supplied by Germany under the Paris agreement of 1954. These divisions were all to be armed with 'modern' (i.e. atomic) weapons and NATO planning was officially based for the next ten years on the principle that nuclear weapons would be used tactically from the outset in response to almost any aggression. Where the major powers were concerned, limited war was inconceivable.

But despite the enthusiasm that greeted this decision and the American undertaking in 1957 to accelerate delivery of suitable weapons, their arrival was in fact very slow, only really getting under way at the end of the decade. The make-up of the 'shield' force of 30 divisions was set out in the supposedly confidential but in fact much publicised NATO document MC 70 of 1957, but the reality never quite caught up. The tally in 1962, for example, came to 23.33 divisions made up as follows: Germany 8 (with four more to follow), US 5, UK 3, France, Belgium, Netherlands each 2 and Canada one brigade. In principle all these were to be equipped and trained with nuclear weapons. As Fred Mulley commented in 1962; (6) 'Twenty-eight full strength divisions would be enough to discharge the tasks allotted to the Shield forces, but unhappily it is unlikely that the additional forces will be forthcoming in the near future. The present paper force of 23.33 divisions represents a fighting equivalent of no more than 16 to 19 divisions'. No wonder, as The Times commented. (7) 'the nuclear artillery has been enthroned in the training manuals as the queen of the battlefield, and the infantry and the armour are now regarded as its supporting arms. Through no fault of its own, the Rhine Army is not organised to react promptly with conventional weapons'. Exercise *Spearpoint* in 1961, the largest manoeuvres of the nuclear epoch until then, revealed that BAOR would be incapable of defending itself even for a short time without nuclear support, even if its strategic posture were to be changed to conform to the developing NATO policy of seeking to 'enforce a pause' by conventional means. (8)

The Americans have always been susceptible to scares and the arrival in orbit of the Russian artificial earth satellite *Sputnik I* in 1957 was a turning point. The huge rocket that had lifted it was relatively crude but it could have delivered a payload over the United States. The development of true Inter-Continental Ballistic Missiles (ICBMs) began at the same time. It was clear that the period of assured US ascendancy was soon to end. With the US itself vulnerable, massive retaliation in response to a conventional challenge in Europe was no longer believable. The arrival of the Kennedy administration in 1961 and the new Secretary of Defence Robert McNamara, brought a new formulation: (9)

> We believe in a policy of controlled, flexible response where the military force of the United States would become a finely tuned instrument of national policy, versatile enough to meet with appropriate force the full spectrum of possible threats to our national security.

At the strategic level, the first response was to emphasise 'counterforce'. Soviet weapons were the strategic targets and senior commanders still talked as though a nuclear war could be 'won'. Then the danger of this approach dawned. As the Soviet Union slowly developed the means of delivering a massive blow against the United States, so the notion of 'riding out' a first strike and then delivering a counter-blow on what could only be empty silos and deserted bomber bases became highly unattractive. The result was a shift back to 'city-busting', holding the people rather than the weapons as hostages. 400 one megaton weapons able to hit area targets would suffice. This totally amoral doctrine was dressed up under the term Mutual Assured Destruction, and its appropriate acronym MAD.

The tactical counterpart to this change of heart took a further five years to mature. It came to be realised that large-scale assault on NATO, while still a deadly danger, was by no means the only nor even the most likely contingency. Attacks with relatively limited objectives must also be anticipated. McNamara's 'flexible response', which became the shorthand title for the whole new concept, clearly required a better balanced mixture of conventional, tactical-nuclear and strategic-nuclear forces. The new policy emerged finally in the NATO Document MC 14/3 (10) known as the 'Athens guidelines' of 1967.

These were later amended by the Nuclear Planning Group guidelines of 1969, the 'first strike' guidelines of 1972 and various biennial ministerial guidelines thereafter. The essence of this policy was to defend at three possible levels: direct defence (which meant conventional defence) against a non-nuclear attack for as long as possible; controlled escalation through the use of tactical nuclear weapons and finally general nuclear response if all else failed. While obviously much more sensible than the preceding 'trip-wire' strategy, this had the unwelcome consequence of requiring NATO to provide larger conventional forces in Germany backed up by immediately available reinforcements. At that time, all the allies were feeling a financial pinch and, apart from the resuscitated Germany, were seeking to reduce spending on defence. The idea of producing expensive additional conventional forces to 'raise the nuclear threshold' was to nobody's liking. Indeed, the size of RAF Germany was sharply reduced in the early 1960s and the French hardly helped by withdrawing from the military structure altogether in 1966. This dilemma was never resolved, though certainly, valiant efforts were made to upgrade the quality and firepower of tanks, tactical aircraft and so forth as well as their logistic backing. In the mid 1980s General Hackett's famous best selling book on the Third World War (11) was expressly designed to point the moral that stronger conventional forces were still needed on the North German Plain.

Whether the book was understood that way is a different question.

Orders of Battle and plans

The British were unique in having a treaty commitment to maintain a minimum number of troops on the continent. Under Article VI of Protocol No II to the modified Brussels Treaty of 1954, the British undertook to keep four divisions on mainland Europe as a confidence-building measure related to the re-armament of Germany. Within four years, despite the extreme reluctance of their partners, the British had whittled the force down to three divisions. In the financial squeeze of the mid-1960s, one of the remaining six brigades was re-located to the UK, but to Britain's credit this was sent back in 1970. The commitment was a large one - some 55,000 men all told, including the brigade in Berlin, or about one third of the British army's strength. The troops were accompanied by an equal number of wives and children and were supported by some 30,000 civilians. On mobilisation, the strength was planned to more than double, with additional regular troops and a host of reserve units and individuals being sent from the UK. It is hard to see how Britain could have done much more.

In 1950, before the build up of forces under NATO had begun, the only Allied formations available to defend the sector between Hamburg and the Harz mountains had been the British occupation forces consisting of the 2nd Infantry and 7th Armoured Divisions, a weak Dutch Corps in the Netherlands, a Belgian armoured division and a Canadian brigade group. It was appreciated by intelligence experts that the Russians, if they ever got around to invading West Germany, would be able to use the greater part of some 50 tank divisions and 30 mechanised divisions. All of these were equipped with the impressive tanks that had recently defeated the Wehrmacht so conclusively. The best the Headquarters British Army of the Rhine (BAOR) could devise was a plan based on trying to defend the Rhine while trusting that the American bombers would come to the rescue in time. By 1952 there were three British armoured divisions on the scene, a British nuclear bomb had been successfully exploded and the first tests of an American

8-inch nuclear cannon shell were imminent. Information from these and earlier test explosions appeared to show that armoured vehicles moving at speed through irradiated areas provided their crews with far more effective screening than any other means of protection, quite apart from shielding against blast and heat. With growing confidence, it was decided to move the main defensive line up to the River Weser. A decade later, the adoption of 'flexible response' required fresh thinking. This had several important connotations. Firstly, against a massed, heavily reinforced thrust from the east, NATO forces would have to win a few days' grace for the politicians by the use of conventional weapons alone. In addition, the idea of hundreds of square miles of ground in the heart of Europe devastated by nuclear explosions had been recognised as military as well as political nonsense. 'Flexible response' also meant that instead of being the means to redress our conventional inferiority and produce a stalemate on the battlefield, tactical nuclear weapons had become, in effect, political weapons whose purpose would be to stop the fighting and produce negotiations to put an end to the war. The Allies therefore had to be prepared to engage in a pell-mell armoured battle from the outset. And in planning terms, the first principal engagements would have to take place further forward than had previously been envisaged. This clearly had great political advantages as far as the Germans were concerned, but meant that the BAOR would have to fight with a major water obstacle at its rear. Forward dumps were needed, and there were other logistical implications. All these were a direct consequence of MC 14/3 and were in train by the late 1960s

Tactical Doctrine

Although the first exercise in the BAOR to practise the tactical employment of atomic weapons was held as early as 1954, there was, as yet, no established doctrine, and commanders had to improvise from their own resources. Then, in 1958, a short booklet appeared, entitled 'The Corps Tactical Battle in Nuclear War': it was nicknamed 'The Purple Pamphlet' because of its garish cover. Its currency lasted ten years, from 1958 to 1968, the only period when the British Army had a genuine nuclear battle-fighting agenda. Its relevance ceased with the 'Athens Guidelines' of 1967 which, as we have seen, laid down the doctrine of 'direct defence', requiring the tactical battle to be fought *without* nuclear weapons; only when defeat was imminent could nuclear 'release' be countenanced.

Nine years earlier, however, The Purple Pamphlet had made some obvious assumptions about the British order of battle. It was strong in armour, with most of the infantry transported in amphibious armoured personnel carriers and, by way of nuclear fire-power, equipped with the 8- inch gun, *Honest John* and *Corporal*. The role of the tactical air force was to destroy the enemy's airfields and nuclear delivery capability and to impede his forward movement and supplies. Direct close air support would be quite exceptional. The life and work of the fighting soldier would not be much affected except for some energetic trench digging. There would be a huge premium on concealment, and on the need to fight and move at night. Up the chain of command there was need to countenance much greater dispersion and a quite new type of battle plan. Some interesting general points were made. First, the possibility of sudden and violent changes in the battle situation called for greater flexibility on the part of commanders and the need to work from broad directives rather than detailed orders and battle procedures as in the past.

Secondly, the effect of ground was redefined. Instead of the long-standing notion of holding ground 'vital to the defence' it seemed that the future value of ground was to provide observation and affect movement. Control of an area would have to be retained by 'offensive mobile' operations. Thirdly, nuclear artillery would become the predominant arm. Planning would centre on the positioning of the nuclear missile launchers. Nuclear target acquisition and analysis became key staff functions, as did the calculation of safety distances and the warning of our own troops when our own strikes were imminent. Time had to be allowed for this and special warning procedures devised. There was much discussion of how to deal with the 'crust' of enemy forces left between our front lines and the nearest enemy positions that could safely be assaulted with nuclear weapons.

The Corps tactical plan was still to be based on a major obstacle, preferably a river line but possibly consisting of demolitions and minefields. This was seen as even more important than before. There were four phases to the projected battle. First, the delaying action beyond the obstacle, carried out by screen forces including engineers. The aim was to identify the enemy axes of advance, cause delay and possibly force the enemy to concertina, thus creating a nuclear target. This was expected to last only a day or so. The second phase, called 'On the obstacle', aimed to cripple the enemy forces so that they could not develop their offensive. This was to be done by using nuclear missiles against unprotected troops (i.e. those doing the assault crossing) and taking toll of their engineers and bridging. If they nevertheless succeeded in crossing in force, there followed a confused phase called 'stabilising' or 'containing' in which the aim was to hold the enemy within five or ten miles of the obstacle by means of rapid anti-tank screens and pre-planned demolitions, maintaining contact if at all possible. The guidelines at this point contained a warning against improper or ill conceived movement which it regarded as hazardous in the extreme. This sat oddly with a doctrine for highly mobile operations. Finally, and most exciting, came the much-debated 'Corps Counter Stroke'. This was in essence a nuclear strike upon an enemy formation preparing to continue the advance, followed on the Allied side by mopping up with an armoured thrust from some unexpected direction. A divisional HQ was normally left out of battle to plan for this. Clearly the selection of the objective, preliminary movement and timing were delicate matters. The question of the 'crust' was of great concern, however. This was to be the British army's last great effort. After that it was assumed that strategic nuclear activity would have forced the enemy to cease fighting and sue for peace.

The Purple Pamphlet reads surprisingly well to-day. It was a brilliant attempt to make sense of an impossible situation. Its ten-year life span coincided with the currency of the Weser Strategy. There really was some depth in the position and a major water obstacle to be defended. The army began to receive the lavish scale of armoured personnel carriers, rapid digging equipment and mechanically laid mines that the plan required. A few nuclear strikes on the Weser crossings would have posed major problems for the Warsaw Pact. The Allies might have held them off for five days or so, which was roughly what the plan required. Once the main defensive position had been moved well to the east, things got much more difficult, and this phase of planning coincided with MC14/3 and the need to forgo nuclear strikes for tactical purposes. But in one sense, planning for this was much more realistic because the great nuclear unknown had been removed from the battle-fighting equation.

However, the main component of battle management the Purple Pamphlet had failed to foresee, at least in so many words, was the concept of the 'killing ground'. This was an ancient idea given a new colour. Before an army can cope with an enemy advance satisfactorily it has to lure the enemy into some kind of dead end and then strike its forces, whether it be by nuclear or conventional means. The mental picture is of a *cul-de-sac*. The killing ground could be located on the near side of an obstacle, as was envisaged in the Purple Pamphlet for the containing phase and corps counter-stroke. In operations east of the Weser, the attacker could use the wooded valleys in that part of Germany, thickened up with well-hidden minefields covered by observation and fire. The model could be applied almost anywhere, and within a few years it became one of the most crucial elements in all planning and discussion; a key concept in the short nuclear-battle-fighting age.

Training

It was very difficult to carry out realistic exercises to practise the nuclear phase of a battle when troops were present. Simulating a nuclear strike meant detailing a party of sappers from the control staffs to light some oily rags in an empty 40 gallon oil drum and produce a loud bang. Then, because neither of these had been noticed by anybody, umpires would be sent round to tell the troops in the notionally affected area that they were either fried, shot blasted or radioactive - or probably all three. Realistically, this meant the end of the exercise for the victims. If there were any woods around, these would have been flattened by blow-down which meant stopping all movement - an obvious difficulty in an exercise which was supposed to involve manoeuvre. It followed that, so far as exercises with troops were concerned, nuclear release tended to coincide with the end of exercise.

One notable exception to this rule had occurred as far back as 1954, when the British Corps attacked a Belgian Corps in Exercise 'Battle Royal'. (12) The Belgians, who were in defence, notionally made use of seven nuclear shells (although of course such things hardly existed at the time) and the list of what they hit provides one of the most instructive visions of the nuclear battlefield. The first, based on good information from a Belgian SAS patrol, hit HQ 7 Armoured Brigade, 6 Field Regiment (SP) and a squadron of the Royals, knocking them out completely, together with 100 other miscellaneous vehicles. The second was accounted a failure, causing only 100 casualties to a motor battalion of 7 Armoured Division; there was no obstacle and the target was largely guesswork. The third, based on the capture of a marked map, hit 61 Brigade at H-hour during an assault across the Ems in their concentration area and the brigade was virtually destroyed. The fourth fell on HQ 1 British Corps which had been accurately located by an agent. Though the HQ was well dispersed it would actually have become non-functional, but for exercise reasons it was allowed to carry on. The fifth was aimed at an assault on the Teutoberger Ridge but hit only one gunner regiment causing 100 casualties. The sixth was aimed at an atomic cannon in the Netherlands sector but ground zero was changed at the last moment and it hit an engineer regiment and some bridging. The seventh was dropped on the British Maintenance Area, causing 40 casualties and destroying 25,00 rations and 1000 tons of fuel. At this stage the exercise was halted and declared a draw.

It is easy to see why, so far as exercises with troops were concerned, this sort of thing was never popular. Reliance was placed instead on Tactical Exercises without Troops, model exercises and Command Post Exercises of various kinds. During the 1960s, major exercises were held each year in the great Exhibition Hall in Luxembourg. The various Corps, Division and Brigade Headquarters were all placed in cubicles, connected by telephone in a realistic way, and the exercise was run to a timetable by an elaborate control staff. One feature was that it ran at double time. The whole day was played between 6am and 6pm, after which the players returned exhausted to their hotels and came back in time for 6am next morning. There was plenty of nuclear play. On one such exercise, the Commander, Royal Engineers of 2nd Division lost a lot of bridging equipment to a Russian nuclear strike but actually succeeded in letting off an ADM. An exercise like that can be very realistic. For many participants it provided by far the most vivid vision they ever had of the nuclear battlefield.

When it came to exercises with troops, an entirely different form of war was played. The big divisional exercises often consisted of long advances to contact and assaults across real water obstacles using real bridging. These were very demanding. Any nuclear episodes would have slowed things to a standstill. It is an open question why exercises tended to take this form. Was it because an offensive exercise was a better test of commanders and troops alike? Or was there a deeper reason? Did everyone, deep down, look on the very idea of a massive Warsaw Pact assault, let alone a nuclear response, as totally unreal. The real action, what the British army always *did* as opposed what they planned and trained for, was offensive action. This was usually undertaken to throw dictators out of lands they had improperly seized. The British had done so in the Second World War, from El Alamein in 1942 onwards and later, in the 1950s, in Korea and Suez. It was what they were to going do in the Falklands in 1982 and the Gulf in 1991. Being trained and ready for it was most necessary, not least on the North German Plain.

Tailpiece

As we have demonstrated, during the second half of the Cold War (i.e. from 1969 onwards), NATO had only a feeble concept of fighting a nuclear battle. The great project of the 1980s was the stationing of *Pershing* and Cruise Missiles in Europe and the harnessing of surveillance and target acquisition to precision guidance and other smart technologies. Once the Russian empire had collapsed, the British were quick to announce that they no longer planned to conduct operations with theatre nuclear weapons. Perhaps the whole notion will come to seem an historical aberration. Certainly there was always room for doubt that nuclear weapons would truly favour the defence rather than the assault, just as one can never know for sure how much the nuclear balance of terror contributed to keeping the peace in Europe. But at the time, the nuclear battlefield seemed all too real - at least in the Luxembourg Exhibition Hall.

References
(1) William F. Burns, 'The future of US nuclear weapons policy, *Arms Control Today*, Vol. 27, No. 7, October 1997, p.3.
(2) Stansfield Turner, *Caging the Nuclear Genie: An American Challenge for Global Security*, Westview Press, Oxford, 1996, pp. 74,5.
(3) *The Corps Tactical Battle in Nuclear War 1958*, The War Office, April 1958, p. 17.
(4) Fred Mulley, *The Politics of Western Defence*, Thames and Hudson, London, 1962, p. 76.
(5) Christy Campbell, *Nuclear Facts: a Guide to Nuclear Weapons Systems and Strategy*, Hamlyn, London, 1984, p. 131.
(6) Mulley: *The Politics*, p. 128.
(7) *The Times*, 25 Jan. 1961, quoted in Mulley, *The Politics* p. 145.
(8) Mulley: *The Politics*, p. 146.
(9) Campbell: *Nuclear Facts*. p. 33.
(10) Campbell: *Nuclear Facts* p. 132.
(11) General Sir John Hackett, *The Third World War August 1985: A Future History*, Sidgwick and Jackson, London,1978, *passim*.
(12) Lt. Col. I.R.Graeme, 'Northern Army Group Exercise Battle Royal', *British Army Review*, No.2, March 1955, pp. 9-22.

3. TECHNOLOGY, TESTING SAFETY, SECRECY

...the public impression that we live in exceptionally risky times is new... The bomb... and the push for nuclear energy, accompanied as it was by much official secrecy, misstatement of risk, and downright falsification has done vast damage to the credibility of governments who continue to issue sedative statements. Lies have always been told and risks played down in the interest of profit, but when we are reminded that coal mining and natural gas storage also pose risks to the workforce and the public, we have to point out that release of radioactivity from a nuclear plant is the only event, at least at the civilian level, that could make a country the size of Britain permanently uninhabitable as a result of a single accident. Clearly the nuclear story, both civil and military, has done immense damage to the credibility of all official statements about public safety...To the man in the street, whose suspicious nature is itself a sovereign risk reducer, 'perfectly safe' in the mouth of a minister or an official spokesmen is taken to mean 'dicey but with reasonable luck we will get away with it', the meaning of such platitudes at the time of Chernobyl. (Editorial, *The Lancet*, 14 July 1990)

We now look into a number of the more technical issues related to nuclear weapons, beginning with a short description of what the weapons consist of and how they work. We look, too, at some problems connected with the dangerous materials from which the weapons are made, and the need for testing. We follow with a resumé of safety and environmental issues. Finally, we outline how decisions on nuclear weapons are made in government and on the need for secrecy.

Fission weapons

Fission weapons use the isotopes uranium 235 (U235) or plutonium 239 (Pu239) as their explosive material. U235 occurs in natural uranium but sparsely. constituting only some 0.72% of the natural metal. To be useful for a weapon, this concentration has to be increased to some 90%, at which stage the material is normally referred to as Highly Enriched Uranium (HEU). The process of enrichment requires a huge industrial effort. Plutonium is an entirely man-made product, which arises when U235 is consumed in a nuclear reactor and has to be extracted from the residue by a system called re-processing - another complex and difficult technology. As it emerges from this process, plutonium consists of a mixture of isotopes. Nuclear weapon designers prefer plutonium with a large concentration of the isotope plutonium 239 (Pu-239). Plutonium containing more than 93% of this isotope is called weapon-grade plutonium. Plutonium containing less than 93% Pu-239, and therefore higher concentrations of other plutonium isotopes, can be used as a nuclear explosive but presents designers with problems. For example, the isotope Pu-240 is liable to detonate too early in the explosive cycle, thus reducing the yield of the explosion (pre-initiation). (1)

To trigger an explosion, it is necessary to put together a quantity of fissile material large enough to ensure that not too many of the high-energy neutrons that are spontaneously generated within it escape from the surface. A sufficient number of neutrons need to hit other heavy atoms within the material, causing these to release more neutrons and so set up a chain reaction. The smallest amount of the material that will produce this effect is called the 'critical mass' and depends on the purity and density of the material and on its surroundings. This mass has first to be assembled and then held together long enough for the chain reaction to take place. The Hiroshima bomb fired two slugs of U235 into each other, using high explosive as the propellant and producing a yield of some 15 kilotons. The same method was used ten years later to produce the early nuclear artillery shells. The other way to make a nuclear weapon is to use segments of high explosive arranged around a hollow sphere of fissile material weighing rather less than the critical mass. When the high explosive is detonated it produces a shock wave that compresses the sphere (implosion). The effect is to reduce the volume of the sphere and so increase its density. (The critical mass is inversely proportional to the square of the density). Matters are so arranged that after compression the original less-than-critical mass of fissile material becomes super-critical, a fission chain reaction begins and a nuclear explosion ensues. This was the type of device that was fired experimentally at the test called *Trinity* on 16 July 1945 and then dropped on Nagasaki the following month, resulting in explosions with yields equivalent to 18.6 and 22 kilotonnes of TNT respectively.

In a nuclear weapon of the latter kind, the fissile material is surrounded by a spherical shell of material - such as beryllium - to reflect back some of the neutrons that escape through the surface of the sphere. The use of a neutron reflector significantly reduces the amount of fissile material needed. The beryllium shell is surrounded by a casing of heavy metal - like natural uranium - that acts as a tamper. The tamper is surrounded by the conventional high explosive. When the latter is detonated, the shock wave causes the tamper to collapse inwards. Its inertia helps to hold the fissile material together during the explosion and prevent its premature disintegration, thus obtaining a larger explosive yield. The chemical explosive surrounding the fissile material is formed into segments or explosive lenses. The timing of the detonations of these components to produce the shock wave is crucial for the efficient operation of the weapon. Accuracy to the nearest thousandth of a millionth of a second is required. The shapes of the explosive lenses are complex and need to be meticulously calculated. The high explosive must be extremely pure and of constant consistency throughout its volume. For greatest efficiency, the fission chain-reaction must be initiated at precisely the moment of greatest compression i.e. maximum super-criticality. Initiation is achieved through a burst of neutrons produced by a small electronic device called a neutron gun. A typical nuclear fission weapon would use three or four kilograms of weapons grade plutonium surrounded by the reflector, tamper and around 100 kilograms of high explosive. The weight of the device would be about 200 kilograms.

Fusion weapons

In a nuclear explosion, very high temperatures of hundreds of millions of degrees centigrade and very high pressures of millions of atmospheres build up in about half a millionth of a second. In this time, about 55 generations of fission take place. Within less than a millionth of a second, the fissile material has expanded so far and its density has so reduced that it becomes sub-critical and the chain reaction stops. The maximum explosive yield of a fission weapon is limited by the factor of critical mass to a figure of some tens of kilotonnes of TNT equivalent. However, the very high energies generated in a fission explosion are enough to trigger its opposite - the fusion of light atoms into heavier ones. For instance, the heavier isotopes of hydrogen (deuterium and tritium) can be fused into helium, generating a further huge release of energy. The result is a fusion or thermonuclear explosion. In theory, since no critical mass is involved, there is no limit to the size of a thermonuclear explosion - indeed the reaction is precisely that which generates the huge outflows of energy from the interior of the Sun. But to make this process work, temperatures in excess of 100 million degrees centigrade are needed to overcome the positive-positive repulsion between the component nuclei. The fission trigger which is used to create these energies must deliver them to the fusion material in a time much shorter than it takes for the explosion to occur. This makes the design of fusion weapons even more problematic than that of fission weapons.

An intermediate stage is possible whereby the yield of a nuclear fission weapon is boosted by injecting some fusion material during the explosion. The resulting fusion is used as a source of neutrons to produce more fission in the plutonium or HEU. The fusion itself produces an insignificant amount of energy, so the explosive yield from the weapon still comes from nuclear fission. Hence this explosive process is referred to as boosted fission. In a typical boosted fission weapon, about five grams of a pressurised mixture of deuterium and tritium gas are injected into the centre of a plutonium sphere from a reservoir placed outside the main core of the weapon. When the fissile material explodes, the pressure and the temperature at the centre are high enough for nuclear fusion to take place in this gas mixture. The neutrons so released produce additional fission in the plutonium before the weapon disintegrates, thus increasing its efficiency. In an un-boosted fission weapon, about 100 fission generations are produced per microsecond, in a boosted fission weapon, about 1000 per microsecond. Boosted weapons are therefore about ten times more efficient than un-boosted ones. With boosted nuclear fission, the maximum explosive power of a militarily usable weapon is about 50 kilotonnes of TNT equivalent. Militarily unstable boosted weapons have explosive yields up to ten times as great.

For a true fusion or thermonuclear weapon, it is often convenient to use lithium deuteride, a solid, as the fusion material, because tritium and deuterium are gases at room temperature. The lithium deuteride is placed inside a nuclear fission trigger. When neutrons from the fission bombard nuclei in the deuteride this produces tritium nuclei. The tritium nuclei fuse with unchanged deuterium nuclei to produce fusion energy. In a typical thermonuclear weapon, a cylinder of HEU known as the spark plug is placed co-axially with a cylinder of lithium deuteride. Neutrons from the trigger produce fission in the uranium spark plug and this ignites the fusion process. If higher explosive yields are required a second fusion stage can be placed under the first. In principle, any number of fusion stages can be added. Typically each stage of a thermonuclear weapon explodes with a power roughly ten times that of the preceding stage. If the fission trigger explodes with an explosive yield of a few tens of kilotonnes the first fusion stage will explode with a yield of several hundred kilotonnes and the second fusion stage, if present, would yield several thousand kilotonnes (one thousand kilotonnes is known as one megatonne, abbreviated to 1mt.).The fusion process in a thermonuclear weapon is probably about 30 % efficient. If so, each kilogram of lithium deuteride would produce an explosion equivalent to about 25 kt. of TNT. A 500 kt. weapon would require about 20 kilograms of lithium deuteride.

Fissile material

There is a direct link between the proliferation of nuclear weapons and the spread of nuclear technology for peaceful purposes. (2) Countries which use nuclear power reactors to generate electricity, or who operate research reactors, inevitably acquire the necessary technical knowledge and scientific and engineering expertise to build nuclear weapons. Such countries also necessarily accumulate plutonium in spent reactor-fuel elements that could be used to make nuclear weapons. (Non-Nuclear Weapon States party to the Non-Proliferation Treaty have, of course, specifically undertaken not to do so). Some elements of the nuclear fuel cycle are considerably more prone to misuse in this way than others. Uranium enrichment plants and reprocessing plants used to remove the plutonium from spent reactor-fuel elements are particularly sensitive. (3)

The sheer size of this problem can be put into perspective when it is realised that the world inventory of plutonium produced by civil and military reactors to date is estimated at 1100 tonnes, while only a fraction of that is required to produce a nuclear device. Some 250 tonnes are contained in the military inventory, the vast majority of which is weapon-grade. The other 850 tonnes have been produced in civil nuclear power reactors and about 150 tonnes of this have been separated from spent reactor-fuel elements. The plutonium produced in this way by nuclear power reactors which operated normally for the generation of electricity is known as reactor-grade plutonium. Typically, it contains only about 60 per cent of Pu-239 but it *can* be used to fabricate nuclear weapons, subject to the reservation mentioned earlier. The critical mass of reactor-grade plutonium metal is in the region of 13-20 kilograms.

Large commercial reprocessing plants are currently operating in the Britain, France and Russia, and one is currently under construction in Japan. Smaller plants are operating in India and Pakistan. A typical modern commercial reprocessing plant can reprocess about 800 tonnes of spent reactor fuel a year, separating about 8 tonnes of plutonium. By the year 2000, according to current plans, about 310 tonnes of civil plutonium will have been extracted by reprocessing. Of this plutonium, about 205 tonnes will be in store: 60 tonnes in the United Kingdom, 50 tonnes in Japan, 40 tonnes in Germany, 40 tonnes in Russia and 15 tonnes in France. Part of this will be used in fast reactors and part as a mixture of plutonium oxide (PuO2) with uranium oxide (UO2) to create a fuel -known as MOX - for use in light water reactors. This type of recycling reduces the amount of fissile plutonium in the fuel by 40% and is the only large-scale use of separated plutonium currently planned. In addition, about 100 tonnes of weapons-grade plutonium is expected to have been removed from dismantled American and ex-Soviet nuclear weapons. (4)

A number of methods of disposal have been proposed by scientists. (5) These include such far-out methods as launching the material into the Sun, or exploding the nuclear material removed from weapons in a rock cavity which would dilute the plutonium in the rock to about one part in one thousand. Other, more likely, methods include mixing the plutonium with high level radioactive waste produced by past reprocessing before incorporating it into a suitable solid material and placing it in permanent storage in geological depositories. High level waste is already being embedded in glass for final disposal in France, Britain and Japan. Another suggestion, which is less desirable from a proliferation perspective, is to embed the plutonium in special materials - such as silicate glass - without the addition of high level waste. This would add to the cost and hazard of any attempt to recover the plutonium. (6) Another major problem with large commercial reprocessing plants is the extreme difficulty of detecting theft or other diversion of plutonium. Even with the best available safeguards, only 97% of the plutonium can be accounted for, leaving considerable scope for the clandestine accumulation of weapons-usable plutonium. It comes as no surprise to learn that some fissile material at Dounreay is unaccounted for, and some may have been diverted to the weapons programme. A further problem is that there is very little transparency about stocks of civil fissile material. (7)

The amount of HEU in existence is currently estimated at around 1700 tonnes, nearly all of it in military hands. The British share of this has been officially given as 21.9 tonnes. The problem of dealing with the growing stocks of HEU from dismantled weapons is much less acute than that of dealing with plutonium. A small percentage of the

HEU in existence could be used in research and isotope production reactors. But the easiest method to dispose of it is to blend it with natural uranium, or that from which U-235 has already been extracted, to produce low enriched uranium (LEU) which can then be used as fuel in nuclear reactors. Such material is not usable in nuclear weapons. Spent naval reactor fuel will probably be disposed of in geological repositories. (8)

Production Cut-Off
In 1992, US President George Bush officially announced that the Americans would no longer produce HEU or plutonium for nuclear weapons, thus giving formal effect to a policy which had already been in existence since 1988 for HEU, and since 1964 for plutonium. HEU production also ended in Russia in 1987 and most of its military production reactors have been shut down. In 1994, Russia formally agreed to shut down the rest as soon as replacement sources of heat and electricity (which the reactors also provide) could be found with American help. This formal agreement included arrangements for verification. These are to include on-site inspections (OSI) of the currently operating Russian reactors as well as of Russian and American reactors that have produced weapons grade plutonium in the past. When these reactors are finally shut down in a few years' time, Russia, the last of the five NWS to produce material for nuclear weapons, will have left the stage.

In his first speech to the United Nations General Assembly on the 27 September 1993, US President Bill Clinton outlined a new non-proliferation plan, which included a comprehensive approach to dealing with the increasing amounts of fissile material from dismantled nuclear warheads and from civil nuclear programmes. He proposed a multilateral convention aimed at prohibiting the production of fresh HEU and plutonium for explosive purposes and seeking to eliminate existing stockpiles. The British supported this proposal, and announced that Britain would not produce any more fissile material for explosive purposes. At the end of 1993, the UN General Assembly adopted a consensus resolution in which it recognised that a non-discriminatory, multilateral and internationally and effectively verifiable treaty banning the production of fissile material for nuclear weapons or other nuclear explosive devices would be a significant contribution to nuclear non-proliferation in all its aspects. (9)

In 1994,the Russian President Boris Yeltsin also supported President Clinton's proposal and it became accepted that the appropriate forum for negotiating a fissile material cut-off would be the 61-nation UN Conference on Disarmament in Geneva (CD). The Conference appointed a special co-ordinator on the issue, but a year later there was still no consensus on a mandate. (10) The 1995 Review and Extension Conference of the Nuclear Non-Proliferation Treaty (NPT) called for 'the immediate commencement and early conclusion of negotiations on the lines of the General Assembly resolution'. (11) The CD duly agreed a mandate for negotiations on a cut-off convention, and the way seemed open for rapid progress on this matter. The nuclear weapons states and their allies, mostly Western states, were prepared to discuss and negotiate. But a cut-off treaty *per se* would clearly not promote disarmament; its chief merit would lie in checking proliferation, for example in south Asia. The so-called Group of 21, now consisting of 30 states, mostly non-aligned, were prepared to negotiate for a cut-off treaty, but only as one element in a complete programme leading to the elimination of nuclear weapons by the year 2020. Understandably, they wanted any cut-off convention not only to restrain future production of fissile material, but also to bring the large and growing existing stockpiles under international supervision and control. In other words, they wanted the convention to be a step towards disarmament, not simply a measure of non-proliferation. But the nuclear weapons states insisted that the cut-off should apply only to future production and should not be linked to any other measure of nuclear disarmament. A further problem is that the approach being taken in the CD does not affect civil nuclear programmes producing plutonium in western Europe and Japan. It does, however, seek to constrain the production of fissile material in regions of instability and high proliferation risk. This double standard has been much criticised. (12) Nevertheless, the time is now ripe for negotiating a fissile material production ban. Both North and South Korea have already pledged to stop constructing facilities for its production, Argentina and Brazil have informally agreed not to enrich uranium to weapon grade and South Africa has stopped producing fissile materials. India and Pakistan, following their nuclear tests in May 1998, have agreed to engage in negotiations. In August 1998, the Israeli government finally dropped its objections to doing so, while not committing itself to any specific outcome. Substantive negotiations are expected to start by 1999, but this is far from certain to take place.

Safeguards

Meanwhile, it is clear that stronger international safeguards need to be put in place covering civil and military fissile material that can be used to make nuclear weapons. The conclusion of the Nuclear Non-Proliferation Treaty in 1968 caused a safeguards system to be put in place on a multilateral basis. This system aims to detect any diversion of a significant quantity of nuclear material from peaceful nuclear activities to the manufacture of nuclear weapons, and to deter such diversions by the risk of early detection. The arrangements made with the International Atomic Energy Agency (IAEA) (13) cater for three safeguarding methods - material accountancy, containment and surveillance - and makes use of four procedures - design review, inspection of plant operating records, reports on plant operation and on-site inspection (OSI). By their very nature, these methods are open to criticism as insensitive, intrusive, discriminatory and liable to misuse for espionage, and they are not as effective as they should be. Increased safeguards and verification mechanisms could give assurance and help to create confidence. So long as surplus military plutonium remains outside the scope of international safeguards, it will much reduce the effectiveness of a fissile material cut-off treaty. Moreover by the end of 2002 civil plutonium stocks world-wide will exceed the stock of military plutonium. Hence a fissile material cut off will be ineffective if it does not include existing civil fissile material. (14)

In the summer of 1993, the IAEA embarked on a major initiative known as Programme 93+2 intended to lead to a strengthened and more cost-effective safeguarding system. (15) The aim was to implement better transparency measures, such as improved data collection and inspections, affecting all aspects of nuclear activity. The point was to provide the IAEA with a means of comparing information derived from material accountancy activities with that from other sources. (16) The Board of the IAEA approved these proposals in 1995, and some of the measures have been implemented. The more far-reaching measures have been set out in an agreed protocol to be added to states' existing safeguards agreements. When in force, they will give access beyond nuclear materials and reactors, including the entire nuclear fuel cycle from mining to waste, as well as research and development and decommissioned facilities. Procedural improvements will include environmental sampling and provision for surprise inspections. (17)

Nuclear Testing
In September 1996, one of the most sought after and elusive arms control agreements of the nuclear age was signed at the United Nations in New York. The Comprehensive Test Ban Treaty (CTBT) bans all explosive tests of nuclear weapons. The historical background to it is worth examining. From the mid-1950s, a series of protests began against nuclear weapons testing, and there was public pressure for an enforcement of limits. Surveys of the health of children had a huge influence. For example, a survey carried out in Wales in 1957 into children dying of natural causes found that they had levels of radioactive strontium 90 in their bones four times higher than adults, apparently derived from atmospheric testing. (18) There was much general public horror at fallout-strontium 90 in mothers' milk. (19) Formal talks for a complete ban on testing started in 1958 at the Conference on the Discontinuance of Nuclear Weapon Tests (CDNWT) in Geneva. The conference met in almost continuous session until January 1962. The main questions at issue concerned how to detect and identify nuclear explosions anywhere in the world. The scientific experts agreed that it was feasible to set up an effective control system to detect seismic events. The experts also devised provisions for on-site inspection (OSI) of events not identified as earthquakes. The conference was, however, divided on the number of OSIs that would be needed and whether they could amount to legalised espionage.

After President Kennedy came to power in 1961,the negotiations took on new life. On the 4 March 1962, an Eighteen Nation Disarmament Conference (ENDC) was set up. However, the Cuban Missile Crisis followed in October, taking the US and the Soviet Union to the brink of nuclear confrontation. This represented a turning point in superpower relations. Shortly afterwards, the Conference of Experts resumed and the possibility of a treaty became apparent. Lord Hailsham, who led the British side in the negotiations, says, 'Britain's role was crucial. We all agreed that we wanted a Test Ban Treaty and my instructions were that when I engaged on the negotiations, I should get a total ban on tests if I could, but if not, to make do with a Partial Test Ban Treaty. That is to say a test ban for the environment providing that nothing could reach the atmosphere'. (20) Unfortunately a comprehensive ban could not be agreed. The Partial Test Ban Treaty (PTBT) was signed on the 5 August 1963 by the British, the Americans and the Soviet Union. The treaty entered into force on 10 October, and it banned all nuclear test explosions in the atmosphere, in outer space and under water. France and China refused to sign. France argued that the treaty had only limited practical importance and reaffirmed its decision to proceed with its own nuclear build-up. China criticised the treaty as not encompassing general disarmament or a ban on underground tests. Nevertheless, both countries *did* finally adhere to the treaty: France in 1974 and China in 1980. (21)

In 1977, tripartite negotiations resumed on nuclear testing. John Edmonds was the leader of the British delegation at that time. He says that by late 1978, Britain had made progress in negotiation with the Americans and the Russians, and there was a serious prospect of achieving the aims of these governments by means of a CTBT. At this point. however, people in the United States responsible for procuring nuclear weapons, supported by their colleagues in Britain, began to cast all kinds of doubts on the desirability of a test ban. US President Carter did not have a firm enough grasp of policy to force the issue. He tried to compromise with the doubters and Prime Minister Callaghan went along with him, though reluctantly. But the ultimate effect was to undermine the possibility of a treaty, and the negotiations eventually failed because vested interests in the United States and Britain did not want them to succeed.

When the Cold War ended, the rationale for developing

and testing new nuclear weapon designs all but disappeared. In 1992, US President George Bush found himself drawn into joining a Russian moratorium on nuclear testing. The French, for the first time, followed suit. The British were dragged reluctantly into this process because all their tests were taking place in Nevada, courtesy of the USA. But the British government made extraordinary efforts, at the end of the Bush presidency in 1993, to discourage renewed American interest in a test ban. (22) In 1993, the Conference on Disarmament (CD) in Geneva was given a full mandate to conduct negotiations for a CTBT, and these began January 1994. The election of President Clinton in 1992, and his decision to focus on nuclear non-proliferation, added impetus to the negotiations. President Yeltsin was keen to make progress and President François Mitterand of France was inclined towards a far more positive attitude. Britain was left dragging its feet, and no doubt damaged its reputation amongst the vast majority of non-nuclear weapons states, including allies in NATO and the Commonwealth. But at some point in 1994/5 Britain shifted position, and the British Government under Prime Minister John Major came around to President Clinton's way of thinking. The CTBT was finally agreed'; but only after intense negotiation. John Edmonds says: 'It was almost as if Britain was dragged kicking and screaming towards supporting a CTBT. We were virtually the only government to support the French resumption of nuclear testing in 1995, and we were among those who insisted on unsatisfactory 'entry into force' conditions in the treaty eventually negotiated and signed in 1996.' (23)

Now that the CTBT has been signed Britain has promised to play a constructive role in its implementation. There are, however, problems about 'entry into force'. Under the treaty, this will take place when 44 nominated states have ratified. These are effectively those with nuclear programmes subject to inspection by the International Atomic Energy Authority (IAEA) and include, of course, Israel, Pakistan and India. India said categorically that it would never ratify, in part because the treaty does not rule out non-explosive testing (including computer modelling) and partly because it does not commit the nuclear weapons states (NWS) to a timed programme of nuclear disarmament. This is quite true, but not helpful, and it is ironic, because India had been a principal advocate of a test ban pact for over 40 years. But if India does not ratify, what then? It is obvious that anyone who signed the treaty and subsequently tested would incur enormous odium. Meanwhile, much of the International Monitoring System (IMS) is being set up. The treaty provides for a global network of 170 seismic stations and an international data centre. The latter has been working since 1996 and 130 seismic stations are already operating. When complete, the system will measure vibrations passing through the earth, the oceans and the air; will monitor radio-active gases and particles in the atmosphere and will provide for on-site inspections and overflights when triggered by national technical means. If all 44 states have not ratified by 2002 a special conference can be called to decide by consensus how to make further progress. That is vague, but the best that could be managed. (24) In April 1998, Britain and France became the first two NWS to ratify the CTBT. Robin Cook, British Foreign Secretary, said it signalled Britain's commitment to the goal of a Nuclear Weapon Free World. (25) It came as a shattering blow to these high hopes when, during the month of May 1998, India and Pakistan both carried out short programmes of tests, some of which were certainly nuclear. The Indian tests were carried out at Pokaharan in Rajasthan and, by their account, included a fission device (of the Nagasaki type), a boosted fission device using tritium fuses and a low-yield device suitable, perhaps, for a tactical weapon. All were plutonium based. The Pakistani tests were carried out in the Chagai Hills in South West Pakistan and reportedly involved fission devices using HEU. All the tests on both sides were carried out underground. Both sides have test-fired long range surface-to-surface missiles: India's, called *Agni,* was tested in 1994 to a range of 1400 km.; Pakistan's, called *Ghauri,* was test fired to a range of 1500 km. in April 1998. The high cost of these missiles, combined with their inaccuracy, makes them suitable only for use with non-conventional (i.e. presumably nuclear) warheads, though whether either side is going to 'weaponise' their nuclear devices in this sense remains far from clear. India claims to require a 'minimum' nuclear deterrent against China. Pakistan follows in

India's footsteps. The danger of a nuclear missile arms race in South Asia is obvious. (26)

These tests brought almost universal condemnation from the international community, and the application of sanctions on the part of the US and Japan. India has officially declared a moratorium on testing and has said she is willing to convert that into a *de jure* obligation. Reportedly, India is ready to drop her condition that all nuclear powers must first commit themselves to a schedule for reducing and eventually eliminating their nuclear arsenals. But she will no doubt seek a *quid pro quo*, if only in the form of the lifting of sanctions. India has also announced strict adherence to, and a stringent tightening of, export control measures on nuclear, missile, chemical, and biological weapons-related technologies. She has agreed, too, to stop blocking the negotiations for a fissile material cut-off. (27) No doubt Pakistan would follow suit. This, however, would be to make something of a mockery of the arms control process. The real reason for India's testing was the desire of a weak and unstable government to seek popular support by means of banging the nationalist drum. By doing so regardless of the diplomatic isolation and economic penalties which follow India is setting an example of the worst possible kind. Non-proliferation policies need to be examined and strengthened to avert the temptation of other threshold states to do likewise.

Nuclear Weapons Safety

Nuclear warheads and their component parts are subjected to many tests during their design, development and production stages to ensure that they satisfy the important requirements of safety, performance and reliability. This means looking at all events that can occur during the transport, handling, launch, flight and re-entry phases of its life. The warhead, and, where relevant, its transport container are exposed to a wide range of tests that simulate the vibration, shock, temperature, and acceleration conditions that it will experience during its whole service life. It is also tested against a series of credible accidents, including multiple impact and fire. The environments applied are in many cases extremely severe and require the use of powerful test equipment. The machines that apply the vibration use up to a half a megawatt of electricity. Acceleration tests, which are conducted on the centrifuge, apply forces that make the warhead weigh up to 200 times its own mass. (28)

In July 1992, the Ministry of Defence scientific advisor Sir Ronald Oxburgh published a report on British nuclear weapon safety. He drew on the report of a US panel of experts - the 'Drell Report' released in December 1990 - which had addressed concerns that an accident involving a missile system could lead to the dispersal of plutonium or even a low-yield nuclear explosion. The essence of the Drell Report was concern over the Trident II (D-5) missile system and its warhead, the W-88. The reason was that W-88 warheads are not equipped with insensitive high explosive (IHE) - a material which is less susceptible to detonation by fire or impact than ordinary high explosive - and are mounted in close proximity to the third stage motor rocket that uses a high energy propellant. Drell had concluded that new assessments needed to be made on the possibility that accidents could occur in handling the D-5 system (the Trident missile system bought by Britain) which could lead to dispersal of harmful radioactivity. (29)

The D-5 missile can carry two types of re-entry vehicle: the Mark V which carries a warhead known as W-88 and the Mark IV which carries a lower yield warhead, W-76. The British warhead for Trident has a lower yield than the US W-88, but a similar yield to the W-76. The design specifications for a warhead to fit into the Mark IV re-entry vehicle, including payload, centre of gravity and centre of inertia as well as the physical shape of the nose cone, are stringent. It follows that the British Trident warhead design cannot be very different from the US 100-kt W-76 warhead, which also lacks IHE. The Oxburgh Report, however, did not address the specific concerns outlined in Drell, particularly the physical proximity of the sensitive high explosive to the third stage rocket motor. Instead Oxburgh concluded by arguing that Trident incorporated the most modern and advanced safety technologies that were available *when designed*, and that it was comparable to and safer than *Chevaline*. The report recommended acceptance into service, provided that British safety case assessments were completed. It also suggested a number of institutional safeguards - principally that a Nuclear Weapons Safety Group be established, and that a research programme should be set up at AWE towards continued improvement in the area of warhead safety. The report recommended that so long as Trident remained in service, there should be a design review every seven years and that the Ordnance Board should revisit its guidelines for nuclear weapon design assessment on a regular basis. It made clear that a strategy for the safety justification of any future nuclear weapon must be defined. (30)

Apart from IHE, two other major safety features have been incorporated into state-of-the-art nuclear warhead's. Enhanced nuclear detonation safety (ENDS) reduces the chance of a warhead's detonators being fired electrically in an accident. Fire resistant pits - the fissile cores - (FRP) reduce the possibility of dispersal of plutonium if a warhead catches fire. Given the lead time for a nuclear weapon system, some of the latest safety features will always be absent from weapons in service. The British government has not revealed which, if any, of the above have been incorporated into the Trident warhead, but the US W-76 has only ENDS and it is reasonable to assume that the same applies to the British warhead. The Ministry of Defence has, however, confirmed that the Trident warhead meets the crucial criterion of One Point Safety. This means simply that if a detonation did take place at any one point in the conventional high explosive array, the probability of this causing a nuclear yield of more than four pounds of TNT equivalent does not exceed one in a million. So far as it goes, this is reassuring.

The Environment

While the environmental consequences of Britain's nuclear programmes are not a major focus of this book, the very basic issues must be introduced. These are highly controversial, but it is notable that environmental expert groups such as Greenpeace take the question of dangers from British nuclear weapons very seriously indeed. They believe that a nuclear missile system deployed on nuclear-powered submarines such as Trident can never be entirely safe. Their fears can be summarised as follows. (31)

1. Reactors at sea are at even greater risk of accident than those on land, because of the additional risk of collision or wreck to an ocean- going vessel and the much greater difficulty of dealing with a nuclear accident at sea. Greenpeace asserts that there are already some eight nuclear reactors at the bottom of the sea as a result of accidents to US and Soviet submarines. A serious accident to a Trident submarine reactor could cause major environmental damage, polluting the oceans for thousands of years to come.

2. The Trident submarine reactor, like all nuclear reactors, routinely pollutes the environment with radiation and radioactive waste, posing a continual hazard to crews, ports, the public and marine life.

3. Nuclear warheads require some of the most radioactive materials on Earth, such as plutonium and uranium, to be produced, transported and processed into nuclear bomb components. The manufacture of these warheads produces large quantities of highly toxic radioactive waste. The warheads for Trident are regularly transported back and forth across the country on public roads between their assembly plant at Burghfield in Berkshire and the Firth of Clyde in Scotland, where the submarines are based. A serious accident that damaged the warheads could release radioactive material, thus poisoning both people and the environment. In the USA, the government became so concerned at the possibility of such an accident that it ordered a federal enquiry and subsequent changes to warhead transport procedures.

4. When the Trident submarines are decommissioned, their reactor sections will still be radioactive and will remain so for thousands of years. There is no known safe method of disposing of these radioactive sections, and the government has put off a decision on what to do with the

submarines that are already retired.

Casualties from radiation date back to the early pioneers: Röntgen died of bone cancer, Becquerel burned his skin by pocketing a vial of radium, Marie Curie and her daughter Irène Joliot-Curie died of aplastic anaemia (bone marrow failure). By 1908 the American Röntgen Society had heard over fifty reports of radiation poisoning. During the 1920s, there was a second wave of deaths amongst pioneer radiologists and their patients from blood diseases and cancers with long latent periods. Despite all this early evidence of danger, the long-term effects of radiation on health were ignored for decades. (32) The Manhattan Project opened the door to new and unprecedented radiation hazards by creating hundreds of new and previously unknown fission products. It was discovered, for example, that plutonium is five to ten times more toxic than radium. The project exposed 150,000 workers to radiation. Nevertheless, it was the dropping of atomic bombs on the civilian populations of Hiroshima and Nagasaki that provided most of the evidence on which safety limits have since been based. It has now become clear that this evidence led to underestimation of the biological impact of ionising radiation. (33) It was uncertain what radiation doses were received, because no measurements were made until fifteen days after the event. Wind and rain produced variable fall-out in different areas. Military restrictions on scientific study remained until 1951. As to the genetic effects, any mutations that were recessive would need several generations to be expressed. (34) Moreover certain radioactive materials that are inhaled or ingested do not pass through the body, but accumulate in various organs and continue to irradiate surrounding tissue. For years, the importance of these 'internal emitters' was ignored.

The fire at Windscale in 1957 provided an interesting object lesson. It was the worst accident of its kind anywhere in the world until the disaster at Chernobyl in 1986. A mistake by the operator of a military reactor led to a fire involving the graphite moderator and 11 tons of uranium. By the time this was noticed 48 hours later, the fire was out of control. Three days after it started, massive quantities of water were used to quench the fire. This contaminated the water in question and risked an explosion, but it worked. The public was told nothing for 24 hours and was then reassured falsely that the weather conditions were carrying the radioactivity out to sea. In fact the wind was carrying the radioactivity inland. The British government, authorised by Prime Minister Harold Macmillan, minimised the accident and covered up important facts, notably that a polonium-triggered hydrogen bomb was being built. This omission to mention one of the most dangerous radionuclides concealed the inadequacy of emergency responses, and falsified later calculations of the biological impact of the radioactivity. In the event, some 20,000 curies of radioactivity were released. Fallout travelled to Denmark, Belgium, Holland, Germany and France. Milk sales and consumption were banned in an area of 200 square miles for 25 days. It was 26 years before the National Radiological Protection Board (NRPB) assessed the consequences of this accident. Even so, it is believed that because vital information was concealed, they underestimated the effects. (35)

In 1981, the MOD asked the Medical Research Council (MRC) to investigate mortality amongst nuclear workers. Several studies took place at different sites in Britain. In 1985, the results were published of a study on 40,000 occupationally exposed workers of the United Kingdom Atomic Energy Authority (UKAEA). Their health had been monitored for an average of sixteen years. The only cause of death which showed a clear association with increasing radiation dose was prostatic cancer. (36) In 1986, a study at Sellafield (Windscale) followed the history of 14,327 workers employed from 1947 to 1975. There was a positive association between radiation dose and death rates from bladder cancer, multiple myeloma, leukaemia, lymphatic and haematopoietic neoplasm. (37) These studies left little doubt that previously accepted risk estimates were substantially understated, although the wide margin of error in such calculations was emphasised. In 1987 a study by the Office of Population Censuses and Surveys (OPCS) compared cancer incidence and mortality around nuclear plants in England and Wales with regional averages in control areas. The study covered the years from 1959 to 1980 and found no general increases in cancer except for leukaemia in the age group 0-24 years. (38) In 1988 the mortality of workers at AWE was analysed, using a sample of 22,552 workers employed between 1951 and 1982 and followed up for 18.6 years (average). The average exposure to external radiation had been very low. But in sub-samples which were also monitored for internal exposure to multiple radionuclides there was an increased incidence of malignant neoplasms, lung and prostatic cancers. It is of interest that the nuclear workers studied were in general healthier than the general population against which they were compared. This makes the incidence of cancer all the more significant. (39)

In 1989, the MRC investigated leukaemias diagnosed between 1950 and 1985 in the Sellafield area. The team, headed by an epidemiologist, Dr Martin Gardener of Southampton University, found that the only significant statistical association amongst many possible factors was the fathers' occupation. Children were seven to eight times more likely to develop leukaemia if their fathers had received a substantial dose of radiation in the period prior to their conception. This would suggest that the fathers' sperm had been damaged by radiation. If this were substantiated, it would explain one link between cancer and nuclear plants. Follow-up studies to the Gardener Report have been carried out and similar studies have taken place at Dounreay and Aldermaston/Burghfield. The Royal Navy has opened its thirty-year records on workers in nuclear submarines and dockyards to a specialist working group set up by the MOD. (40) The general trend of these investigations has been to substantiate some causal link between ionising radiation and childhood leukaemia, although the exact nature of the link remains elusive and important discrepancies remain. It seems however that, apart from workers in the nuclear industries and their offspring, no risk to the public at large has come to light.

One of the latest studies carried out by the NRPB, in 1996, assessed the radionuclide levels around the former air base at Greenham Common, Berkshire. This followed the release of a confidential report that indicated the presence of enriched uranium in leaves and leaf-mould in the area. Because of concern over leukemias in Newbury the NRPB adopted an approach that would determine general radionuclide levels. Samples of undisturbed soil were collected from eighteen points around the former air base complex and from 29 locations in the surrounding area. Many of these locations were close to or within centres of population. According to the findings of the report there was no evidence of enriched uranium in or around the former air base and levels of natural uranium were consistent with published values for the area. Consequently the findings show that the doses received were no different to those received in other areas of the country. (41)

Secrecy

> A potential for destruction on a scale hitherto undreamt of lies in the hands of a few aging individuals who, in terms of personality, motivation, and of stress and cerebral efficiency, should hardly be trusted with the weekend shopping. (42)

It became clear from the overview of Britain's nuclear history given in Chapter 1 that from the beginning, there has been a veil of secrecy surrounding nuclear weapons policy decision-making. Decisions about the A-bomb, the H-bomb, Polaris, *Chevaline* and Trident were taken in secrecy and sometimes in direct contradiction to the manifesto pledges on which governments had been elected. It has also long been the Westminster tradition that discussions in government on nuclear weapons policy are a matter for an elite inner circle of decision-makers drawn from selected members of the cabinet, senior civil servants and eminent government scientists. Only a handful of ministers have ever been cleared to receive all the vital information provided by nuclear scientists. Often, the rest of the Cabinet is not even told that the work is under way. This process has ensured that facts and opinions put forward by a small group of interested scientists and other support staff have been given excessive weight and have rarely been criticised within Whitehall. This same emphasis on secrecy makes it impossible to open up for peer-group review the opinions of those who set themselves up as experts. It makes the views put forward by such people to some extent self-fulfilling. Ministers come to see themselves as privileged to have access to such information, and to take decisions of such importance. Questioning the authority of these in house experts therefore becomes very difficult. Governments generally see the whole area as fundamental to their political strategy, and not one on which they are prepared to accept advice from anyone else. (43) Commander Robert Green writes, 'In 1980 I was a fly on the Whitehall wall when Thatcher insisted on having Trident, despite disagreement among the Chiefs of Staff and without consulting the Cabinet. Admiral of the Fleet Sir Henry Leach, First Sea Lord at the time, was the first to call it 'a cuckoo in the naval nest'. (44)

The Ministry of Defence has the main responsibility for the development and production of nuclear warheads in Britain. Its head is the Secretary of State for Defence (Defence Secretary) supported by the Minister for Defence Procurement. His principal Civil Service aide is the Permanent Under Secretary for Defence (PUS), who is likewise supported by the Chief of Defence Procurement (CDP). The Procurement Executive is the corporate body responsible for nuclear weapon procurement. An important group working within the Ministry is the Defence Scientific Staff who in turn control the Atomic Weapons Establishment (AWE). Ministry and AWE scientists have links with the US laboratories in America, particularly with Los Alamos and Lawrence Livermore. They also have control over the flow of information on nuclear weapons. Anyone dealing with such information has, of course, first to be positively vetted and then given special access. (45) Another group involved in decision-making is the intelligence community upon whose annual estimates of enemy capability the threat assessment is based, and who therefore have an input into future nuclear weapons requirements. Other influences on nuclear weapons decision-making are the Treasury, the Foreign and Commonwealth Office and the Cabinet Office. Despite their all-pervasive influence upon government generally, these bodies can have only a minor impact on technical decisions about types of new weapons or the requirements they are designed to meet. The Foreign Office in particular very rarely takes an independent line where nuclear policy is concerned. (46)

Both the Conservative Party and the Labour Party have been involved in major political decisions to build and maintain a British deterrent and there appears to be a high degree of cross-party consensus. Efforts to influence or throw a different emphasis on this process come from outside. Westminster is surrounded by influential lobbies and Non-Governmental Organisations (NGOs), some of which are, in effect, part of the wider establishment while others remain on the fringes. Nevertheless most inputs from these groups on defence related decisions are given little more than polite attention. While popular attitudes cannot be ignored in Whitehall and concerns which directly affect the public, such as safety, have to be listened to, this rarely affects decision-making. The decision to forswear anti-personnel land mines appears to be a commendable exception, though this was largely effected by the emotional pressure exercised by the death in 1997, of Diana, Princess of Wales, who had been a high profile campaigner in this field.

Is secrecy still important today? Is it in the interest of national security to remove classifications? Obviously this would be going too far. However on less sensitive issues, it would be better to engage in a much more open debate which could involve the media and the public. There could be more co-operation with the parliamentary opposition and the Defence Select Committee. There is no reason why decisions on nuclear weapons should not be made in a more open and accountable fashion. Learning from the United States, perhaps a Freedom of Information of Act could bring about some improvement? In an interview with Denis Fakeley, he attempts to throw some light on why there has been so much secrecy within the British nuclear weapons Establishment and why it has surrounded nuclear weapons decision-making in the past. He says 'I suppose I would have to say that there has been undue secrecy surrounding nuclear weapons decisions but, given the sensitivity of the technologies that are involved in nuclear weapons development and production, it is not *that* surprising if secrecy has spilled over from that area to the political area. I think more could have been said without detriment to the UK security interest, but the way in which the nuclear programme started and was built up almost automatically meant that there was a shroud of secrecy surrounding everything. There was always the fear that if you talked about something, you would say too much, and therefore it was better to say nothing. It was such a politically sensitive subject. You could understand that politicians did not want to air it, because of the criticisms they would face, simply because they supported some parts of the nuclear programme. It made for a quieter life to do things quietly behind closed doors...however, there is room for an open debate and it would be more democratic.' (47)

A non-governmental organisation called the Oxford Research Group (ORG) is particularly concerned with excessive secrecy in defence decision-making. Scilla Elworthy, Director of the ORG, argues: 'There is an unacceptable degree of secrecy over defence matters in Britain under the present system. The result is that Parliament, and hence the British public, is denied information which could substantially alter options and votes. Money is wasted, and the excuse of risk to national security is used as a screen behind which information on inefficiency and corruption can be concealed. There are three aspects to this problem: the need on the part of Parliament for more information; a lack of proper accountability; and the absence of any clear definition of what may and may not legitimately be kept secret.' (48) The need for information was highlighted in a survey conducted in 1988 of members of Parliament from the Conservative and Labour parties who claimed they found it difficult to gain reliable and accurate information on defence. After the 'Options for Change' exercise in 1992, Prime Minister John Major decided to tackle the problem of excessive secrecy and bureaucracy, and since then the situation has improved slightly. But the need for greater freedom of information remains. Martin O'Neill says: 'As the Opposition shadow defence secretary I made several requests to be allowed to visit the Aldermaston Weapons Research Establishment (AWRE) and was refused every time by the Conservative ministers through whom I had to go. It was only after the Labour Party changed its position from unilateralism to multilateralism that the government was prepared to let me into the Establishment. Indeed, Alan Clark was extremely helpful, but it was only after the Labour Party's change of policy that I was able to see a great deal of the work going on.' (49) In an interview before the 1997 election, Bruce George said: 'Even on the Defence Select Committee, where in theory we should have access to 'NATO Top Secret' documents, the Ministry of Defence is notoriously unwilling to give us the necessary information to do our jobs. NATO is reluctant too. They are excessively secretive. I am not calling for all our secrets to be made public, but they should better define what is best kept under wraps. There is a large area that is currently designated Top Secret that should not be.' (50)

Scilla Elworthy argues that the following changes are necessary for a more open debate. Defence budgets should be more detailed, particularly over expenditure for weapons procurement which should be broken down into research, development and production stages. Agreements with other nations, including those for collaborative procurement projects, should be subjected to full parliamentary debate before signature. This could include agreements with other nations on defence and nuclear issues, especially on research and development, including the texts of nuclear agreements with the United States and France. All defence export licences granted by the Department of Trade and Industry should be made public. Officials in charge of procurement should be named and made subject to the usual sanctions through courts of law if they are negligent. Finally it is important to define and list what is currently kept secret and to debate whether it is appropriate. (51)

Time will tell whether the Labour government elected in 1997 will be more open on the issue of secrecy generally. (52) On the nuclear issue, Labour has made several welcome breaks with tradition. It has disclosed the number of nuclear missile bodies to be bought, the load to be carried by each Trident submarine and the maximum arsenal of operationally available nuclear warheads. It has been more forthcoming about aspects of previous systems such as WE-177, *Polaris* and *Chevaline*. It has given much fuller information about the running costs of the submarine, missile and warhead programmes. It has declared the size of holdings of nuclear materials held outside international safeguards. And it has promised to produce, by spring 2000, an initial report of defence fissile material production since the start of Britain's defence nuclear programme in the 1940s (53) These are limited gestures, however, and the question is whether such changes continue and further ones are made. Clearly, the government wants to make an impression and is perhaps not as steeped in tradition as the Conservatives were. It is still too early to judge.

References
(1) Frank Barnaby, *Acquisition of Nuclear Weapons, Technical Details of What is Required, Strengthening the Non Proliferation Regime in 1995*, Oxford Research Group, Briefing Number One, 1995.
(2) Interview with Frank Barnaby, 5 March 1997.
(3) The United Kingdom Atomic Energy Authority (UKAEA) originally concentrated on molecular separation as a form of uranium enrichment technology. In 1984 however, Britain decided in favour of the atomic separation process, and British Nuclear Fuels (BNFL) initiated a laser isotope separation programme in 1982. By 1986, BNFL felt it would be in a position to consider a plant installation in the late 1990s. Development work with the UKAEA is currently under way. Information from Richard Kokoski, *Technology and the Proliferation of Nuclear Weapons*, Swedish International Peace Institute SIPRI, Oxford University Press, 1995, pp.95-96.
(4) Kokoski: *Technology*, pp.84-95.
(5) Thomas B. Cochran, 'Plutonium: the international scene', Paper presented at the Pugwash Conferences on Science and World Affairs, Public Discussion Meeting on Plutonium Management and Control, at the Royal Society, London, 8 December 1995.
(6)Interview with Frank Barnaby, 5 March 1997.
(7) Frank Barnaby, *Civil Fissile Materials, Their Potential Use in Weapons, Strengthening the Non Proliferation Regime* , Oxford Research Group, Briefing Number Two, 1995.
(8) Barnaby: *Civil Fissile Materials*.
(9) Kokoski: *Technology* pp.92-95.
(10) Kokoski: *Technology* pp.92-95.
(11) Quotation from the Principles and Objectives for Nuclear Non Proliferation and Disarmament NPT Review and Extension Conference 1995. Christopher R. Hill, R. Sebastian Pease, Rudolf E. Peierls, Joseph Rotblat, *Does Britain Need Nuclear Weapons?* Report from the British Pugwash Group, 1995, p 27.
(12) Kokoski: *Technology*, pp.92-95.
(13) Kokoski: *Technology*, pp.147-176.
(14) Kokoski: *Technology, pp 147-176*.
(15) *SIPRI Yearbook*, Oxford University Press, Oxford, 1995, p.667.
(16) 'Nuclear Non Proliferation after the NPT Review', *Non*

Proliferation, Arms Control, Disarmament, 1995, p.585.

(17) Suzanna van Moyland, 'The Non-Proliferation Treaty: strengthened review, strengthened safeguards', *Trust and Verify,* Issue 79, March 1998, VERTIC, London, p.5.

(18) *Ionising Radiation,* Medical Educational Trust Report, Background Paper, August, 1990, p.6.

(19) Correspondence with Lady Kennet 20 April 1998.

(20) Interview with Lord Hailsham 17 February 1997.

(21) G. Allen Greb, *Survey of Past Nuclear Test Ban Negotiations,* Institute on Global Conflict and Cooperation, University of California, San Diego, La Jolla, California, pp.101-103.

(22) Interview with John Edmonds 5 February 1997.

(23) Interview with John Edmonds 5 February 1997

(24) Stephen Young, *A Test Ban Treaty that Doesn't Ban Tests?* British and American Security Council, BASIC Document Number 53, 23 September 1996.

(25) *The Guardian* 7 April 1998.

(26) Ben Sheppard, ' How far has South Asia gone out of control?' *Bulletin of Arms Control,* No. 30, July 1998, pp. 20-26

(27) John F. Burns, 'India's Line in the Sand: "Minimum" Nuclear Deterrent against China', *International Herald Tribune* 8 July 1998, p. 4. 'For India, Disarmament or Equal Security', Jaswant Singh, *International Herald Tribune* 5 August 1998, p. 6.

(28) *Environmental Testing at AWE,* AWE Briefing Paper, 1993.

(29) Hill: *Does Britain need Nuclear Weapons?* p.11.

(30) Hill: *Does Britain Need Nuclear Weapons? p.12.*

(31) Greenpeace, *The True Cost of Trident,* 1995.

(32) *Ionising Radiation,* pp.2-1, 2-2.

(33) Sir Kevin Spencer, former Chief Scientist, Ministry of Power in the UK, speaking in 1983, cited in C. Caufield, *Multiple Exposures: Chronicles of the Radiation Age,* Penguin, 1989.

(34) *Ionising Radiation,* pp.2-3, 2-4..

(35) *Ionising Radiation,*.pp.8-9.

(36) Beral *et. al., British Medical Journal,* 17 August, 1985, p.440,quoted in *Ionising Radiation.*

(37) Beral: *British Medical Journal,* p.845.

(38) Cook-Mozaffari *et. al., Cancer incidence and Mortality in the vicinity of Nuclear Installations in England and Wales,1959-1980 Series: Studies on Medical and*

Population Subjects, No.51, HMSO, 1987.

(39) Beral: *British Medical Journal* p.757.

(40) *Ionising Radiation*, p.22.

(41) F.A.Fry and B.T.Wilkins, *An Assessment of Radionuclide Levels around the former Air Base at Greenham Common, Berkshire*, National Radiological Protection Board M752, 1986.

(42) Quotation from Norman Dixon in Scilla Elworthy, *Power and Sex*, Element, Shaftesbury, Dorset, 1996, p.70.

(43) Interview with Clive Ponting 6 March 1997, also Clive Ponting, 'Defence decision making and public opinion, a view from the inside', in Catherine Marsh and Colin Fraser, (eds), *Public Opinion and Nuclear Weapons*, Macmillan, London, 1989, pp.177-190.

(44) Commander Robert Green RN (Retd.) (quoting Sir Henry Leach) in *Questioning Nuclear Deterrence, the Military Point of View*, 1996. Conversation with George Fairbrother, World Court Project, 17 October 1998.

(45) Scilla Elworthy, 'Nuclear weapons decision making and accountability', in Marsh: *Public Opinion*.

(46) Elworthy: *'Nuclear weapons'*.

(47) Interview with Denis Fakely, 1 April 1997.

(48) Scilla Elworthy, 'How secret do defence decisions need to be?' in John Gittings and Ian Davis, (eds), *Rethinking Defence, Britain in the Twenty First Century*, Bertrand Russell Press, Nottingham, 1996, pp.153-161.

(49) Interview with Martin O'Neill 6 February 1997.

(50) Interview with Bruce George 6 February 1997.

(51) Elworthy: 'How secret?' pp.153-161.

(52) A Labour Government was elected on 1 May 1997. George Robertson became Defence Secretary and Lord Gilbert Defence Procurement Minister. Richard Mottram remained the Permanent Under Secretary and was succeeded in July 1998 by Kevin Tebbitt.

(53) *The Strategic Defence Review*, Cm. 3999, The Stationery office, London, July 1998, Supporting Essay Number Five, pp. 5-2 to 5-10.

4. CHANGING DOCTRINE IN A POST COLD WAR ENVIRONMENT

> Weapons themselves are not the root of conflict and the real risk of war can only be eliminated when international conflict itself is moderated.(1)

The political realities we face today bear no resemblance to those of 1945. Russia is now a Partner for Peace and no NATO weapon is targeted against any other state. Yet old ways of thinking die hard. The purpose of this chapter is to discuss the ways in which thinking about nuclear weapons in particular is changing in the post-Cold War environment.

For some, nuclear weapons and the essentially robust form of deterrence they provide seem safe enough. However, as the threats have receded since the end of the Cold War, it is becoming clearer that the risks involved in keeping these weapons are potentially high. Nuclear weapons have the potential to destroy civilisation, a capacity which has been well entitled 'omnicide'. (2) The end of the Cold War has greatly lessened the possibility of a large-scale conflict and has brought into serious question the value, even in political terms, of nuclear arsenals of the type held by the five nuclear weapons powers. With the break-up of the former Soviet Union, Britain is no longer under mortal threat, and the conflicts that cause most trouble, mainly ethnic and internal, are not affected by and do not require possession of nuclear weapons. The same type of analysis now needs to be applied to them as to other costly weapons systems. (3)

When the decision to replace Polaris was taken, the Soviet Union seemed to be more dangerous than ever before. It made sense to procure an advanced system that could penetrate future Soviet defences. The decision for Trident was driven in part politically, in order to strengthen Anglo-American relations, but Trident was also the system that best served Britain's needs. It now provides Britain with a destructive capability far in excess of what could ever be required. There are various reasons why it has survived calls for its cancellation from various quarters. Partly as a legacy of the Cold War and partly as a consequence of the continued uncertainty over the stability of the international environment, strategic nuclear deterrence is still perceived to be an integral part of the defence policy of Britain. In this respect, the doctrine has remained essentially the same. However some of the underlying assumptions have changed, particularly in regard to the tactical utility of nuclear weapons. New generations of precision-guided munitions are coming up that are capable of performing most of the military roles for which there were no credible non-nuclear substitutes in earlier decades. This has removed the military rationale for almost all the war-fighting roles that could be performed by nuclear ordnance. But not all states have access to, or can afford, these weapons, and some countries still see nuclear capability as an affordable alternative to deter the superior conventional military might of their enemies. By arranging for *Vanguard* class submarines to go to sea with missiles carrying a mixture of loads, Britain will be able to maintain a tactical and strategic deterrent on a single type of platform. This has combined well with a move away from deterring specific threats to insuring against unspecified risks. It also fits well with the need not so much to check Soviet expansion, as to provide some counterbalance in Europe to Russia which is still one of the world's great nuclear powers.

Government Policy
The 1996 Statement on the Defence Estimates says of nuclear weapons: 'The Government remains committed to maintaining a credible and effective minimum deterrent for as long as is necessary for our security. Our operationally independent nuclear deterrent forces continue

to provide the ultimate guarantee of our national security and make an important contribution to NATO's strategy of war prevention, a strategy that has prevented major conflict in Europe for almost fifty years. All of our nuclear forces are assigned to NATO and form an integral part of the Alliance's nuclear posture, but could, if necessary, be used independently of the Alliance in the defence of our supreme national interests.' (4)

The NATO Alliance's strategic concept states that 'Nuclear Weapons make a contribution in rendering the risks of any aggression incalculable and unacceptable. Thus, they remain the preserver of the peace ... the fundamental purpose of nuclear forces is political: to preserve peace and prevent coercion and any kind of war.' (5) And in similar vein NATO's defence ministers have said, 'We reaffirm that the fundamental purpose of NATO's nuclear forces is political; to preserve peace and prevent coercion...we reaffirm that nuclear forces continue to fulfil an indispensable and unique role in the Alliance'. (6)

British nuclear doctrine is thus based on the notion that nuclear weapons can be used both independently *and* under the aegis of NATO. Trident will be deployed in a multi-purpose role, including a capability to use it in a limited nuclear war, whatever that might mean. The reasons the government gives for keeping nuclear weapons can be separated into three main components. The first is to confront any possible threat from a resurgent Russia. The second is to be available for a sub-strategic strike. The third is because nuclear weapons cannot be disinvented. The British government does not regard these purposes as inconsistent with a policy designed to control the proliferation of nuclear weapons to other states. (7)

Britain, like the other nuclear weapons states other than China, has always refused to give an assurance of 'no first use' (NFU) of nuclear weapons because it believes that such a commitment would inevitably weaken deterrence and perhaps invite attack. In other words, Britain in principle reserves the right to use nuclear weapons in response to an overwhelming non-nuclear assault if there were no other way of defeating it. Britain has in the past deployed nuclear weapons in regional crises involving non-nuclear powers. For example both during the Falklands war in 1982 and in the Gulf war in

1991, Britain had the means to escalate to nuclear use. But it is hard to believe that such use was ever remotely considered. This is not only because there was no serious prospect of losing either of these wars. A much more powerful consideration will have been the immense political odium that would have been incurred. It is easy to imagine the relish with which the media would relay the side effects of any use of a nuclear weapon. Hiroshima has erected a vast taboo against any repetition, let alone one initiated by a Western power against a member of the developing world. This may not be very logical. We learn of the massacre of 500,000 Tutsis by their fellow-countrymen in Rwanda and do nothing. But nuclear weapons, together with chemical and biological ones, are regarded with unique revulsion.

Moreover any such use would be subject to the important undertakings given by Britain along with the other nuclear weapon states never to use, or threaten to use, nuclear weapons against a state party to the NPT (or a similar regional treaty) which does not itself posses nuclear weapons, unless it commits aggression as the ally of a nuclear weapon state. This so-called 'negative security assurance' protects almost every country in the world other than the nuclear weapons states themselves, along with Israel, India and Pakistan. It is very difficult indeed to imagine any credible scenario where a British Prime Minister would *initiate* the use of nuclear weapons against any of these countries. This means that Britain comes very close, as it should, to a 'no-first-use' posture, where its nuclear weapons serve only to deter the use of nuclear weapons against Britain or her allies.

Sub-strategic role
When this role was originally defined the Cold War was still at its height. The military requirement for a sub-strategic system was to penetrate Soviet air defences with an accurate long-range, air-launched missile, while Trident stayed behind in the Atlantic as the final arbiter. But what does sub-strategic mean now? It is clearly intended to mean something different from the battle-fighting role that was previously envisaged for tactical or theatre nuclear weapons. While the Americans and particularly the Russians have kept large stocks of such weapons, the British have disposed of theirs. The idea

perhaps originated in France, which always eschewed any concept of nuclear war fighting, but devised the notion of 'pre-strategic' use for their ground-based short range nuclear missile systems *Pluton* and *Hadès*. The idea was that if there were a major invasion threatening to engulf France, the French could unleash their pre-strategic strike (hopefully against the invader while still outside French soil, as the Germans used to scornfully observe) for a kind of final shot across the bows of the invader, warning that he must cease and desist or bear the full weight of French retaliation. What part a concept of this kind could play in British policy is far from clear. The answer probably is that no one knows. Cautious planners in the Ministry of Defence argue that some day in a game of international bluff, a deterrent may have to be called into play, and Trident is the only available option, strategic or otherwise. But this is hardly a satisfactory answer.

A role for Trident?

We have lost the Soviets and discovered the Rogue States.(8)

Britain faces no clear threats from any country today, and Trident is not aimed at any particular enemy. Yet there is always the danger, however unlikely, of a revanchist Russia. Nuclear anarchy in the former Soviet Union has made the security of nuclear components and materials a matter of concern. And there are over fifty states. with the capacity to acquire nuclear weapons in the longer term, some of which are unstable. A nuclear war that involved the Korean Peninsula, the South Asian subcontinent or any of the Middle Eastern states would disrupt the world economy and completely destabilise the international system. Not only would it have profound repercussions for Britain's commercial interests, but it would also have a disastrous psychological effect by breaking the norm of non-use.

In such potential contexts, it would seem, then, that there are four possible uses of Trident.

(1) In response to a nuclear attack against British terri-

tory or forces, the latter most likely during a crisis, say in the Middle East.

(2) In response to an attack on the UK or on UK forces using chemical or biological weapons. Today, about fifteen countries of interest to NATO are developing or fielding chemical weapons (half of whom maintain stockpiles) while ten states also have some form of biological weapon in their programmes. These weapons are comparatively cheap to produce and states with an aggressive ambition that outruns their industrial and scientific resources can resort to CBW as 'the poor man's answer to a nuclear bomb'. Presumably, most states engaged in such programmes are doing so to enhance their regional power. But as the range of delivery vehicles increases, so do the implications for international stability. More than a dozen states possess ballistic missiles suitable for delivering these weapons and several more are developing them. The SCUD missile has long been commonplace in the developing world, and several states are engaged in their local manufacture. A new generation of longer-range ballistic missiles is under development in the Third World. Despite the provisions of the Missile Technology Control regime (MTCR), which are designed to prevent such proliferation, there is no doubt that technology relating to missiles is being exported. (9)

(3) As a demonstration shot to deter an enemy from taking a particular course of action.

(4) As a nuclear response which might be made to a state which had refused to desist from a specific course of action, for example a major conventional attack.

It is very important to repeat, in connection with the last three possibilities, that the use of nuclear weapons in any of these circumstances, except against Russia, China and their close allies or India, Pakistan or Israel, would run flatly counter to the negative security assurances given by Britain. (10)

Deterrence

The issue of nuclear deterrence has some

what fallen off under the changed circumstances of the end of the Cold War. When it does arise, it is usually in the guise of public debate on the risks of weaponry, as with the protests against French nuclear testing, rather than an understanding of the continuing security advantages. (11)

The basic concept of deterrence - that weapons exist to prevent wars rather than to fight them - originated in the early theories of strategic bombing. Such theories came to prominence during the inter-war years. The terrible sufferings in the trenches during the First World War of 1914 to 1918 caused strategists to seek for a more humane method of warfare. With the aircraft, then relatively new, showing promise as a powerful weapon, the answer seemed to lie in bombing raids that could, in theory, provide a quick end to wars. By threatening the destruction of the war-fighting potential of the enemy and the collapse of the enemy society, strategic bombing would, it was argued, avoid wars or at least bring them to a relatively clean end. By the 1930s what was by then known as the 'deterrent', the threat of an immediate aerial counter-offensive against the enemy homeland, was believed to be the only means by which Britain could protect herself against the Germans.

Strategic bombing was conducted by all parties throughout the Second World War. An ugly consequence was that, because the attack on enemy morale became a legitimate objective, so did attacks on civilian populations. In the case of Britain, a further reason was the need to be seen to be hitting back at the Germans at a time, after 1940, when they had occupied most of western Europe and aerial bombardment was almost the only available means. Lacking any form of accurate bombsight, at least in the early years of the War, there was no option but to go for area bombing. Later, in 1944, German use against London of inherently random rocket weapons, the V-1 pilotless 'plane and the V-2 stratospheric missile, added a further gruesome, and frightening, dimension. Elsewhere, the damage done by strategic bombing was not without effect; arguably, it would have brought about the surrender of Japan within a few more months, obviating the need to use the atom bomb.

However, strategic bombing always caused less disruption to war production than expected, and the effects on the morale of civilian populations has usually been to strengthen their resolve: this, in fact, is precisely what happened among both British and German civilians subjected to bombing during the War. The arrival of nuclear weapons, however, introduced something entirely novel and unique. Their virtually unlimited destructive power, and the unpredictable danger of escalation once they were available to both sides, changed the nature of the equation completely. By obliging states to exercise the utmost caution in their relations with potential adversaries, nuclear weapons could very plausibly be presented as a deterrent to attack and so a preventative against war.

Between 1946 and 1989, the Soviet system appeared to be threatening Western Europe. In previous periods of history where there were two ideologically opposed camps, this often led to war. During the cold War, this did not happen, even though there were many points of friction and areas of potential dispute. Many people believe that the two sides were mutually deterred by the knowledge that any kind of war between them would have been likely to risk escalating to the nuclear level. They argue that nuclear deterrence in this way stabilised the world system. Of this, we can never be sure. What is certain, however, is that nuclear deterrence brought with it a unique moral dilemma: whether the saving of thousands of lives by deterring major conventional wars was worth the small, but unavoidable, danger of a nuclear holocaust (12)

Today this dilemma has taken a different form because NATO now has more than sufficient conventional strength to defeat any potential adversary or group of adversaries. But at what cost? No one can deny that it is far better to deter aggression than be forced to defeat it. There is also no evidence to suggest that conventional forces, however large or capable, could in isolation always deter a determined and ruthless adversary. Those in favour of nuclear weapons argue that only nuclear forces have that potential. At the same time, it has become clear that nuclear deterrence could not be used to deter aggression that threatened less than the survival of the state.

> The idea of deterrence, of deterring someone
> from acting in unacceptable ways is, whether
> we like to admit it or not, built into inter-state
> relationships just as it is built into regulating
> inter-personal relationships and ensuring
> behaviour within the law in civil society. (13)

One of the most rational voices arguing for retention of British nuclear weapons today is that of Sir Michael Quinlan. As a leading apologist for nuclear deterrence, he argues that there are too many reasons for not ridding the world of nuclear weapons. (14) First he believes that it is unrealistic to expect that Russia and France (two examples) would sign up with genuine intent to an abolitionist goal. He reasons that it is not feasible to base future policies on the hope that other countries have the motives we would like. Secondly Sir Michael highlights the impracticality of verification. He argues that it is utopian to expect every nuclear-capable state to lay itself open to rigorous and intensive verification backed by the threat of international sanctions. He regards it as an obvious fallacy to suppose that nuclear weapons were just a Cold War phenomenon. It is over-optimistic to assume that there could never again be an all-out war between developed states. Nevertheless, Quinlan believes that because of their virtually limitless power, nuclear weapons have brought about the *reductio ad absurdum* of such war. Paradoxically, their purported abolition would serve in effect to re-rationalise warfare. He believes that instead of pursuing the visionary and unrealistic goal of total abolition, we should continue to pursue the constructive arms control agenda which is already in hand. (See Chapter 9).

At the heart of Quinlan's argument lies the obvious point that we can never forget to how make nuclear weapons. But the British Pugwash Group led by Professor Rotblat believe that this argument is not, of itself, decisive: 'There are many products of the advances in science and technology that have turned out to be hazardous to people or harmful to the environment. A feature of a civilised society is that it attempts to control the undesirable creations of science and technology through national laws and international treaties...The impossibility of disinvention is not a conclusive argument against nuclear disarmament...' (15) Moreover the impossibility of disinvention is itself only a half-truth. 'Few pieces of conventional wisdom run deeper than the notion that 'you can't disinvent nuclear weapons'. Like most conventional wisdom, it is part true, part false. Knowledge of the physics that makes nuclear weapons possible is humanity's permanent inheritance. But that is not true of the assembled, partly tacit, largely engineering-based skills that make nuclear weapons technological realities rather than drawing-board concepts. Once the infrastructures are dismantled, the teams split up and key individuals die, rebuilding a programme is not a lot easier than creating it in the first place - especially if testing is impossible'. (16)

Political issues
In the past, the Labour Party suffered at the polls because the British public did not believe that Britain could be independent and free if it did not have its own nuclear weapons. Nuclear Weapons proved to be a crucial focus of internal party strife in the Labour party in the late 1950s, and again in the early 1980s. Analysts of public opinion believe that the party's commitment to unilateral nuclear disarmament was one of the contributory factors to its defeats in 1983 and 1987. As Bruce George has put it: 'The campaign by the government and the MOD against Labour's defence policy in the 1980s was both sophisticated and crude and it helped to destroy Labour's election prospects. I think that Tony Blair has recognised over the last few years, as did John Smith and eventually even Neil Kinnock, that you do not go into an election with a defence policy that is perceived as incredible as Labour did in 1983 and 1987, and the responsible possession of nuclear weapons is something that is required by most of the British electorate'. (17)

The Labour party abandoned unilateralism under Neil Kinnock in 1989, when a policy review document was approved by its annual conference. But conference consistently faced both ways by also passing motions to scrap Trident and cut defence spending. In 1994, the motion to scrap Trident was carried by 54 per cent to 46 per cent. At the Labour Party Conference in 1995 Tony Blair secured a decisive vote *not* to scrap the Trident nuclear missile system. The shop workers union USDAW, which carried five per cent of the vote, had voted to scrap Trident in 1994, but changed its position to support the leadership. There also appears to have been a substantial shift in opinion amongst local party delegates. The vote by 55.8 per cent to 44.2 per cent, represented a decisive rejection of unilateralism.

During the election campaign of 1997, the Labour Party promised a Strategic Defence Review and since their victory, this has been completed. This review was supposed to place long-term thinking at the centre of policy-making and aimed to create a coherent strategic framework in which to reassess Britain's security interests and defence needs. In large measure, it has succeeded and the intellectual coherence of the resulting reports is impressive by any standards. But the question whether or not to retain nuclear weapons was not at issue in the Review. This meant that while the exact number of missiles and warheads could be reconsidered, the government had decided *a priori* to keep the independent British deterrent Trident for the duration of its useful life. The question of its ultimate replacement was left open. In other words, if instability across the world were to create conditions where Britain once again became subject to a plausible nuclear threat, the government would still have the option of replacing Trident at the end of its life.

Fresh Thinking

> Everyone knows that a British Government of whatever colour, if it were starting with a clean sheet of paper today, would not be embarking upon Trident...As a nation, we are marginally safer but we gain a great deal more importance as a result of our continued nuclear status. Trident is here to be milked for international influence ... (18)

If the international climate remains as calm as it is now, attacks on retaining Trident are likely to be heard increasingly within the Ministry of Defence as the government tries to maintain the existing force structure within the Treasury's cash limits. So far, this argument has been confined to a debate about the numbers of war heads Trident submarines should carry, and the number of missile bodies to be purchased, which in both cases has resulted in a small reduction. But the idea that Britain no longer needs nuclear weapons has become less revolutionary. Over the past few years, a body of opinion has grown up within defence circles which argues that these weapons are of declining importance, certainly unfashionable and perhaps unnecessary. It is commonly accepted from almost all sides of the defence debate that were Britain to be faced with the decision to procure Trident in today's climate, that decision would probably not be taken. As political attention has focused on international peace-keeping efforts in areas such as Bosnia and central Africa, the nuclear issue has been pushed aside as peripheral. Michael MccGwire, an ex-naval officer and intelligence specialist, argues that since the Gulf War and disintegration of the former Soviet Union, the idea of eliminating nuclear weapons has become respectable. An influential body of opinion has grown up in the American national security community that nuclear weapons have no military utility except to deter their use by others. If so, it would be logical to take the further step of concluding that the general abolition of these weapons would be in everyone's interests. If no one has them, there is no need for anyone to deter their use. (19)

The most cogent reasons for eliminating nuclear weapons are:

1. The existence of nuclear weapons makes nuclear war possible. This could begin as the result of a deliberate decision by governments. More probably it would be triggered by unauthorised action, miscalculation, misunderstanding or sheer technical malfunction.

2. A major nuclear war could destroy civilisation and jeopardise the survival of the human race.

3. Human fallibility means that so long as nuclear weapons exist their use is ultimately inevitable.

> We have had thousands of false alarms of
> impending missile attacks on the United

States, and a few could have spun out of control. (20)

These considerations lead to the clear conclusion that nuclear weapons should be abolished. Governments should act now to set this process in motion, which could well take 20 to 30 years to complete. The aims of such a policy would be to reduce the possibility of a major nuclear exchange to zero, while decreasing the probability that nuclear weapons could ever be used at all to as low a level as possible. According to Michael MccGwire, the aim of a nuclear weapon free policy is not in itself to eliminate war, to achieve complete disarmament, to resolve regional conflicts or to enhance global stability. But he believes that if the Nuclear Weapons States adopted the policy of working towards a Nuclear Weapon Free World (NWFW), we would begin to see the effects at once as the number and variety of co-operative policy measures involved would impact upon the evolving international system.

1. The treaty-making process would act as bridge to the non-aligned nations and be a force for compromise. By renouncing nuclear weapons the Nuclear Weapons States would be making a great concession. The transparency required to ensure control and verification of the NWFW regime would apply to all, and the universal goal of stopping a nuclear catastrophe would generate an unusual mutuality of interest amongst participants.

2. Adoption of this policy would dissolve dissatisfaction with the Non-Proliferation Treaty, because the principal argument against it has been its so-called discriminatory effect of dividing the world into 'haves' and 'have nots', apparently for ever.

3. It would meet a key objection to the Comprehensive Test Ban Treaty raised, for example by India, and, based on the same argument, would make it easier to police the Chemical and Biological Weapons conventions.

There are many reasons for delay in this process however. It is clear that geo-political conditions quite different to the present would have to be met before the goal of abolition could be safely accomplished. One of the most obvious dangers is that while moving ostensibly to the goal of total abolition, one or more states would secretly retain either a small stockpile of weapons or at least the means to re-manufacture weapons very quickly. This is known as the problem of breakout and is difficult to resolve. The necessary degree of surveillance and verification is hard to envisage so long as nations remain basically suspicious of each other. The final stage of elimination would no doubt require the resolution of regional conflicts and wide-ranging renunciation of regional force. Thus, moves towards a nuclear weapon-free world can only be made safely as parts of a wider move towards regional and global stability and security. Michael Quinlan says: 'We can, of course, postulate political conditions in which none of these disagreeable questions arises - a New World Order in which entrenched good sense and accepted global authority have made war apparently and dependably obsolete, even under stress, as a way of conducting international business among major states (as has been plainly achieved in the European Union). But this would be a world vastly unlike the world we now live in, or can base our policy upon; and there is no plausible ground for supposing that commitment to nuclear abolition will prompt an all round Damascene conversion to its creation. We must hope to travel in that direction, but abolition will be cart not horse.' (21)

A conventional alternative?
Some experts argue that the military functions for which nuclear weapons were formerly required can now be better performed by modern conventional weapons. According to Robert O'Neill, while the international system has been changing, the power of conventional weapons has hugely improved. For example, the conventional weapons used during the Gulf War were both highly accurate and extremely destructive - if less dramatically so than some enthusiasts told us at the time. He argues that if, in the future, the West has to use force to confront or deter even nuclear threats by lesser powers, it will certainly prefer to use conventional force rather than nuclear. It is generally agreed that nuclear deterrence, in the form that operated during the Cold War, is

unlikely to work at all against smaller rogue nuclear states and groups. Modern conventional weapons have a much better prospect of doing so. Their effectiveness is more readily demonstrated in tests, and from a political and moral standpoint, Western nuclear powers face far fewer inhibitions about using them. (22)

It could accordingly be argued that if Saddam Hussein had known in August 1990 the size of forces that would be ranged against him and the destructiveness of some of their weapons, he would have been deterred from invading Kuwait. But the fact remains that he was *not* deterred, just as President Galtieri of Argentina was not deterred from invading the Falkland Islands in 1982. If either of them had anticipated a *plausible* prospect that Britain would use her nuclear weapons against them, they would assuredly have held their hands. From this reasoning, a pro-nuclear conclusion can be drawn. The lower the destructiveness of one's retaliatory force, the more likely one's bluff is to be called. The price of nuclear abolition might therefore be an increase in the number of conventional wars, exactly as Quinlan has argued. The point cannot be proved either way, however.

Europe and NATO

> Britain is perhaps the most committed European member of NATO. It has a capability that is more professional, certainly as well equipped, and it has made a point of placing itself in the European structures in such a way as to be closer to the United States. (23)

A big question is how Britain will fit in with any future European security policy. Europe is a wider community of nations than those represented in the European Union (EU) or NATO. Crises such as Bosnia and the Gulf have forged co-operation between this wider group of nations and NATO has worked hard through the Euro-Atlantic Partnership Council and the Partnership for Peace programme to give institutional form to this wider community. But NATO remains the primary and much the most effective body for defence. Alternative efforts to forge co-operation within Europe, either through the development of a European Security and Defence Identity (ESDI) or via the Organisation for Security and Co-operation in Europe (OSCE), have so far had little success. Very few of the 54 member governments of the OSCE seem ready to give that organisation a leading role in European security and to resource it accordingly. NATO members in particular have seemed determined to keep the OSCE as low-key as possible. And despite some interest on the part of the present British government, the whole idea of a Common Foreign and Security Policy (CFSP) within the EU has failed to make much headway. So the question becomes rather how to organise an increasing European co-ordination within NATO. This brings into focus the future of the Western European Union (WEU). At present, the WEU stands outside the EU; there is no formal treaty link and it is not answerable to any of the EU's democratic mechanisms. But the WEU is described in the Maastricht Treaty as an integral part of the Union, charged with working out a European defence policy and implementing those decisions of the EU that have defence implications. In practice, because of the special position of the neutrals within the EU, (Ireland, Finland, Austria and Sweden) and because two of the WEU members are nuclear powers, the possibility of creating a common defence policy, much less a common defence, seems many years away at best. (24)

For many years, Britain has wanted to bring the French back into NATO as fully as possible, but has been frustrated by France's dispute with the US over command in southern Europe. The underlying problem is that the French are determined to create a serious European entity as far as possible independent of the US, while the US still want to use NATO as an extension of their own security system. Despite these difficulties the French and the British are becoming more closely involved in their approach to nuclear matters. A Joint Commission on Nuclear Policy was established between the two countries in 1995 at a meeting between President Jacques Chirac and Prime Minister John Major. They agreed to a strengthening of nuclear co-operation, particularly on technical matters. (25) The October 1995 joint statement said: 'We do not see situations arising in which the vital interests of either France or the UK could be threatened without the vital interests of the other also being threatened...We have decided to pursue and deepen nuclear co-operation between our two countries. Our aim is mutually to strengthen deterrence, while retaining the independence of our nuclear forces.' A French diplomat emphasised that 'the British must understand that unless we co-operate neither of us will be able to withstand pressures for cuts in our arsenals or afford to maintain a deterrent.' (26) So Britain is working closely with France, co-ordinating activities in such practical areas as patrolling. But it is doubtful if nuclear planning can be concerted much more closely. It makes sense for Britain to work in co-operation with France over administration, patrol planning and the sharing of targets. But the ability to use the weapons and the decision to do so is perhaps the most important power that any country possesses, and this power will remain firmly in the hands of individual governments.

In 1995, the French and British began to consider devising a common approach to nuclear issues with the Germans, which in turn might lead to a common nuclear doctrine. Despite their traditional insistence on the independence of the *force de frappe*, it was the French who launched the project for a European nuclear consensus. Their aim, it seems, was to ward off mounting international pressure for nuclear disarmament, not least from within the EU. Anti-nuclear sentiment in the community has been significantly strengthened with the accession of Sweden and Austria. But the evolution of a European nuclear doctrine would be fraught with problems. Among the issues to be considered are:

1. The conditions which might cause Europe to have resort to nuclear weapons,
2. Whether the use of nuclear weapons other than for the direct defence of a member state is conceivable
3. Whether all EC members would have the right to call on British or French nuclear weapons?
4. Whether the Bundestag would accept a European nuclear arrangement with no national veto over use of nuclear weapons
5. If every nation had such a veto what possible credibility could such a deterrent threat possess?

With such considerations in mind, the military planners and civil servants in Paris and London insist that a common deterrent is out of the question. But this has not stopped the European Parliament calling for one. The Parliament's Foreign Affairs and Security Committee has argued for a common system of deterrence. In a public drafting session in 1997, the Committee made it clear that they envisaged such a deterrent would be nuclear. They did not foresee the EU acquiring nuclear weapons of its own, but taking over nuclear weapons now owned by France and Britain.

British Members of the European Parliament were not supportive, and argued that a European nuclear deterrent would violate Article I of the Non Proliferation Treaty, which prohibits countries with nuclear weapons from transferring these to any other recipient. (27) Besides that, what threats would a common deterrent address? Since it is hard to think of any, perhaps the European deterrent would only exist as a symbol of the Union's superiority over its neighbouring states. This would play badly with the Russians, the Eastern Europeans and the North Africans, who would quite correctly view themselves as the outsiders in this context. The possible creation of a European Union nuclear force raises other serious questions about defence policy in the post-Cold War Europe, and about how and where Britain will choose to stand. For example, will Britain really wish to play along with any Common Foreign and Security Policy (CFSP)?

Martin Butcher has written: 'CFSP is a process for policy making rather than an actual policy. It is intergovernmental in its nature and very few central resources are available for it. Europe has had little success with the CFSP because the mechanism is cumbersome and there is no central information gathering and analysis centre, nor a mechanism for taking the necessary action.' (28) Whether in the future Britain will be prepared to become a stronger European partner, remains to be seen. If Britain decides against committing herself fully to a European security option, then another problem will confront British policy makers. Bearing in mind the strong British political tradition of seeking security within an alliance framework, with whom will the British align themselves? The obvious solution is to stick with the Atlantic Alliance that has proved such an effective agent of collective security for fifty years. Self-evidently, NATO is only viable in a military sense when backed by

American military power. This raises the question whether the European segment of NATO can continue to enjoy the certainty of US military support in future. For the time being, the answer to this question is quite clearly Yes. But as the centre of gravity and interest for the USA shifts more and more westwards to the Pacific, and voices are increasingly raised to question why a power of the size and economic weight of Europe should not accept full responsibility for its own security, perhaps this reassuring answer will not hold for much longer.

References
(1) Gerald Segal, *The Nuclear Weapons Revolution, Guide to the World Today*, Simon and Schuster Limited, London, 1988, p.77.
(2) The main crisis involving a threat of nuclear war was the 1962 Cuban Missile Crisis. There was one minor alert during the 1973 Arab-Israeli war and in 1969, the Soviet Union threatened a pre-emptive strike against Chinese installations.
(3) Segal: *The Nuclear Weapons Revolution*,
(4) *Statement on the Defence Estimates 1996*, Command Paper 3223 London: HMSO, 1996.
(5) *The Alliance's Strategic Concept* 1215/91, Paragraph 39 and 55.
(6) *DPC/NPG Ministerial Communique*, June 1996.
(7) *Statement on the Defence Estimates 1996*,
(8) Interview with David Fischer, International Atomic Energy Agency, 18 May 1997.
(9) Andrew G.B. Vallance, 'New thinking about the unthinkable, air power', *Air Clues*, January 1997.
(10) Paul Rogers, *The Role of British Nuclear Weapons After the Cold War*, BASIC Research Report 1, November 1995.
(11) David Omand, 'Nuclear Deterrence in a Changing World: The View from a UK Perspective', *Defence and International Security, RUSI Journal*, June 1996, p.15.
(12) Vallance: 'New Thinking'.
(13) Omand: 'Nuclear Deterrence in a Changing World..." p.15.
(14) Sir Michael Quinlan, 'Nuclear Abolition and the Arms Control Agenda', *Bulletin of Arms Control*, Number 26, June 1997, p.6-10.

(15) Hill: *Does Britain need Nuclear Weapons?* p.46.

(16) Donald Mackenzie. 'Moving towards Disinvention'. *The Bulletin of the Atomic Scientists.* Vol. 52, Part 5, September/October 1996, p.4.

(17) Interview with Bruce George, 6 February 1997.

(18) *RUSI Newsbrief*, Volume 16, Number 6, June 1996, p.42.

(19) Michael MccGwire, 'Nuclear Abolition and the Arms Control Agenda', *Bulletin of Arms Control*, Number 26, June 1997. pp.11-15.

(20) Stansfield Turner. *Caging the Nuclear Genie: An American Challenge for Global Security.* Westview Press, Oxford, 1997, p. 17.

(21) Quinlan: *'Nuclear Abolition'*, p.6-10.

(22) Robert O'Neill, 'Britain and the future of nuclear weapons, *International Affairs*, Number 4, Volume 71, 1995, pp.747-761.

(23) Interview with Martin O'Neill 5 February 1997.

(24) Martin Butcher, 'How does Britain fit into the European security system?" in John Gittings and Ian Davis, (eds), *Rethinking Defence and Foreign Policy*, Bertrand Russell Press, Nottingham, 1996. pp.39-51.

(25) *Statement on the Defence Estimates, 1996*, Command Paper 3223, HMSO, London, 1996.

(26) *Sunday Telegraph*, 6 August 1995.

(27) *Sunday Telegraph* 2 June 1996.

(28) Martin Butcher, 'Nuclear weapons dividing the new Europe', *Alert*, Number 8, Centre for European Security and Disarmament, October 1995.

5. PROTEST AND DISSENT

Early dissenters

During and immediately after the Second World War, there was very little public opposition to nuclear weapon development. The nuclear programme was highly secretive; everything was under wraps and had been since 1939 (1) The first seed of public dissent began with the Labour MP Bob Edwards who, early in 1943, wrote a pamphlet warning of the possible development of the atomic bomb and the military uses of atomic fission. This was largely ignored. By 1945, Britain was utterly weary of war and Christopher Driver in 'The Disarmers' recalls that only 21 per cent of the British public disapproved of the nuclear bombing of Japan. After six years of fighting, the atomic bomb seemed like a blessing, and there were only a few who questioned its moral implications. (2) The first action of the General Assembly of the United Nations, in January 1946, had been to call for the abolition of atomic weapons, and later that year, a detailed report was produced by a British mission sent to study the effects of the bombs at Hiroshima and Nagasaki. But these created little parliamentary or public interest. (3) It was against this background of public indifference that in May 1948, the decision to make a British atomic weapon was formally announced in the House of Commons.

When the testing of the first Russian nuclear device

was announced in September 1949, the whole idea of civil defence came under attack as seemingly useless. Dr Alex Comfort, biologist and pacifist, wrote a leaflet called 'Civil Defence: What You Should Do Now' which sold 45,000 copies. An organisation called the Peace Pledge Union set up a Non-Violence Commission to explore the possibility of direct action to achieve its objectives. By this they meant, as we shall see, something more forceful than a simple demonstration. (4) A further argument was developed by leading lights in radiation biology and medical physics, such as Sir Henry Dale. They explained how the testing of atomic weapons in the atmosphere could lead to the formation of radioactive isotopes that could enter and fatally contaminate the human body. (5)

In January 1950, the US announced that it was developing the H-bomb, but few people were greatly concerned, and protests were isolated and sporadic. Bishop Ernest William Barnes of Birmingham, well known as a maverick theologian, demanded that Britain should not follow the US example. A hundred Cambridge scientists petitioned the government asking that Britain should give the lead in not making H-bombs, and from this, a movement called Atoms for Peace developed amongst the scientific community. Pacifist bodies organised a gathering of 3,000 people at a Hiroshima Day commemoration in Trafalgar Square, which was addressed by the Reverend Donald Soper. The so-called British Peace Committee (BPC), which was backed by the communist-led World Peace Conference, gained more than 1 million signatures for what it called the 'Stockholm Peace Appeal'. This demanded unconditional prohibition of the atomic weapon as a weapon of aggression and mass annihilation of people and strict international control for the implementation of this decision. The Appeal declared: 'We shall consider as a war criminal that government which first employs atomic weapons against any country'. But because of its communist connections, this group never gained wide influence. (6)

Although 1952 saw the first instances of 'direct action', this approach did not appeal to more than a few committed pacifists. Eleven people sat down outside the War Office, 30 demonstrated outside the Atomic Weapons Research Establishment (AWRE) at Aldermaston and two demonstrators lay down, non-violence fashion, outside the US Air Force bomber base at Mildenhall. (7) During the next few years, numerous small meetings were held all over Britain, particularly by the Quakers and other religious groups and societies. (8) These were among the first to explore the moral implications of nuclear warfare. They claimed that it was impossible to wage a nuclear war successfully, save as an aggressor. This would flatly contravene the 'just war' tradition to which many of the churches adhered. (9)

The 'Lucky Dragon'

Public concern about the radiation damage from atmospheric nuclear testing was first aroused by the US hydrogen bomb test that took place on 1 March 1954 at Bikini Atoll, in the Marshall Islands of the central Pacific. The bomb went off with a yield of 15 mt., which was over twice the amount intended. Robert Divine explains in his book *Blowing on The Wind* how unexpectedly strong winds resulted in radioactive fallout being distributed over 7,000 square miles of the Pacific. A Japanese fishing boat named the 'Lucky Dragon' sailed unknowingly into the nuclear fall-out area. Although it was well outside the declared danger zone, all members of the crew were covered in white radioactive ash and when the boat finally docked in Yaizo Harbour 23 of them were suffering from radiation sickness. One subsequently died. The fallout also affected inhabitants of the Marshall Islands 110 away from the explosion, as well as US servicemen stationed on other nearby islands. Divine believes that over 300 people received doses of radiation. Radioactive fish were later found off Japan, and radioactive dust particles were also detected. Divine asserts that the US Atomic Energy Commission (AEC) played down the effects of the radiation, claiming that preliminary data showed no cause for alarm. The Commission asserted that the danger of nuclear testing was no greater than that involved in manufacturing conventional explosives, or in transporting flammable substances. They claimed that none of the tests had resulted in residual radioactivity being detected anywhere outside the testing areas. They were, of course, lying, and despite their best efforts to allay public concern, a debate on nuclear testing got under way. (10)

News of the accident broke in Britain, and a few weeks

later the government became concerned about the possible impact on public opinion. Both the British and the American governments woke up to the hazards of radioactive fallout and the prospect of public opposition to their nuclear programmes. Both were convinced that without the H-bomb in their hands the West would become immediately vulnerable to pressure from the Soviet Union. 'We have to prevent the hot war and win the Cold War. What are we to do? Until the passions of mankind can be cooled by reason or by love they must be chained by fear, and there is no other way.' (11) An official serving in the Ministry of Defence at the time has said: 'It was the Japanese fishing boat accident which hit the news and made the intelligent world at large conscious of the effects of tests. Officialdom had more information, and to the best of my knowledge it seeped into official consciousness that something had to be done. There were a lot of agitators around the world keen to play up the effects on health of nuclear testing and manufacture and so on'. (12)

The accident brought a sudden realisation that nuclear weapons not only caused destruction at the time they exploded, but also had long lasting and lethal side-effects. It was now apparent that these weapons could potentially destroy not only whole cities, but even complete populations. This marked the beginning of a moral revulsion that gave rise to the anti-nuclear movements later in the decade. It sparked a world wide campaign for an end to tests, which were now seen to be an environmental as much as a political problem. The governments of Japan and India issued calls for suspension of testing. In July, the UN Disarmament Commission submitted a formal call for a stand-still on testing. Individual scientists, including members of the Soviet scientific community, also rallied to the test ban cause. In an interview, the Russian diplomat Professor Oleg Grinevsky claimed there was a strong anti-testing lobby in the USSR, where practically all the struggle or the sentiments were expressed under the auspices of a committee - the Peace Committee'. (13)

Political reactions
Early in April 1954, Labour MPs introduced a motion into Parliament asking the government to seek a summit

meeting with the Soviet leadership, and Churchill promised to act on this. It was then that the first British protest group was set up with the help of Tony Benn. Known as the H-Bomb National Committee, it focused political attention on the prospect of an end to the arms race and to nuclear proliferation. The aim of the six MPs on the Committee was to meet church, peace and labour organisations, and to launch a petition aiming at a million signatures by the end of the year. This was to call for a top-level disarmament conference and the strengthening of the United Nations. However, the campaign was wound up after only one year. (14) In the words of Tony Benn: 'A group of us got together in April 1954 and we set up the H-bomb National Committee... This was not explicitly a Campaign for Nuclear Disarmament organisation, as this was a long time before CND was formed. What we did was to take Attlee's proposal for a summit meeting, and embody it in a petition, the H-Bomb petition. We were hoping to get a vast number of signatures, but in the end we only got 150,000. We took the Albert Hall in 1954. We had Sir Richard Acland, who was a member of the Labour Party, George Thomas, Sidney Silverman, Anthony Greenwood, Donald Soper, and Fenner Brockway. We organised petitions around the country and then in December 1954, we presented the Petition to No. 10 Downing Street. Then it went down the tubes, and we were very disappointed at the response.' (15)

All this was causing problems for the British government. On 2 December 1954, the Defence Minister, Harold Macmillan, presented a Top Secret memorandum to the cabinet based upon British scientific assessments of the American H-bomb tests in the Pacific. (16) They estimated that a 10-megaton explosion could affect 5000-6000 square miles, and that there would be an inner zone of approximately 270 square miles in which radiation would be so powerful that all life within it would be extinguished. The government was thus made well aware of the effects of the H-bomb, and realised that the general public was more likely to worry about fall-out than direct damage. For the first time, serious political opposition began to be feared in the guise of strong anti-testing sentiment at the very time when Britain was in the process of working up its own H-bomb programme. This fear of domestic opposition proved to be well founded. Widespread public concern grew about the effects of radioactive by-products. This had the effect of creating support for the idea of a test ban. In an interview with Professor Joseph Rotblat he said: 'The total radiation exposure of the population was increasing as a result of nuclear detonations, the discharge of radioactive waste from nuclear reactors and a rise in the use of X-rays and radio isotopes for medical and industrial purposes. There was, therefore, a general problem of radiation hazards and nuclear tests made this visible to the whole population. Bikini was the catalyst that focused fears'. (17)

While the H-bomb National Committee had not been very influential in shaping opinion it *did* serve to heighten public awareness about the H-bomb. After the Committee's demise, small pockets of protesters began forming across the country. From these, an informal network was gradually created, and in 1957 a National Committee for the Abolition of Nuclear Weapons Tests (NCANWT) was formed by Sheila Jones and Ianthe Carswell. Their aim was to co-ordinate the efforts of these local groups, warning of the dangers of nuclear tests in the atmosphere and consequent pollution. NCAWNT blossomed during 1957, and was eventually to merge into the soon to be formed Campaign for Nuclear Disarmament. (18)

Public Opinion
The British government felt it imperative to develop the H-bomb, but realised that it now faced national and international pressure to halt testing before it could reach this goal. After the first Soviet thermonuclear test - not a true H-bomb - in August 1953 it was clear that their scientists had found a cheap way of making a fusion weapon, using solid lithium deuteride. It was this situation, along with the fact that there was an impending weapons testing moratorium, which made the British work rapidly to complete their own thermonuclear weapon.

In the next few years, the full implications of nuclear policy for civilian populations began to become known. Use of the H-bomb would not simply destroy a large number of people; it could end life on the planet. Alan Brooke-Turner, a member of the British delegation to the Nuclear Tests Conference in Geneva, 1962, said in an interview: 'At first, people thought that radiation effects from fall-out were just short-term. Then it was realised that radioactive iodine was concentrated in cows' udders and people started finding out about Caesium 137 as well as Strontium 90 and how it had very long half-life and was concentrated in food lines. Report findings were published and then achieved headlines and that, of course, increased the concern being felt and put pressures on Members of Parliament'. (19) In 1955, a committee was set up by the Medical Research Council (MRC) to investigate 'the hazards to man of nuclear and allied radiations'. This committee reported in June 1956 at much the same time as the much bigger Bronk Report appeared in the USA. These were informative documents which received wide press coverage, and the issue was debated at length in parliament. (20) The United Nations also set up the UN Standing Committee on Atomic Radiations (UNSCEAR) which in 1958 issued an authoritative report with a substantial British input. The public had every reason for confidence in the professional judgments set out in these reports.

Recently, there have been suggestions that British and American Governments of the 1950's and 1960's were consistently less than honest with the general public on the dangers of radioactive fall-out from the tests. Throughout this time, the British government was maintaining that the effects of fallout were negligible. In their concern to minimise the effects of radioactivity. it is suggested that the government set up misleading safety standards and recommended impossible Civil Defence Plans. In an interview, Professor Rotblat claims that significant evidence was concealed by the Macmillan government. (21) It is important to remember however, that in the early 1950s there was no satisfactory consensus, even among scientific authorities, on whether there was a safe threshold of radiation tolerance and if so, what it was. Until the MRC and UNSCEAR reports were published, there was little general understanding of the mechanisms of distribution of the long-lived isotopes, how they entered the food chain and then penetrated the human body, and how damaging their effect would be when they did so. Today, we are all aware of the risks from excessive exposure to ionising radiation and of the hazards of nuclear materials and nuclear waste. The spectacular disaster at

Chernobyl in 1986 has made many people suspicious of the nuclear industry in all its forms. Against today's situation, it is difficult to grasp how contemporary attitudes to nuclear matters stood 40 years ago, when public knowledge of radiation was rudimentary. Whether the Government *did* attempt to conceal, distort, contain or put an unjustifiably reassuring gloss on the evidence of the dangers of radiation remains an open question.

As information about radiation grew more widespread, pressure groups emerged whose aim was the ending of tests. In February 1957 two Quakers, who belonged to a religious group longstanding in its pacifism, sailed a boat around Christmas Island in the Pacific. Their exploit gained world-wide publicity. (22) There was also growing dissent from influential figures such as Prime Minister Jawarharlal Nehru of India, the famous missionary doctor Albert Schweitzer and the English philosopher Bertrand Russell. On 12 March 1957, the World Health Organisation (WHO) published a report on the dangers of genetic damage from radiation. It proposed that the UK cancel forthcoming tests on Christmas Island and instead open negotiations with the Americans and the Russians on an agreement to ban tests. On the 19th March 1957, in an important Parliamentary debate, Macmillan argued that the WHO report had not added any new information to the MRC Report, and that the Disarmament Conference meeting in London was already dealing with agreements to ban tests.

The United Nations had naturally become a focus of debate on this issue. In 1957, as Macmillan had informed Parliament, the Russians and the Americans had discussed the major issues involved in a possible cessation of tests at the London Disarmament Conference. During this period, members of the Eisenhower administration gradually began shifting their views. Simultaneously, the Soviet government under Nikita Khrushchev adopted foreign policy goals quite different from those of the late Josef Stalin, and affirmed its belief in peaceful co-existence. It drew attention to the dangers of nuclear war, and showed a willingness to move away from the all-encompassing model of Russo-American competition.

By now, the Conservative government in Britain was facing serious opposition to development of the H-bomb, not least from the Labour Party. But the government was determined to ensure that Britain possessed a usable thermonuclear weapon, and quietly rode out all domestic protest until this goal had been achieved. It was not until after the first successful test of a megaton device had been carried out that the British Establishment showed any enthusiasm for a test ban. British public opinion during this period was in transition. The trade unions were holding conferences against tests, urging meetings of the nuclear powers, pressing for abolition of nuclear weapons under international control and for undertakings not to use nuclear weapons first. At the Labour Party Annual Conference in October 1956, the Party declared itself opposed to continuation of nuclear explosions.

The new H-Bomb Committee

Alongside official party policy, there was growing dissent from individual members of Parliament such as Michael Foot. In the summer of 1957 30 Labour MPs joined a new Labour H-Bomb Campaign Committee, and in September they rallied 4,000 people in Trafalgar Square to oppose British manufacture of the weapon. A composite resolution proposing British unilateral renunciation of nuclear weapons was put to Labour's Annual Conference, but failed. Members of the Labour Party then set up a body which they called the Non-Nuclear Club, with the aim of urging the Government to end tests and abolish nuclear weapons. This was not generally regarded as of great importance, the opinion being that the efforts of the Government to prevent war were more likely to achieve that end. But the club *did* come to the attention of the American press, and the *New York Times* commented that the Non-Nuclear Club is a direct contradiction of the defence policies, not only of the British government, but of the whole North Atlantic Alliance. (23)

Duncan Sandys, then Defence Secretary, set out a new policy in the Defence White Paper of February 1957. In this, he announced the ending of conscription, the proposed demise of manned aircraft in favour of missiles, and new importance attached to independent nuclear deterrence for Britain. It was hoped that this would halt Britain's decline as a world power, as underlined by Suez, or at least allow NATO to be developed in ways that would best serve British interests. In May and June 1957, Britain detonated one very large fission device and two H-bomb devices yielding less than one megaton. In November a third H-bomb test yielded 1.8 mt; almost twice as much. In October 1957, the Soviet Union launched the first artificial Earth satellite, *Sputnik I*, which not only demonstrated Soviet prowess in the field of rocketry. but also sent shock waves through America. For the first time. the USA had to face the prospect of being within range of Soviet nuclear warheads, a situation that Britain had known for years. *Sputnik* represented a golden opportunity to persuade the US to enter into collaboration, and Prime Minister Macmillan took full and prompt advantage of it. Meanwhile, Britain completed her thermonuclear weapon programme with a series of four shots in the autumn of 1958.

Pugwash
Up to this time the role of scientists in public protest had been minimal and the scientific community was itself divided. Experience on the Manhattan project had convinced some British scientists of the necessity for nuclear weapons, and heightened tensions between East and West had led some to conclude that the use of these weapons was imminent. Such people saw a new nuclear-armed threat arising from the Soviet side, and believed that this could only be countered by a strong Western defence. But others who had worked for the allied project took the opposing view and became vigorously opposed to nuclear weapons.

Bertrand Russell and Albert Einstein had not worked on the Manhattan project, but they were strongly opposed to nuclear weapons, even though it had been Einstein who influenced the start of the Project by writing to President Roosevelt in 1939, urging him to a speed up research in case the Germans made an atom bomb first. After the explosion of the hydrogen bomb on Bikini Atoll in 1954, Russell was horrified at the failure of politicians and people to recognise that the yield was nearly 1000 times greater than that of the Hiroshima bomb. He had a long negotiation with the BBC, trying to get air time to talk about this development, and eventually obtained a slot on 23 December of that year. His broadcast had a substantial impact, and Russell turned his mind to further moves. He drafted a Manifesto that was essentially an edited version of the broadcast. He sent a copy to Einstein who signed it just before he died in April 1955. Three months later, the document was published, having been signed by a total of eleven internationally prominent scientists, nine of them Nobel prize winners. (24) The Russell-Einstein manifesto, as it came to be called, described radioactive fallout and the ensuing damage. It urged, in dramatic terms, an end to nuclear testing, the rolling back of the nuclear arms race and the early abolition of nuclear weapons in the interests of common humanity.

One immediate effect was to stimulate links between scientists in many different countries, including the Soviet scientific community. In 1957, there began a series of unofficial meetings of scientists to discuss their role in the world, and, in particular, questions connected with disarmament and nuclear energy. The first of these was held in July 1957 at the small village of Pugwash, Nova Scotia, and the series subsequently became known as the 'Pugwash Conferences on Science and World Affairs'. Their purpose was to bring together from around the world scientists and scholars concerned with reducing the danger of armed conflict and seeking co-operative solutions to global problems. Russell was mainly responsible for inviting participants to the first conference, and for some years acted as chairman of the Pugwash committee, which issued invitations to later conferences. The meetings were attended by scientists of widely differing political views, meeting in private as individuals. British invitees were selected by Joseph Rotblat, who encouraged responsible British scientists to attend. American scientists may have been chosen for their influence, avoiding strong dissenters. The participation of Soviet scientists was made possible only by the death of Josef Stalin in March 1953, and the Academy of Sciences showed a modicum of independence.

In an interview Lord Kennet, an early participant at Pugwash, said: 'Pugwash was of unusual origin. In its early years, it brought together the bomb makers on both sides who were driven by their own conviction that their governments were on a disaster course and couldn't get that conviction through to those responsible. After one or two meetings, the chief scientists in the government, as well as the actual bomb physicists, began to come privately to meetings. Then, after that, they became more open and nobody got into trouble for going to Pugwash'. (25)

Lady Kennet, herself a writer on arms control matters, confirms that the Pugwash conferences were attended by the most eminent scientists: 'At the time, Pugwash was as high powered as it could be, but it had something of the former secret organisation about it, feeling its way forward. The two sides had the opportunity to speak to each other and found that neutrons behave the same way on either side!' (26) The senior civil servant previously quoted said of Pugwash: 'The first two or three Pugwash meetings were considered very subversive and scandalous and the attitude was how could a Canadian millionaire (Cyrus Eaton, who financed the early meetings) be 'allowed' to talk to the Russians freely? As soon as defence scientists from America and Britain had been to a Pugwash meeting or two, however, they realised the virtues of being able to talk freely to Russian equivalents. The development of Pugwash coincided with a growing consensus in the Foreign Office and the defence establishments of the West that something must be done, and perhaps could be done, over the control of nuclear testing. It was this consensus that led to the growing acceptability of Pugwash. It was a considerable shock to find senior Russian academicians being so frank about Russian nuclear developments, nuclear strategy and nuclear control. The hitherto unknown Russian great men in the nuclear world caused considerable surprise when they were so open'. (27)

The historian Sir Michael Howard puts a different slant on the story. He says that the American scientist Jerry Weisner persuaded John F.Kennedy that Pugwash was a useful forum. He believes that Pugwash was given credibility only by Kennedy's support. Before 1960, when Kennedy was elected president, it was regarded with scepticism. He says 'The group has always been associated with enthusiasts, not so much left-wing as in the best sense of the word peaceniks, people who were desperately worried about the bomb and refused to be discouraged'. The British and Americans regarded it as a serious attempt by which a logjam could be broken and bureaucracy by-passed. As far as the Russians were concerned, however, it was another element in their propaganda against the West. 'It was useful to be able to tell people at home that the major scientists on the other side were in agreement, contrary to the views of their own military-industrial complex'. The able Russian scientists did not have much of a speaking part, and Michael Howard believes that they were fielded very largely for show. He adds: 'I was vaguely conscious that the Intelligence Services were interested in what was going on, and I remember that at the Oxford Conference, there was a great flap because it was thought that one of the Russian scientists was going to defect. So there was clearly a level at which other people about whom we knew nothing were involved. I have no doubt whatsoever that the Russian delegation contained serious intelligence agents from the KGB. Probably there would be intelligence reports from MI5 and MI6 that would give the names of Russians. That is only my hunch, as Pugwash meetings were closed.' (28)

Was Pugwash then working on two levels? On the first, it appeared to be a respectable forum for serious academic debate, attracting eminent scientists and academicians from all over the world; on the second, was it used for propaganda purposes or even subversion? (29) Frank Blackaby vigorously denies that Pugwash could be used for propaganda purposes. He says: 'The sessions were closed, no media present. There were standard rules, no attribution of any statement to any individual. The conclusions of the conferences were given strictly limited circulation; they were sent to Governments but no attempt was made to interest the press in them. As a result the knowledge that Pugwash existed was limited to a pretty small circle. Pugwash was not a campaigning organisation.' He further argues: 'The Soviet side did not use Pugwash for propaganda. It put the Soviet point of view to Americans who might be in a position to influence policy, and the same thing the other way around. The USSR Pugwash scientists kept well away from the World Peace Council and all that.' (30)

It is fair to say that, unlike other bodies mentioned in this chapter, Pugwash was not a movement of protest and dissent. In so far as it worked at all, it did so at very different level, by way of ideas percolating through to policy makers on each side. Although it was founded by a British peer - Bertrand Russell was 3rd Earl Russell - and for many years run by a British citizen - Josef Rotblat and Pugwash were virtually synonymous - it was essentially an operation of contact between Americans and Russians. It was an exercise in high-level infiltration of ideas rather than part of the British protest movement. Pugwash reflected the mood of the times, and its success or failure depended less upon technical questions, more upon whether there was a genuine desire to get an agreement by the governments involved. It remains an open question, however, to what extent ideas originating from Pugwash found their way into the negotiating briefs of those working on the Partial Test Ban Treaty, and how far they served to advance the negotiations.

The Campaign for Nuclear Disarmament

In late 1957, Bertrand Russell wrote a strong article in the *New Scientist* about the evils of nuclear weapons. This provided the spark which melded the separate informal anti-nuclear groups into the Campaign for Nuclear Disarmament (CND), which was founded in the UK in January 1958. In February, CND organised a four-day march to Aldermaston. The British government called this march subversive, but that was overstating the case. The march was an anti-war demonstration, seeking to stir up popular opinion against nuclear weapons, and consisting for the most part of ordinary people airing their point of view. The Aldermaston march was broadcast around the world, challenging the secrecy of the H-bomb programme and highlighting one branch of grass-roots opinion. As CND grew, a parting of ways occurred between Russell and Rotblat. It was agreed that Russell would carry on the campaigning side and Rotblat would remain in academia. In an interview with Sir Oliver Wright, at the time Private Secretary to Lord Home, he said of the movement's origins: 'CND provided the forum in which people made clear that they wanted evidence that the Government had this terrible destructive weapon under control. We had moved from an A-bomb to an H-bomb and the general public was worried as it was perceived that these matters were not under control.' (31)

The Labour Party

During the next three years, CND was undoubtedly successful in getting nuclear disarmament onto the political agenda, with a second Aldermaston march and local demonstrations. By 1960, the Labour party conference at

Scarborough passed a resolution from the Transport and General Workers Union (TGWU) supporting CND's call for unilateral nuclear disarmament. For a while, it looked as though CND might change the nuclear policies of this country, but this was not to be. The Scarborough decision was soon to be reversed and internal conflicts within CND began to dominate. In April 1960, the government cancelled the British Intermediate Range Ballistic Missile *Blue Streak*, and by 1962 they had decided to go ahead with *Polaris*. A decline set in for CND and the organisation did not pick up for another ten years. The reason for this is not clear. but it was probably in part because of internal divisions. and in part because of general public apathy. (32) In 1963. the signing of the partial Test Ban Treaty did much to defuse public concern over the issue of testing. At all events, by the mid-1960s CND was being dismissed as a fashion that had passed.

It has been suggested that the British government made deliberate attempts to undermine protest groups. The senior civil servant quoted above sees the issue as follows: 'There were times when the government of the day felt that the public at large ought to have a balanced view of the issues CND agitated about. I expect that there were bouts of information plus argument to inoculate the voter against what the Government perceived as the excesses of the CND position. I don't remember, but I wouldn't be surprised to hear that there were periods when a good deal of Central Office of Information material was being pushed out against the CND position, but on the basis of giving a more or less objective assessment of risks and plenty of facts. When there is an alarm about some part of the nuclear business, the government of the day tends to push out an explanatory piece of information along the lines that the agitators have got the wrong information, or they have a genuine point, but are exaggerating it'. (33)

Was CND a front organisation?
Bruce Kent says, 'CND has always maintained independence, and there is no question about that. Within CND, however, there has always been a small element, we call them 'tankies', that is to say the kind of Communist Party members, the Stalinist element who supported everything that happened in Eastern Europe. These were a

very small element. An enormous engine of vilification was, however, mounted by the right wing in this country, the right wing of the Labour party and of the Conservative Party, to vilify CND. So any kind of a hint or suspicion or any impression that there was sympathy for the Eastern position was immediately blown up as a sign of treachery. I don't think objectively that those in CND who maintained a position that the Soviets were only responding to Western pressures and that their arms race was explicable, were a large enough element in themselves to create a defamatory climate, but I think that their presence was used by the Right wing for their own purposes. CND always kept at arm's length from the World Peace Council which was the official organ of the Soviet Union'. (34)

In an interview, Christopher Rootes, a writer on CND, said of this issue: 'Communists and fellow travellers are a very small and marginal part of the British peace movement, and to the extent that there were once Marxists involved, they were more likely to be Trotskyites than friends of the USSR. The peace movement appears to have represented genuine worries among people who were free-thinkers, Christians, moralisers, pacifists, socialists, anarchists, and overwhelmingly supporters of the Labour Party'. Rootes argues: 'It is doubtful that the peace movement was a tool of Moscow, and while some of the protests coincided with Soviet interests, they were motivated by a genuine fear and threat of nuclear war. Clearly, supporters and apologists for the USSR could quite un-cynically embrace CND to the extent that they genuinely believed, as a great many did, that theirs was the path to lasting peace and CND a vehicle for at least defusing one part of the armoury which threatened peace. Such people, again un-cynically, justified the USSR's possession of nuclear weapons as purely defensive and looked forward to the day when they would be unnecessary. Nevertheless, my overwhelming impression is how unim-portant communists were to CND, and how little they affected its public image. After all, from the beginning, CND was an elite campaign set up by people who were clearly not communists, so attempts to label them so can-not carry a lot of weight.' (35)

The Committee of 100 (C100) was formed in 1960 to oppose what it regarded as the growing menace of nuclear war, using the technique of violent civil disobedience as an integral part of its activities. C100 was founded by Bertrand Russell who was then President of CND. It was opposed however by Canon John Collins and the majority of the CND executive, and relations between CND and C100 were famously fraught. C100 was active for only two years, although in name it continued to exist until 1968. The other change to the structure of CND in the 1960s was the formation of specialist groups, e.g. youth CND, colleges and universities CND etc. A large number of trade unions also became affiliated. (36)

Arms control

> The Partial Test Ban was almost certainly due to the general public horror at fallout, strontium 90 in mother's milk. Once the Partial Test Ban was signed and the Americans and the Russians were content to carry on with underground testing (and the British necessarily so too), CND indeed lost the authority it had temporarily enjoyed. Its immediate job was completed, the international clear air bill achieved, an environmental success, rather than an arms control one. (37)

Ever since the mid-1950s, there had been discussions and some international negotiation aimed at curtailing, if not putting an end to, nuclear weapons testing. But until the early 1960s, these had failed to produce agreement. It is widely believed that the defining moment which was to change public opinion was the Cuban Missile Crisis of 22-28 October 1962. President Kennedy demanded the removal from Cuba, only 90 miles from US territory, of newly installed Soviet missiles and offered in exchange to withdraw US nuclear weapons from Turkey. After a long week of negotiations, during which nuclear war seemed all too likely, Khrushchev backed down and agreed to remove his missiles. Two years later, Khrushchev was dismissed as Russian leader for 'hare-brained scheming'. Many of those directly concerned with the Cuban Missile crisis now believe that it was only by the slenderest of chances that nuclear catastrophe was averted. In the aftermath, people came to see more clearly that there were no circumstances in which it would be possible to use a nuclear weapon sensibly. Various confidence-building measures were set in place, for instance the installation of a hot line between the presidential offices in the USA and the USSR which was to serve as a means of crisis communication to avert misunderstandings.

In July 1963, Khrushchev put forward a proposal for a treaty banning tests in the atmosphere, under the sea and in outer space. A similar proposal had been put forward by the West as early as 1959. In these three environments, there was no real disagreement about the possibility of detecting tests. Making use of the work already completed during years of negotiation, the parties found it possible to draw up, agree and sign a treaty within a few weeks. The Limited (or Partial) Test Ban Treaty of 1963, whose sponsors were the governments of the United States, the Soviet Union and Britain, committed the parties not to carry out any nuclear weapon test explosion in the atmosphere, under water or in outer space. (38) France and China both tested nuclear weapons in the atmosphere after 1963, but they and most other countries have since acceded to the treaty. A clear line of cause and effect can thus be traced from the public concerns over testing born in the early 1950s, to the first in the series of test bans which were to culminate in the Comprehensive Test Ban Treaty of 1996 over 40 years later.

By 1964, the Vietnam War began to claim increasing international attention and public interest in nuclear matters declined. In 1964,the British Labour government endorsed its predecessor's decision to acquire the *Polaris* system, and this meant that Britain would now have a new nuclear weapon system with an expected life time of a further 30 years. Attention shifted to the negotiation of a Nuclear Non-Proliferation Treaty (NPT). This Treaty was to divide the nations of the world into two classes. The first class, known as Nuclear Weapons States (NWS), consisted of the five permanent members of the UN Security Council - the US, the Soviet Union, China, France and Britain - all of whom had serviceable and tested nuclear weapons at their disposal. They promised not to transfer nuclear weapons or related technology to any other countries, but to help them acquire nuclear technology for

peaceful (power-generation) purposes. They also promised to pursue among themselves negotiations in good
faith towards nuclear disarmament. The second class,
called Non-Nuclear Weapons States (NNWS), promised
not to acquire nuclear weapons or related technology by
any means, and to accept regular inspections by the
International Atomic Energy Agency (IAEA) together with
other safeguards covering their nuclear plants. The NPT
was signed in 1968 and entered into force in March 1970.
(39)

By the late 1970s however relations between the US
and the Soviets had once again deteriorated. The most
serious bone of contention was Russian deployment in
1977 of SS-20 Intermediate Range Ballistic Missiles.
These were mobile systems with a range of 3,700 km.,
carrying three independently targeted warheads on each
missile. Deployed in western Russia, these missiles posed
a direct threat to the whole of western Europe, whereas
in western Europe itself, there were no countervailing
systems. In October 1977, Helmut Schmidt, then
Chancellor of West Germany, made a notable speech at
the International Institute of Strategic Studies in London
pointing out the resulting imbalance. After lengthy and
difficult debate, NATO ministers agreed in December
1979 that American *Pershing II* launchers and Ground
Launched Cruise Missiles (GLCM) should be stationed on
their territory. A fortnight later, the Soviet Union invaded
Afghanistan . This put an end for the time being to any
talk of détente. With a return to vitriolic rhetoric between
East and West, the anti-nuclear interest groups re-
emerged.

Cruise Missiles
Britain was one of the countries which agreed in 1979 to
accept American cruise missiles but it was not until mid-
June 1980 that the government announced where they
were to be based, namely Greenham Common in
Berkshire and Molesworth in Cambridgeshire. From this
point on, while the government remained solidly in favour
of retaining nuclear weapons, all was not entirely plain
sailing where public opinion was concerned. People had
misgivings about the decision to deploy US ground-
launched Cruise missiles (GLCMs) in Britain and as a
consequence, there was increasing cynicism about the

appropriateness of American nuclear policies. And the same was true of other European countries. In October 1981, there were large-scale anti-nuclear rallies not only in London but in Paris, Madrid, Oslo, Brussels and Helsinki.

Towards the end of 1983, the American GLCMs began arriving at Greenham Common and the base was declared operational on 31 December. It was against this background that the Greenham Common Women's Peace Camp was set up. These ladies took strong exception to Britain's submission, as they saw it, to the offensive designs of the US, arguing that this would make Britain an early target for Soviet nuclear attack in the event of war. Over 30,000 women became involved in non-violent direct action. Their tactics included squatting outside the Greenham Common base, surrounding the perimeter, talking to and sometimes jeering at the soldiers and police guards, repeatedly cutting the wire, entering the base, dancing on the missile's protective bunkers, and painting the buildings. (40) They kept this up for more than ten years. On several occasions, additional troops had to be called out to cope with them.

Lady Olga Maitland says that she spent some time with women at Greenham Common such as Helen John, in order to write an article for the Conservative Bow Group magazine Crossbow. She was impressed with the infrastructure of the protesters. Yet she thought that many of the women were confusing the issues of nuclear weapons with other emotional issues such as feminism and women's liberation. In her article for Crossbow, she argued that the whole nuclear debate had spun out of control and was now based on distortions and misinformation about nuclear weapons and their role and purpose. She concluded that the anti-nuclear campaign was a campaign to destabilise the West, as there was no rational argument for one-sided nuclear disarmament. As she tells the story: 'With the help of Sir Alfred Sherman, head of the Centre for Policy Studies, in 1983 I launched the pro-NATO grass-roots organisation Women and Families for Defence in direct opposition to the Greenham protesters and CND. I set this up with the support of Virginia Bottomley, Angela Rumbold, Angela Browning and Ann Widdecombe, none of whom were members of Parliament at the time and all of whom felt that the anti-nuclear debate was distorting issues and promoting one-sided nuclear disarmament at a time when the Soviet Union still had SS-20s.' The group supported NATO and the right to defend the country with nuclear weapons. (41)

The Greenham Common protest, although mainly peaceful, managed to create a large amount of controversy and some outrage. Arguably, the fact that the pronuclear lobby in the shape of Women and Families for Defence felt the need to set up their own group is testimony to the strength of the protesters. While the latter were not successful in preventing the deployment of Cruise missiles, or securing their removal, there is no doubt that they were effective in raising awareness of the issues involved and in causing some concern to the government of the day. (42)

CND - *The Second Phase*

A revival of CND in the early 1980s was also due to the prominence given by the media to their protests against the decision to station American Cruise missiles in the UK. In March 1980, the Conservative government published a nuclear weapon survival guide *Protect and Survive* which attracted much ridicule. In July, the government announced its decision to spend £5,000 million on a four-submarine Trident force to replace Polaris when the latter became obsolete in the 1990s. The Home Secretary, William Whitelaw, further announced that the government planned to spend an extra £45 million on civil defence over the following three years. Design outlines for private fall-out shelters were made public by the end of the year. At the time of anti-nuclear protests in October 1981, the membership of CND had reportedly passed 300,000. But while CND was successful in giving organisational form and continuity to the anti-nuclear protests of the 1980s, it never managed to move beyond being a vehicle for protest to being able to shape and maintain public opinion in competition with more conventional political forces. This is not surprising; it merely shows the strength of organised institutional interests, and the difficulty of radical new groups in competing with them. It is fair to say that CND, both originally and during its revival in the 1980s, was, like all peace movements, a reaction to international political conditions.

CND has been a remarkable survivor. A small nucleus of the organisation survived years of demobilisation between 1963 and 1979, and similar kernel will probably survive for at least another decade. While nuclear weapons still exist and Britain possesses them the basic raison d'être of CND remains.

European Nuclear Disarmament

In 1980, a movement called the European Campaign for Nuclear Disarmament (END) was founded by another group of British protesters. END supported other European groups under a broad anti-nuclear umbrella, and campaigned for a demilitarised zone in Europe. END also took the lead in criticising the Soviet Union for quashing the unofficial East European wing of the movement, and campaigned strongly against the deployment of Russian SS-20 missiles as well as American Cruise missiles and Pershing 2. With the arrival of the American missiles in November 1983 and the evident determination of NATO governments to continue with their deployment, the leadership of END was unsure where to direct its next campaigning focus and accepted defeat. Although END was an entirely logical and predictable extension of CND, it was always viewed with suspicion and its east European peace activists and contacts were constantly harassed by the Soviet bloc regimes. (43)

Independent Groups

For completeness' sake, a number of other small groups deserve mention. For example, there were organisations set up within the professions such as Psychologists against Nuclear Arms, International Lawyers against Nuclear Arms, the Medical Campaign against Nuclear Weapons, Scientists against Nuclear Arms, Journalists against Nuclear Extermination and Teachers for Peace. These smaller groups did useful work in their own way by exposing the consequences of the use of nuclear weapons. For instance, International Physicians for the Prevention of Nuclear War brought home the devastating results derived from analysis of the casualties at Hiroshima. Other specialist groups included Families against the Bomb, Women Oppose the Nuclear Threat, Tories against Cruise and Trident, ex- Services CND, and even Babies against the Bomb. (44) Bodies such as the

United Nations Association (UNA) fostered support for the UN and its policies, publicised resolutions on disarmament and pointed out the failure of governments to comply with them. The National Peace Council (NPC) is an umbrella group to which virtually all peace organisations are affiliated, and a clearing-house for coordinating activities. Finally, the World Disarmament Campaign (WDC), which was formed in 1982 to work for the success of the second UN Special Session on Disarmament in that year, has remained active ever since. (45)

Ecology Movements
Apart from the pro- and anti-nuclear interest groups that have been concerned with shaping opinion on nuclear weapons, ecological organisations have also played an important role. There has been some overlap between these and the peace organisations and there have been joint campaigning activities. On the whole however, these groups prefer to preserve their separate identities. Until quite recently nuclear power was generally regarded as a good thing, an area of advanced scientific endeavour in which Britain was a world leader. The opening in 1956 of Calder Hall, Windscale and, subsequently, other nuclear stations did not become an issue of concern for many years. Indeed, so far from worrying about any possible negative aspects of nuclear power, most people who took an active interest in such matters were keen that it should be further developed. Britain was also interested in research into nuclear fusion technology for peaceful purposes. Ecological movements, however, were the first to highlight other dangers connected with nuclear power stations, such as unintended radioactive emissions and industrial accidents. A new dimension to the debate thus emerged.

In 1977, Greenpeace established itself in Britain, and since then has campaigned tirelessly against nuclear weapons, nuclear testing, the transport of nuclear material, and the dumping of radioactive and toxic waste at sea. In 1979, Greenpeace became an international organisation with offices in Europe, the Pacific and North America which, together, constitute Greenpeace International. The organisation has undertaken a variety of tasks ranging from scientific research to promoting solutions to environmental problems, political lobbying and direct action. Greenpeace has a policy of complete independence from any political party, business interest or outside organisation. Between 1977 and the end of the Cold War, Greenpeace activists were involved in many non-violent direct action protests. These included highlighting hazards from nuclear tests which might have otherwise gone unnoticed, entering nuclear test zones, blocking toxic waste pipes and sailing in rubber dinghies around ships discharging hazardous radioactive waste drums. Its mainstay is a fleet of six ships that carry out campaigning tasks all over the world. The most famous of these was the ex-fishing vessel *Rainbow Warrior*. On 10 July 1985, while preparing to leave for a peaceful protest against French nuclear tests on the Pacific island of Mururoa, this ship was bombed by French secret service agents and sank, causing the death of a Greenpeace photographer. This event became a focus of worldwide publicity and caused great embarrassment to the French government. (46)

Friends of the Earth (FOE) was established in 1971, and has also played a small role in influencing public opinion on nuclear matters FOE is opposed to any activity involving radioactivity, nuclear technology, and the construction of nuclear power plants in Britain. Their main argument is that nuclear power is linked to human illness and environmental contamination and the radioactive discharges from power stations are polluting the global environment. They claim that nuclear power is obsolete, uneconomic and unsustainable, and that nuclear technology has diverted resources from the promotion of self-sufficiency and alternative energy options. However, FOE has never played a great part in opposing nuclear weapons as such. (47)

According to Bob Worcester, Director of the polling organisation MORI, 'Nuclear weapons become of interest only when there is a crisis, as for example during the Gulf War, or the Chernobyl nuclear disaster'. (48) Nuclear weapons as an issue of public concern tend to sink out of sight when there is no specific nuclear or security shock to provoke interest. It would seem, therefore, that interest groups rarely manage to shape opinion during periods when nuclear affairs are not the main news. This is not to say that such groups are purely dependent upon external events. They are working all the time in the background to achieve influence through political lobbying, patient campaigning and investigative journalism into events that can popularise their campaign's aims and widen their own agenda. Nevertheless, the dismal fact remains that the best chance of making progress on these matters comes out of some form of catastrophe.

CND today

In a revealing interview with Bruce Kent, a former director of CND, he agreed that the organisation needed security shocks to provoke public opinion, and he cited the example of the French tests of 1995: 'The French tests certainly gave CND new impetus, not just CND but all around the world. This was a real case of an episode that no one had planned for acting as a real regeneration. When the French stopped testing however, this impetus stopped and the general public went quiet again'. (49)

Christopher Rootes argues, 'Since the end of the Cold War, it is difficult to see what could now excite the development of CND. The threat element so important to CND's revival is now absent. The moral element remains, but since the wars and conditions of oppression to which they are most relevant are usually quite remote, this is more likely to generate humanitarian aid than a social movement in Britain. To some extent this concern has been subsumed into the Green movement'. (50) Yet Bruce Kent is optimistic about the future of the peace movement: 'I think there is still an enormous job for peace and disarmament movements. The situation has changed, in that we are now concentrating considerably on international structures, and the framework within which security is possible. So we are a little more wideranging than just opposing Cruise missiles, but the need for it is clear. One cannot talk about environmental protection, as many do, unless we take into account the element of militarism in the world which I think is the greatest single polluter. Wars and the preparation of wars, nuclear testing, consumption of land, climate change, and resources of oil...this is the key to it. The other link is the poverty link: there is enormous public opinion with us on that, but we have still have to get people to accept that hospital failures and school failures are due to a militarist budget. The other thing that I think that CND will have to get into is the whole reform of the UN structures, genuine common security, because you cannot take away the weapons and leave the psychology and inadequate structures standing. We have to have something that fills people's need for security.' (51)

The World Court Project

One small victory for the section of public opinion which is profoundly anti-nuclear was the opinion handed down by the International Court of Justice on the Legal Status of Nuclear Weapons. On the 15 December 1994 the United Nations General Assembly adopted a resolution asking the ICJ to give its opinion on the question: 'Is the threat or use of nuclear weapons in any circumstances permitted under international law?' After considering written and oral submissions from a large number of participating states, the Court released its Advisory Opinion on the 8 July 1996. The ICJ found that the threat or use of nuclear weapons would 'generally be contrary' to international law. But there was no definite conclusion as to whether the threat or use of nuclear weapons was legal in an extreme case of self-defence 'in which the survival of the state would be at stake'. The Court did conclude, however, that a commitment existed to pursue and finalise negotiations leading to nuclear disarmament: 'The obligation here is an obligation to achieve a precise result - nuclear disarmament in all its aspects - by adopting a particular course of conduct, namely, the pursuit of negotiations in good faith'. (52)

The fundamental issue to be determined by the ICJ had been whether the illegality of nuclear weapons was absolute or conditional. If the ICJ had decided that the use of nuclear weapons was absolutely unlawful this would have had a direct bearing on the possession, preparation for use and testing of nuclear weapons. Although the Court determined that the use of nuclear weapons would be *generally* unlawful it did not determine that use would be *absolutely* unlawful. Thus, by implication, it did not outlaw possession, at least *ad interim*. Both sides of the argument could claim to have won, and it is hard to see in what way the judgment will have any immediate practical significance. But it may turn out to have been an important symbolic gesture and helpful in the long run for those in favour of the abolition of nuclear weapons. It has reiterated with great force the obligations undertaken by the nuclear weapons states to get on with the process of nuclear disarmament and stop dragging their feet.

The Canberra Commission

In the latter part of 1995, the Australian government established the Canberra Commission on the Elimination of Nuclear Weapons, with the aim of examining what the prospects were for a nuclear weapon-free world. The Commission included members from a wide range of states, NWS, NNWS, West, East, and Non Aligned. Former Secretary of Defence Robert McNamara and General Lee Butler, former head of Strategic Air Command, were leading American participants. Field Marshal Lord Carver was a prominent spokesman for the UK. In an interview with Lord Carver he said of the Canberra Commission: 'What it recommended was that the nuclear states and the undeclared nuclear weapons states should make an unequivocal statement that under the Non-Proliferation Treaty, they were committed to the eventual elimination of nuclear weapons. They should make an unequivocal statement that this was their definite aim and that they intended to move towards it as rapidly as was safely possible. The commission believed that now was the time to make a definite effort in this direction, because the relations between the two major nuclear powers, without whose agreement you couldn't make any progress at all, were at the moment fairly good. There was no serious matter of tension between them and if they could resolve the START-2, START-3 argument and get going on further reductions, this was the time to make that effort. There was no guarantee that this period of comparatively relaxed relations between the United States and Russia would last. One thing the commission was absolutely clear about was that unless you can persuade the United States and Russia to take the initiative and to move vigorously in the direction of getting rid of nuclear weapons, then you would never get there at all'. (53)

The Canberra Commission no longer exists. The Australian government that set it up has been replaced by another which is not so committed. The new government shows little enthusiasm for pushing the report forward, so there is no machinery and no money from any source to continue pressing for its implementation.

Attempts are being made by the American representatives on the Commission to try and raise both financial and political support for it, but they have not yet had much success. Robert O'Neill has said, 'The Canberra Commission has done its work. The Australian government regard it as having done its part, it was presented at the United Nations General Assembly, it is out in their public debate as one more contribution...' (54)

Nobel Prize

The Nobel Peace Prize of 1995 was awarded to Professor Joseph Rotblat and the Pugwash Movement of which he is President. Professor Rotblat is a nuclear physicist. He was one of the community of scientists who created the first atom bombs but left the Manhattan Project before the end of the Second World War in 1945, and since then has been committed to the abolition of nuclear weapons. He was a founder member of the Atomic Scientists' Association and the Pugwash Movement as described above. He has recently set out proposals for disarmament in a Pugwash monograph entitled 'A Nuclear-Weapon-Free-World Desirable? Feasible?' In this, he envisages that the United Nations Security Council would outlaw nuclear weapons. There would be a nuclear weapons convention with safeguards and verification systems. The latter would include 'societal verification', by which he means the placing of an obligation on every citizen to 'blow the whistle' on any suspected breaches of the convention by any government.

A military call

> One of the most encouraging developments is that the move to zero has become intellectually respectable. (55)

Support for this contention has come from a number of senior military people who were once committed professionally to supporting nuclear weapons. These are people of integrity and they command respect. Now, by their support for nuclear disarmament, they have brought the debate to a new stage and have given it credibility which the peace groups on their own have never been able to command. In 1996, *The Times* said of this phenomenon

'A global coalition of retired senior generals and admirals from countries, including Britain, America and Russia yesterday issued a joint demand for the complete and irrevocable elimination of the world's nuclear arsenal. Field Marshal Lord Carver, former Chief of the Defence Staff and General Sir Hugh Beach joined nearly 40 senior officers from America and Russia, including General John Galvin, the former Supreme Allied Commander in Europe, and General Aleksandr Lebed in calling for the eventual abolition of nuclear weapons. In Washington, General Andrew Goodpaster, a former Supreme Allied Commander and advisor to President Eisenhower, joined General Lee Butler, former Commander in Chief of the US Strategic Command, in issuing their own joint statement. The United States and other nations, they said, should take steps to align nuclear weapons policies to match their diminished role and leading to multilateral disarmament as rapidly as possible. The generals added that nuclear weapons were no longer necessary in a post-Cold War World, and merely provided an option to respond in kind to any nuclear threat or attack by others, including rogue nations. Other risks included accidents, unauthorised launches, and the theft of weapons or weapons materials by international and domestic terrorist groups. Despite the Nuclear Non Proliferation Treaty, nuclear arms could spread to other nations to cause a war. Conventional capabilities offered a sufficient deterrent and defence against conventional forces and, combined with other defensive measures, could curb the threat of chemical and biological weapons. Although the former military chiefs were not advocating immediate elimination of nuclear weapons, they believed that, unless the five official nuclear powers make a substantial gesture in cutting to minimum their nuclear inventory, countries with the capability to produce nuclear weapons and maverick nations intent on having their own atomic bombs will have no incentive to surrender such ambitions'. (56) Field Marshal Sir Nigel Bagnall, Chief of the Defence Staff from 1985 to 1989, urges that the entire Trident fleet should be decommissioned. He argues that, 'We should take them out of service, mothball them, and have one as a training ship.' (57)

Ian Doucet, writer on psychology and nuclear weapons, has said of these developments: 'In the past, military and political leaders grasped nuclear weapons to their breast because they dared not let them go. One thing that is clear over the years is the near impossibility of having a rational debate over nuclear weapons, though many people have tried, including some of the scientists who invented them. What is more remarkable is that the people who made possible nuclear technology, possibly some of the most intelligent people of this century, have almost all come out against nuclear weapons in the end. (Perhaps with the exception of Edward Teller, the Manhattan Project physicist who developed the thermonuclear bomb). They have gone from a scientific curiosity, interest and fascination with these weapons to a much larger moral condemnation, a very mature judgment by very intelligent men, to the rejection of them. The fact that this has made no difference is remarkable, and I think it attests to the difficulty of having any rational discussion about nuclear weapons until now, over fifty years on, and that is why this is an exciting time. It is a generational thing. One generation of scientists is dying out and losing influence, and a new generation is coming up which is freer to enter what was once unthinkable territory. The condition of needing absolute protection from an absolute threat to one's psychological survival can only be dismantled piece by piece. It cannot be argued against. One cannot stand back and look at it on a rational level and discard it.' (58)

Conclusion

In this chapter, we have argued that protest movements have always been small, but that is not to say that they have been a total failure. For example, in retrospect, it is clear that CND came close to converting the Labour Party to a non-nuclear stance, and it was probably only an accident of timing that it failed. Labour Party leader Hugh Gaitskell's battle against the unilateralists - 'We shall fight, fight and fight again' - was hard won. The successful conclusion of the Partial Test Ban Treaty was almost certainly due to public pressure based on recognition of the hazards of fallout. Today, the World Court Project has been a notable achievement. The Labour government elected in 1997 has been converted to accepting the idea of a world-wide ban as a serious objective of policy. Opinion polls have shown that the majority of the British public is against the possession of nuclear weapons, and a very large majority is in favour of negotiations for a Nuclear Weapons Convention. (59) Today CND is the largest single-issue peace movement in Europe. There now also appears to be a move towards internationalism, with a network of over 1000 organisations campaigning for a world-wide ban. Finally, it is fair to say that the main achievement of the protest movements was to keep the issue alive, and in this they succeeded. Had it not been for the protest movements, nuclear weapons might now be so embedded in military structures as to be virtually inextricable.

References
(1) Correspondence with Lady Kennet 20 April 1998.
(2) Christopher Driver, *The Disarmers*, Hodder and Stoughton, 1964, cited in the introduction to John Minnion and Philip Bolsover, (eds), *The CND Story*, Allison and Bushey Limited, London, 1983, p.11.
(3) One hugely significant influence on American and also British public opinion, however, was John Hersey's book *Hiroshima*, (Penguin, London, England, 1946), which was a vivid and shocking account of life and death in the Japanese city after 6 August 1945. The "New Yorker" magazine devoted an entire issue to printing the full text of Hersey's book in August 1946, and the book was soon afterwards published in Britain. It was one of the first sources from which the general public came to learn that the atomic bomb was much more that an unimaginably powerful explosive - the impression the British public received from newspaper reports on the 9 August 1945.(Correspondence with Alan Brooke Turner, member of the UK Delegation to Nuclear Tests Conference, Geneva 1962. 22 March 1998.)
(4) Minnion: *The CND Story* pp.11-12.
(5) Correspondence with Lorna Arnold, 8 April 1998.
(6) The Stockholm Peace Committee Appeal, cited in Minnion: *The CND Story* pp.11-12.
(7) Minnion: *The CND Story p.*12.
(8) John Cox, *Overkill*, Pelican Books, 1981, p.195.
(9) See Chapter 6 for further details.
(10) Divine, Robert.A., *Blowing on the Wind, The Nuclear Test Ban Debate 1945-1960.*

New York, Oxford University Press, 1978, p.29.

(11) Harold Macmillan, House of Commons, 2 March 1955 cited in M. McIntosh, *Managing Britain's Defence*, Macmillan, London, 1990.

(12) Interview with an unnamed official serving in the Ministry of Defence during this period. See Nadine Gurr, *Arms Control Negotiations and Middle Powers; The Role of the UK in the Partial Test Ban Treaty Negotiations, 1952-1963*, Southampton University, 1995. (unpublished PhD.thesis).

(13) Interview with Professor Oleg Grinevsky, 1991. See Gurr; *Arms Control*.
The Soviet "Peace Committee", and similar Soviet organi sations including the word "peace" in their title, cannot be viewed in parallel with the non-communist organisations of the West. It is now generally acknowledged that these were Soviet front organisations responsive to directions from Party sources, and the writings of those who worked in the system or have had access to the archives of the time have now confirmed this. No doubt many ordinary Soviet citizens who belonged to these movements, like countless ordinary people in many countries, earnestly desired peace and the ending of nuclear tests. Amongst the published statements of the front movements, however, there is never any criticism of the actions of the Soviet government.

(14) Cox: *Overkill*, p.197.

(15) Interview with Tony Benn , 1991, in Gurr: *Arms Control*.

(16) *Memorandum on fall-out from the Ministry of Defence 9 December 1954*. CAB 129/69 C(54)250.

(17) Interview with Professor Joseph Rotblat, 1991, in Gurr: *Arms Control*.

(18) Minnion: *The CND Story* p.13.

(19) Interview with Alan Brooke-Turner, 1991, in Gurr: *Arms Control*.

(20) The Medical Research Council Committee reports of 1956 and 1960 laid before parliament as White Papers, were made available to the public and the press. Command Paper 9780 and Command Paper 1225.

(21) Interview with Professor Joseph Rotblat, 1991, in Gurr, *Arms Control*.

(22) Minnion: *The CND Story* p.13.

(23) *The New York Times*, 31 July 1959.

(24) The Russell-Einstein Manifesto (1957) was signed by the following: Max Born, Frederic Joliot-Curie, Joseph Rotblat, Percy W. Bridgman, Herman J. Muller, Bertrand Russell, Albert Einstein, Linus Pauling, Hideki Yukawa, Leopold Infeld and Cecil F. Powell.

(25) Interview with Lord Kennet, 1991, in Gurr: *Arms Control.*

(26) Interview with Lady Kennet, 1991, in Gurr: *Arms Control.*

(27) Interview with an unnamed official serving in the Ministry of Defence during this period, in Gurr, *Arms Control.*

(28) Interview with Sir Michael Howard, in Gurr: *Arms Control.*

(29) Interview with Sir Michael Howard, in Gurr: *Arms Control.*

(30) Interview with Frank Blackaby 28 April 1998.

(31) Interview with Sir Oliver Wright, in Gurr: *Arms Control.*

(32) Cox: *Overkill* pp.203-204.

(33) Interview with an unnamed official serving in the Ministry of Defence during this period. See in Gurr: *Arms Control.*

(34) Interview with Bruce Kent 2 February 1997.

(35) Interview with Christopher Rootes, 4 April 97.

(36) Cox: *Overkill* pp. 200-212.

(37) Correspondence with Lady Kennet 20 April 1998.

(38) Treaty Banning Nuclear Weapon tests in the Atmosphere, in Outer Space and Underwater. *Arms Control and Disarmament Agreements, Texts and Histories of Negotiations,* US Arms Control and Disarmament Agency, Washington D.C. 1982 Edition, pp. 41-43.

(39) *Arms Control and Disarmament Agreements*: pp. 132-154.

(40) Scilla Elworthy, *Power and Sex,* Element, Shaftesbury, Dorset, 1996, p.213.

(41) Interview with Lady Olga Maitland, 8 March 1997

(42) During the early 1980s, a number of groups also sprang up whose members were committed professionally and psychologically to supporting British nuclear weapons within the alliance framework and in the conviction that this linked Britain with America. For example 'Peace through NATO' was a pro - NATO campaigning

organisation which was funded by the Foreign and Commonwealth Office (FCO) to organise debates, distribute leaflets, show videos and organise other pro-nuclear defence publicity. The British Atlantic Committee (BAC), was an officially sponsored charity, which took on the role of disseminating information, organising speakers, and trying to counter some of the facts propagated by CND. In 1983, campaigns in opposition to CND were waged by the Conservative Party, the Freedom Association, and the Coalition for Peace through Security. These groups took the stance that the Labour Party's defence policies (early in the 1980s) meant no defence, and they also claimed that the Labour Party had no good alternative forms of non-nuclear defence. (Paul Mercer, *Peace of the Dead*, Policy Research Publications, 1986, pp.1-2,121,162,183,190,199,202-3).

(43) Gerald Segal, *The Simon and Schuster Guide to the World Today*, Simon and Schuster, London, 1988, p.102.

(44) Minnion: *The CND Story* p.39.

(45) Cox: *Overkill*, pp.224-226.

(46) *Overview of Greenpeace*, Greenpeace Publicity Pamphlet, March 1997.

(47) Interview with a campaign worker from Friends of the Earth 13 February 1998.

(48) Interview with Bob Worcester 18 February 1997.

(49) Interview with Bruce Kent, 2 February 1997.

(50) Interview with Christopher Rootes 4 April 97.

(51) Interview with Bruce Kent 2 February 1997.

(52) The ICJ or World Court has jurisdiction to resolve contentious disputes between conflicting parties if those parties accept the jurisdiction of the Court, or it can give Advisory Opinions requested by Organs of the United Nations. Advisory Opinions are not intended to settle particular disputes: they do, however, reflect international law and to that extent they are binding on all states.

See generally, Nicholas Grief, *The World Court Project on Nuclear Weapons and International Law*, Second Edition, 1993, and Robert Green, 'The World Court decision on the legal status of nuclear weapons', *Bulletin of Arms Control*, Council for Arms Control, Number 24, December 1996, pp.7-12.

(53) Interview with Field Marshal Lord Carver 20 February 1997.

(54) Interview with Professor Robert O'Neill 17 March

1997.
(55) Interview with Mr Frank Blackaby 14 March 1997
(56) Thomas Rhodes and Michael Evans, 'Military elite call for an end to nuclear arms', *The Times*, 5 December 1996.
(57) In a BBC interview, now untraceable.
(58) Interview with Ian Doucet 28 February 1998.
(59) Baroness Symons, Parliamentary Under Secretary of State at the Foreign and Commonwealth Office, speaking in the House of Lords on 17 December 1997, acknowledged and welcomed the latest poll findings. She said, 'We recognise that [nuclear disarmament] is also a question in which there is a high level of public interest. In the Gallup poll which was conducted in October this year 87% of those questioned supported negotiations to prohibit nuclear weapons. We pay close attention to that.' *Hansard* 17 December 1997. Column 684.

6. THE VIEWS OF CHRISTIAN CHURCHES

The trouble is that if Christianity really is incompatible with war, we have to turn our backs on 2000 years of warring Christendom, and assume that during those centuries, God was unaccountably withholding his Holy Spirit from his Church. No: God can only work through his creation: and his Church consists of men and women who are not so much sinful as shaped by their history and culture...The Church is inexorably part of its background of the society around it. It reflects and expresses the changing values and the conflicts of that society. God did not give any of us the power to transcend the cultural limits of our own times. He finds us as we are, and uses us as he sees fit. In His house are many mansions, and there is plenty of room for the warrior priest as well as the Quaker, for the crusader for war as well as the crusader for peace.

The University Sermon delivered at St Mary the Virgin, Oxford on 11 November 1984 by Professor Michael Howard, Regius Professor of Modern History in the University of Oxford.

Nothing illustrates the dilemma and confusions within

the churches over the question of nuclear weapons more poignantly than reactions to the BBC's programme *Songs of Praise*, broadcast from Faslane on Sunday 11 January 1998. This programme showed scenes shot on board a Royal Naval nuclear submarine. The Reverend Maxwell Craig, general secretary of Churches Together in Scotland, the main inter-church body, objected strongly to these scenes being shown on the grounds that they were 'deeply insensitive, bordering on blasphemous'. All the churches in Scotland, he said, had been very clear in their forthright opposition to Trident. Seeing a programme like this will puzzle people, he thought. (1) If so, the puzzlement will only have been compounded by the fact that the submariners in question were Crown servants acting by will of Parliament, and some were keen Christians. Nor is there anything novel in this dilemma. Since its foundation, the Christian Church has been ambivalent towards the state in general, the armed forces in particular and the participation of church members in both or either. And this confusion is rooted in the acts and sayings of the Church's founder as these have come down to us in the canonical scriptures.

Was Jesus a Pacifist?

The situation in Jesus' lifetime was this. Under the *Pax Romana*, the 'Roman peace' that prevailed throughout the vast Roman Empire, of which Palestine was a part, there was no such thing as war between nations, nor could Jesus be expected to have any views on it. There was no national army nor concept of compulsory military service; the soldiers in the Gospels were an alien, Roman, occupation force concerned with internal security. What one can justifiably look for are Jesus' opinions on the use of force in support of public order, attitudes to the occupying power, dual taxation and Emperor-worship; the puppet regime of the Chief Priests, whose role was almost wholly political, the role of armed struggle in support of nationalist goals and how it was possible, in these confused circumstances, to maintain some form of personal integrity. All these indeed we find. It seems that Jesus saw himself as renewing Israel but not, for whatever reason, in direct confrontation with Rome, which was pointless anyway. He accepted Rome's role as the occupying power and the need for law and order. His famous saying:

'Render unto Caesar the things that are Caesar's '
(Matthew 22: 21) was deliberately ambiguous. If he had
said a straight 'Yes' to taxation he would have been in
trouble with nationalist sentiment; a straight "No" and he
would have been in trouble with Rome. What belongs to
Caesar? - the coins bearing his image. What belongs to
God? - our whole being, since people are made in the
image of God. He accepted in principle the puppet regime
of the high priest, and was not a supporter or sympa-
thiser of the resistance movement, let alone the terrorists. Jesus had an overwhelming messianic sense of his
role in the spiritual war. His grasp of the spiritual values
at stake and his unbending integrity led him to see that,
in the last resort, even a religious leader may have to
break the law, may have to countenance violence of a
kind, as he did in throwing money-changers out of the
Temple. In the Garden of Gethsemane, his aims were
almost irreconcilable, he needed the presence and support of his friends without putting at risk their safety and
freedom. With hindsight, it seems strange that he let his
friends come armed but it is beyond reasonable doubt
that he did so. His subsequent arrest took place at the
cost of one Roman soldier lightly wounded. And in Mark's
Gospel (15: 39) a Centurion's is the first human voice to
call him the Son of God.

Early Christian Teaching

It is generally agreed that for about a century after 70 AD,
there is no authentic evidence for the existence of a single Christian soldier. In part, this was due to the idola-
trous environment in which soldiers of the Roman army
had to serve. The soldier's oath of allegiance (*sacramen -
tum*), the cult of Standards, the constant round of military festivals and sacrifices created a climate of pagan
observance which any Christian in the army would have
found hard to live with. But there was more to it than
that. During this period, Christians saw themselves as at
war with spiritual enemies, with Satan and his legions.
Healing miracles and exorcisms were an important part
of their activities and proof of their claims. Their weapons
were the weapons of the spirit. They disapproved not only
of bloodshed, but also of hatred, even anger. Christians
were under an obligation to love their enemies, respond
to curses with prayers and to violence with gentleness,

for in so doing they exercised a greater power. Suffering should be freely accepted, not violently resisted. Such Christians could hardly have regarded service in the Roman army as a suitable occupation, and there was not the slightest pressure on them to serve. The view seems to have been that if you were a Christian you did not belong in - indeed you might have to resign from - any branch of the public service. You were not supposed to join the police or become a magistrate. It was not that the Christians were unpatriotic; a strong tradition grew up that there were better things for them to do. They gave an alternative service of a quite different nature. They worked continuously for the improvement of the moral fibre of the citizens, which was of benefit to the whole state. They provided a power-house of prayer, particularly for the suppression of demons which stirred up wars and disturbed the peace. The Canons of Hippolytus, early in the 3rd century AD, said that a man could not be received as a Christian if he was in the army of the emperor; a catechumen who showed military ambitions was to be rejected because this was 'far from the Lord'. The closest parallel today is probably the pacifist, egalitarian Quakers. But while one can readily admit an individual specialist Christian vocation to steer clear of the public service, this could not possibly apply to the population at large. Origen, then head of the catechetical school at Alexandria, said that the Christian's service, though different from the soldier's, is in harmony with it. He said that one of the objects of the Christian's prayer is 'those who fight in a righteous cause'. There was no strand of Christian thinking that denied the right, indeed the duty, of the state to provide itself with the means not only to cope with wrongdoers within - something on which St. Paul so clearly insisted - but also to defend itself against enemies without. As a matter of hard fact, every state on Earth does this, by one means or another, to the benefit of Christians, as to all other citizens. It is not becoming for Christians to stand aside and allow the burdens of civic and military duty to be borne exclusively by others. Not surprisingly, therefore, from the end of the 2nd century AD, some Christians participated in the military and their number continued to grow thereafter. Some Roman soldiers, too, were converted to the faith.

Constantine and Augustine

Constantine I, who became Emperor of Rome in 312AD, proclaimed Christianity as the official religion of the Roman Empire in 313AD, and the way was open for attitudes to change substantially. Some people believe that everything changed for the worse: it was under Constantine that the church was forced down the slippery slope of compromise. That way, in the future, lay the Crusades of the 11th-14th centuries, bishops commanding armies and the hideous 17th century wars of religion in Europe between Catholic and Protestant. There is some truth in this. But the real key to the problem of war in Christian thinking lay in bringing to bear the precepts of Natural Law. This process was begun by the great intellectual superstar, the berber Bishop Augustine of Hippo (354-430AD), whose diocese was systematically sacked by Vandals. In his letters to Boniface, governor of Roman Africa, Augustine clearly recognised war as part of the human condition and believed that the Christian soldier could be an agent co-operating in God's providential governance of the world. In his tract *Against Faustus the Manichean,* he gave as a possible example of a holy war the struggle of a Christian army against a pagan one. Later, in his book *The City of God,* Augustine set the practice of warfare within the context of the pursuit of the peace of the earthly city. He affirmed the justice of warfare only as one of the tragic necessities to which Christians must at times resort, in order to check the savagery which is liable to break out between, as well as within, political societies. He coupled this, however, with a radical distrust of all existing political structures, their system of institutions and functions, including that of war. The change that occurred with Constantine was less a reversal than a general shift of Christian thinking, made possible by earlier ambiguities and made necessary by the altered political circumstances in which the Christians now found themselves. By his writings, Augustine did more than any other author to shape the pattern of Western thought in Christendom.

The Just War

Augustine died in AD 430. Some 800 years later, his ideas were picked up by another hugely influential writer, the Dominican Thomas Aquinas (1225-1274), and refined by his followers, notably the Spanish theologians Francisco de Vitoria (1486-1546) and Francisco Suarez (1548-1617), into the tradition which came to be known as that of the Just War. This body of thinking acknowledges that under certain circumstances, war is unavoidable if the state is to survive. The moral imperative is to bring Christian insights to bear upon it. These can be grouped under two headings:

1. Jus ad Bellum - which deals with the circumstances in which it is right to go to war, and
2. Jus in Bello - which deals with the means by which war can justifiably be waged.

Under the heading Jus ad Bellum come five considerations:

1. Lawful authority By this, Aquinas meant that it is only the sovereign who has the right to go to war, not barons or private warlords   -   an obvious safeguard at a time when anarchic relations between city states were a curse to the common people. (The question of Just Rebellion against an intolerable tyranny is a separate one, also recognised by Aquinas, but does not directly concern us here). At the present day, the question of lawful authority arises in a different, non-royal, form. It is an interesting question whether, for example, the President of the United States can lawfully go to war without the express mandate of Congress, or the British Prime Minister without a vote in Parliament. This argument has been given a new slant in present day terms by the consideration that if force is going to be used for the sake of peace and international good order, then perhaps only an international authority has the right to authorise it. In Europe this could be the Organisation for Security and Co-operation in Europe (OSCE). Under the United Nations Charter such questions are dealt with by resolutions of the Security Council (UNSCR).
2. Just Cause meant for Aquinas a war to avenge wrongs or to restore what had been wrongfully seized. As de Vitoria put it, there is one, and only one, just cause for waging war - an injury received. In the past half century Just Cause has generally been equated with the right of

individual or collective self-defence against an aggressor, and this is specifically provided for by Article 51 of the UN Charter.

3. The criterion of Last Resort means that war arises only when all other means of coping with the situation have been exhausted, on the face of it a prudent and humane precaution. If a nation is under armed attack, plainly this condition has been met. If it is a question of reversing by force of arms an illegal occupation which is already fait accompli, then it is widely held that other means than military force - for example economic sanctions and their enforcement by sea and air - must be given time to work. Only if they are not working at all, or not quickly enough, is it permissible to expel the invader by force. However, it is a matter of fine judgment how long sanctions should be given to work. It might have to be for five or ten years, during which time the original wrong would have been greatly compounded. Moreover, general economic sanctions exact a heavy price from the common people upon whom they are imposed, including privation of water, electricity, sanitation, medical care and food, leading to hunger, illness and even death. It may, therefore, be preferable to use limited military force against carefully selected military targets as a means of compulsion before applying general economic sanctions. This illustrates a more general point. Just War criteria, while providing a rational, indeed indispensable, framework for considering the moral justification of military acts, provide no cut and dried solutions.

4. A reasonable prospect of success means exactly what it says. Troops should not be committed to battle in a lost cause; that is, unless there is a reasonable prospect that by doing so the Just Cause can be vindicated. It happens that there is a recorded saying of Jesus on precisely this point (Luke 14: 31,2):'Or what king will march to battle against another king without sitting down first to consider whether with 10,000 men he can face an enemy coming to meet him with 20,000. If he cannot then, long before the enemy approaches, he sends envoys and asks for terms'.

5. Right Intention meant for Aquinas either to promote good or to prevent evil. The desire to hurt people, for revenge, an implacable and unrelenting spirit, ferocity in renewing a conflict and a lust to dominate are all, he

said, wrong. There is a nice line to be drawn here since, under the criterion of Just Cause, Aquinas had allowed the notion of avenging wrongs. So much for the categories of Jus ad Bellum. As far as they go these criteria make good sense. The instances given above have shown that they can be directly and usefully applied to modern circumstances. They do not, however, have any particular bearing upon the possession of nuclear weapons as such.

In the category of Jus in Bello there are only two headings:

1. Discrimination. The innocent, who can do no harm, must not be knowingly or deliberately attacked. The elderly, sick, children and handicapped cannot by any stretch of the imagination be part of the war effort, whereas politicians, civil servants and workers in armaments obviously can. This is a very difficult area. It is rare in modern war that no innocents at all are killed. But it is one thing to attack a column of tanks, a bridge or a military air base, killing some bystanders unavoidably in the process. It is quite another thing to attack an opponent's capital city. Moral philosophers attempt to cope with this issue by allowing for double effect - that is, the killing of innocents, provided that it is unintended, when it is a necessary consequence of an otherwise discriminate action. No one, however, could pretend that this is wholly satisfactory. In practice, there is often little option but to merge this consideration with the last criterion of Jus in Bello, namely the issue of Proportion.
2. Proportion. The rule is simple and self-evident: to be just, an act of war must do more good or avert more evil that the harm wrought in the process. An obvious example of an act of war which did not meet this criterion was the bombing of Dresden on the night of 14-15 February 1945. The attack was ordered by the British Chiefs of Staff not only to cause confusion among the German armies evacuating from the East, but also to hamper the movement of troops from the West. In fact, it caused a fire-storm, destroyed the centre of the city and killed an estimated 35,000 people, but quite possibly many more. It was no excuse that the Germans were at that time bombarding London with Vergeltungswaffen - reprisal or

Vengeance weapons, the V-1 'Flying Bomb' and V-2 rocket, both of which were inherently indiscriminate. Dresden was a city of great historic and cultural value, but of almost no military significance. Reservations were voiced at the time, and afterwards. Even Prime Minister Winston Churchill had his doubts. 'The destruction of Dresden,' he said six weeks after the raid 'remains a serious query against the conduct of Allied bombing.' This controversial raid can now be seen as an act of terror directed against the Germans' morale and one which, in the event, did little to shorten the war. The criterion of proportion clearly condemns it.

On 17 November 1993, the Roman Catholic bishops of the United States issued a reflection entitled *The Harvest of Justice is Sown in Peace*. This included a thoughtful restatement of Just War principles, from which they concluded that the criteria taken as a whole must be satisfied in order to override the strong presumption against the use of force. They put a useful and much-needed gloss on the whole attempt to apply Christian moral principles to the messy business of conflict:

> We also recognise that the application of these principles requires the exercise of the virtue of prudence; people of goodwill may differ on specific conclusions. The just-war tradition is not a weapon to be used to justify a political conclusion or a set of mechanical criteria that automatically yields a simple answer, but a way of moral reasoning to discern the ethical limits of action. Policy makers, advocates and opponents of the use of force need to be careful not to apply the tradition selectively to justify their own positions. (2)

Christian Pacifism
Christian pacifists, for example those in the Mennonite tradition, argue that all Christians should be committed to total non-violence and this stand must be maintained in all circumstances as a witness. This has already been noted as an essential strand within Christianity, witnessing to a world very different from the present. In the debate over nuclear weapons, it is the Christian pacifists

that have been most vocal. Canon Paul Oestreicher is well known as a pacifist and is currently the vice-president of the Campaign for Nuclear Disarmament. In his view, 'there is no respectable Christian view that the use of nuclear weapons is morally justified, but there is a quasi-respectable view that their threat, in order to avert the worst, in other words their possession, would actually prevent war. There is a theoretical possibility that is true, that at the height of the Cold War during the Cuban Missile Crisis, when the world was on the brink of nuclear war, nuclear weapons prevented war. However to assume the use of nuclear weapons in the long run is not reasonable'. (3)

Critics of pacifism believe that to use pacifism as an instrument of policy is self-defeating. Whereas pacifists look to Mahatma Gandhi as a hero, critics argue that his techniques of non-violent resistance were forged at a particular time and in unusual circumstances, in a society where spirituality was deeply embedded and a culture where non-violence was already respected. To behave in that way in Stalin's Russia would have simply been both foolish and suicidal. And almost no one believes that Hitler's neighbours should have dealt with his regime non-violently. A critique of pacifism along these lines would probably be accepted by the majority of members of church communities in this country. If it is not often articulated this may be because it is vaguely (if mistakenly) felt to be out of tune with the teaching of Christ himself.

Nuclear weapons

> I think that Christians live between the times. We live within this world, with a need to establish a just order, and because it is a fallen world, we need to use coercion or the threat of coercion. However, we live towards the hope of the Kingdom of God when this will be ended. Interview with Richard Harries, Bishop of Oxford, 3 March 1997.

During the past fifty years, the advent of nuclear weapons has cast a new light over Christian thinking on issues of peace and war. These weapons have a destructive potential greater by orders of magnitude than anything that has existed hitherto. Their invention, together with the missile forces to deliver them, has placed in the hands of large highly developed states what Sir Michael Quinlan describes as for practical purposes infinite destructive power, unstoppable and inexhaustible at any humanly-relevant levels. (4) If the full panoply of nuclear weapons available to the Soviet Union and America at the height of the Cold War had been discharged, it is quite possible that civilised life, in the northern hemisphere at least, would have been obliterated. The conclusion Quinlan draws is that nuclear weapons have brought about the *reductio ad absurdum* of warfare between advanced powers. Like it or not, this is a fact of life. 'It is, to say the least, odd to think 'so much the worse for nuclear weapons rather than so much the worse for war', to suppose that the right inference is to abolish nuclear weapons rather than to value the prevention of war by this route while we look for the day when it can be prevented equally surely by some other more comfortable means'. (5)

It is clear, however, that more than comfort is at stake. So long as nuclear weapons exist, particularly in large numbers, widely dispersed and under varying degrees of control, a finite chance must exist that one will be fired off, leading perhaps to the use of many, whether by political ill-will, the colossal risks notwithstanding, miscalculation or sheer mechanical malfunction. The fact that this has not happened during the first half-century of the existence of nuclear weapons provides no guarantee for the future. Moreover, within the general category of inhumane weapons, the nuclear occupy a place of peculiar horror. This is in part because of the effects of radiation upon human generative powers, and in part because fall-out can remain latent in the ground for decades - as witness the effects of the blow-out at Chernobyl upon Welsh sheep farmers to this day.

Some authorities have maintained, under the rubric of existential deterrence, that the mere possession of nuclear weapons by a state is sufficient to deter any attack upon it, regardless of any intention to use them. Logically, however, the ability to deter must imply at least the capability to use nuclear weapons, and no government possessing that capability could responsibly rest content without devising some doctrine for their use. The question then arises whether it is possible to use nuclear weapons without inevitably breaching the principles of discrimination and proportion. In theory, a nuclear attack upon a warship in the wide ocean or upon a tank column in an unpopulated desert could, if the weapon was a clean one set to explode at altitude (high airburst), be guaranteed to cause little, if any, damage to the innocent. No realistic strategy, however, is based upon such limited use. At the other extreme, the type of attack variously described as counter-value or counter-city makes a virtue of maximising the deterrent effect of the available weapons precisely by threatening the greatest destruction of an adversary's fabric and livelihood. The obvious immorality of such a strategy has led to the abandonment, at least as far as public declaration goes, of earlier doctrines such as those known as 'massive retaliation' or 'mutually assured destruction'. Even such strategies as that ostensibly adopted by the UK - attacking key aspects of an enemy state's power (i.e. Moscow) - would involve vast civilian casualties, highly foreseeable, if strictly speaking unintended. In recent decades, NATO sought escape from these dilemmas by recourse to the policy of 'flexible response'. This means that in response to conventional attack, and if direct defence failed, legitimate military targets would be sought for nuclear attack. Their destruction would do damage to the Soviet system out of all proportion to any benefit its government might anticipate by going to war, and would thus constitute an acceptable policy of deterrence. (6) This was always an unconvincing compromise.

Advocates of the strategy of nuclear deterrence argue that the strategy is justifiable precisely because its aim is to prevent war. The ethical point at issue is whether the possession, preparation and planning for the use of nuclear weapons falls under the same moral condemnation as their actual use. There is, of course, a profound difference between intentions and deeds, at least in terms of their possible consequences. There is also an ambiguity about a threat, especially when part of its effectiveness lies in the uncertainty about whether it will actually be carried out. One cannot avoid the conclusion that the readiness to do something wrong shares some of the wrongness of the action itself. But it would be absurd to claim that the strategy of nuclear deterrence and the weapons on which it depends are as unmitigated an evil as a nuclear war would be. (7)

> We still have to ask the question, however: if an act is immoral, is a threat or conditional intention to commit that act also immoral, especially if the intention is righteous? It will, perhaps, clarify the issue if we eliminate the question of bluffing. When Solomon said, 'divide the living child in two' he was bluffing. If an identical issue had arisen the next day, Solomon's technique might not have worked a second time. States have been known to bluff, of course, but to reach a sound ethical judg- ment we have to assume that nuclear defend- ers mean what they say, that they are not bluffing, that if deterrence fails, nuclear weapons *will* be used. When it comes to the point, authorised decision makers may shrink from mutual annihilation, but their present intention to use nuclear weapons if deterrence fails must be taken as serious and sincere. (8)

In terms of Just War theory, there is no escape from these dilemmas. The only acceptable course is to build down the nuclear arsenals in a controlled and deliberate manner, aiming at zero. This was exactly the approach set out in the Treaty on the Non-Proliferation of Nuclear Weapons (NPT), signed in July 1968. The treaty states, in Article VI, that "Each of the parties to the treaty under- takes to pursue negotiations in good faith on effective measures relating to the cessation of the nuclear arms race at an early date and to nuclear disarmament, and on a treaty on general and complete disarmament under strict and effective international control". It has to be said, however, that the final clause, with its strong flavour of utopianism, undermines the Article as a whole - and was no doubt inserted for this reason by those nuclear weapons powers who were, in any case, in no hurry to see this Article implemented.

Attitudes of the churches

We now examine the attitudes of the Roman Catholic church and the Anglican church towards nuclear weapons. These are the two principal denominations in Britain and as such are the most influential in the nuclear weapon debate. It should be noted that Scottish churches are in general more anti-nuclear than English churches, and free churches more anti-nuclear than Anglican ones.

> Wickedness does not lie in weapons, but in people. We live in a world prone to moral corruption, and the situation which has given rise to nuclear deterrence must be deplored . (9)

As early as 1963, the Roman Catholic Church had come out strongly in favour of nuclear disarmament. 'If one country is equipped with atomic weapons, others consider themselves justified in producing such weapons themselves Moreover, even though the monstrous power of modern weapons does indeed act as a deterrent, there is reason to fear that the very testing of nuclear devices for war purposes will, if continued, have disastrous consequences. [Hence] nuclear weapons must be banned. A general agreement must be reached on a suitable disarmament programme, with an effective system of mutual control.' (10)

So the elimination of nuclear weapons is not new to Roman Catholics, and has for decades been the basic position of their church. But this has by no means laid all argument to rest. In the early 1980s, during the controversies over stationing American intermediate-range nuclear weapons in Europe, there was a confusion of voices and a number of statements emerged that were far from coherent. Various conferences of Catholic bishops, led by those in the United States, issued letters or other documents intended to give some kind of guidance on the nuclear issue. These showed a divergence between the views of bishops who came from countries possessing nuclear weapons and those who lived in states that did not. For example, the Irish bishops differed fundamentally from the Americans.

Perhaps the most important of these utterances was a pastoral letter, produced by the American Roman Catholic bishops in 1983, called 'The Challenge of Peace: God's Promise and Our Response'. In this the bishops presented anew the traditional teaching of the church on war and peace and suggested how these moral principles might translate into governmental policy in the nuclear age. They also discussed pastoral approaches for developing the modern role of Christians as peacemakers. The document went through a number of drafts and the final version was less clear in its position on nuclear weapons than earlier unpublished versions had been. The letter asked, almost plaintively: 'Why do we address these matters fraught with such complexity, controversy and passion? We cannot avoid our responsibility to lift up the moral dimensions of the choices before our world and nation. We are the first generation since Genesis with the power virtually to destroy God's creation. We cannot remain silent in the face of such danger. We are simply trying to live up to the call of Jesus to be peacemakers in our own time and situation.' (11)

The bishops were generally sceptical of nuclear deterrence and the arguments of the military and the government in its favour, but they were not convinced that it was an illegitimate policy in all circumstances. Everything hinged on the intentions of governments that possessed the weapons. The key moral question was, and remains, did nuclear deterrence imply on the part of its proponents an intention to kill large numbers of innocent civilians if deterrence failed? In Catholic teaching, the intentional killing of people who have done no harm is absolutely forbidden. Did nuclear deterrence involve such an intention? This was the heart of the dilemma. 'Protecting human life from nuclear destruction must be pursued in tandem with promoting those values necessary for life to be lived with dignity.' (12)

Into this confused scene, there came a papal intervention. The Vatican Secretary of State, Cardinal Casaroli, delivered a message from Pope John Paul II to the 2nd Special Session of the United Nations General Assembly on Disarmament on 11 June 1982. This message included the following crucial text: 'In current conditions, 'deterrence' based on balance, certainly not as an end in itself, but as a step on the way towards progressive disarmament, may still be judged morally acceptable. Nonetheless, in order to ensure peace, it is indispensable not to be satisfied with this minimum which is always susceptible to the real danger of explosion.' (13)

This formulation created immediate difficulties. People found it difficult to understand how deterrence could be a step towards nuclear disarmament. However, the bishops generally fell into line and did the best they could to clear up the confusion. The American bishops issued two reports updating their original pastoral letter. 'We remain convinced that the policy of nuclear deterrence is not a stable long term method of keeping peace among sovereign states...our conditional acceptance is not an endorsement of the *status quo* that we find inadequate and dangerous. Progress towards a world freed of dependence upon nuclear deterrence must be carefully carried out. But it must not be delayed.' The other noteworthy statement was: 'How do we live with nuclear weapons, politically, strategically and morally, until the day when we can live without them? Some believe such a day is a distinct possibility. Others are equally convinced such a goal is a delusion, or at least a dangerous distraction from more modest objectives of living with nuclear weapons more safely'. (14) Cardinal Hume summed up the majority Catholic position in 1983 when he said: 'The acceptance of deterrence on strict conditions, and as a temporary expedient leading to progressive disarmament is emerging as the most widely accepted view'. He agreed that this view 'places us in a seemingly contradictory position' because of the strength of the case against any actual use of nuclear weapons. (15)

At that time, talk of immediate progress towards elimination of nuclear weapons seemed unreal, but by the 1990s, a very different background was emerging. The Cold War was over. The need to deter an over-mighty and threatening Soviet Union had vanished. Hence, ten years after their first controversial statements, the bishops of the United States felt ready to push their ideas further, saying that the elimination of nuclear weapons was now much more than a moral ideal and had become a policy goal. In a speech given on 15 October 1997 to the United Nations General Assembly the permanent observer of the Holy See to the UN, Archbishop Renato Martino, claimed a direct connection between disarmament and development. 'A new political attitude would say No to investment in arms and Yes to investment in the construction of peace. The relationship between disarmament and development, given short shrift by governments since the international conference of 1987, must be emphasised anew'. The archbishop then gave what appeared to be a genuine change in view from the Vatican on the nuclear issue. 'Those nuclear weapons states resisting such negotiations must be challenged, for, in clinging to their outmoded rationales for nuclear deterrence, they are denying the most ardent aspirations of humanity, as well as the opinion of the highest legal authority in the world. Nuclear weapons are incompatible with the peace we seek for the 21st century. They cannot be justified. They deserve condemnation. The preservation of the Non-Proliferation Treaty demands an unequivocal commitment to their abolition.' So it is clear that nuclear deterrence is now considered as unacceptable and an obstacle to peace. The statement continues: 'There is a gathering momentum of world opinion in support of the complete elimination of nuclear weapons. This is a moral challenge, a legal challenge and a political challenge. That multiple-based challenge must be met by the application of our humanity'. (16)

> The prevailing view from the Vatican is changing. Statements which are coming out from the Vatican and from a number of bishops' conferences around the world are undermining the philosophy of deterrence, and this is very challenging to Britain. In the mid-1990s if there was a political will there is a serious possibility of nuclear disarmament. (17)

Despite papal statements and a general move in favour of nuclear disarmament since the end of the Cold War, the nuclear issue has moved into the background and nuclear weapons have become a less important issue in the public realm. The Roman Catholic bishops in Europe and America, not wanting to upstage the Pope, have concentrated on other issues. Obviously there are exceptions. But it is the Roman Catholic non-governmental bodies, such as Pax Christi, and the peace organisations who are now making the running on the nuclear issue. The bishops are arguing that this is not a theological issue, but rather a matter of strategic, political and military concern. There is much to be said for this view.

> The church has come to realise the power and
> the hold the Cold War had over Third World
> Countries, particularly Africa, India and
> Pakistan, and the crippling economic effects
> the Cold War has had over nation states in
> terms of the arms race. The church saw an
> opportunity for a genuine disarmament to
> bring with it a genuine rehabilitation of coun-
> tries. Now there was an opportunity for a kind
> of security that would not be based upon on
> deterrence, fear and the arms race. (18)

By way of postscript, at the end of 1997 the Malaysian
government put down a motion for the UN General
Assembly First Committee proposing an immediate start
to multilateral negotiations for a Nuclear Weapons
Convention that would ban the weapons and provide for
their early elimination. The British government voted
against the resolution on the grounds that its call for
time-bound multilateral negotiations was unrealistic.
(19) The chairman of the Roman Catholic Bishops'
Commission on Justice and Peace did not follow the
British government's vote. While this had little effect, it is
clear that Roman Catholic Church is now somewhat at
odds with the British government's view.

The Church of England
The Church of England has been engaged in the debate
on nuclear weapons from the outset. After the Second
World War, despite the fact that many in the church were
deeply troubled by these issues, the hierarchy supported
the policy of nuclear deterrence. But as the weapons
became more destructive, so did articulate spokesmen in
the church become more hostile. It must be said, however, that the Church of England is a very broad church
with widely differing views on this as on almost every
topic. The Archbishop of Canterbury's utterances carry
some weight, though far less than those of the Pope in the
Roman Catholic Church. It is in the General Synod,
which is the Church of England's most democratic forum,
that the most vigorous debates are held, embracing a
wide range of opinions. Bishops have on the whole played

a minor part.

A notable exception is John Austin Baker, a well known theologian, who as Bishop of Salisbury in the late 1970s and early 1980s chaired a working party for the Church's Board of Social Responsibility. The report of the working party, which was published in 1982 as a book entitled *The Church and the Bomb*, was of high quality and was widely discussed. It advocated unilateral renunciation of nuclear weapons by Britain on moral grounds. Bishop Baker was influenced by Sydney Bailey, a noted Quaker writer on issues of peace and war, and a member of the working party. *The Church and the Bomb* analysed the technical issues, explored the underlying moral questions and made detailed recommendations concerning NATO's policy and the British nuclear deterrent. The report also tried to come to terms with the criteria of the Just War and the question of how these can be reconciled with the possession of nuclear weapons. It concluded that one cannot in the long run justify continued possession of these weapons because of the implied conditional intention to use them. The working party took the view that the use of nuclear weapons could in no circumstances be accepted as a justifiable form of war. The General Synod debated the report on 10 February 1983, and voted against its conclusion, by a majority of 387 to 49 (with 29 abstaining). It adopted a clause affirming that: 'it is the duty of Her Majesty's Government and her allies to maintain adequate forces to guard against nuclear blackmail and deter nuclear and non-nuclear aggressors'. They qualified this position by adding that even a small scale first use of nuclear weapons could never be morally justified and called on all countries, including members of NATO, publicly to forswear the first use of nuclear weapons in any form. They also called for immediate steps to reduce NATO's dependence on nuclear weapons and to decrease nuclear arsenals throughout the world. (20)

The General Synod of the Church of England had thus come to accept, as had the Pope, that in a temporary and very dangerous situation such as the Cold War, when there was a real prospect of a major conflict, the theory of deterrence was just within the bounds of Christian moral acceptance. It might be morally acceptable, if in possession of nuclear weapons, to threaten to use them in order not to have to do so. It might still conceivably be within the realm of reason for a nuclear weapons power to defend itself, if others have attacked with nuclear weapons, but to use them first would always be immoral. This was a very confused and untidy position. Presumably, everyone regarded it as an interim measure until such time as nuclear weapons could be negotiated away, as the Non-Proliferation Treaty undoubtedly required.

A further report was produced in 1988 by a working party under the chairmanship of Richard Harries, Bishop of Oxford. The resulting book, entitled *Peacemaking in a Nuclear Age*, focussed mainly on the issue of *détente*, and the need for Christians to make every effort towards rec-onciliation between East and West. The nuclear issue played only a small part in this report, which reached an ambivalent conclusion. 'For some of us, this means that deterrence of a minimal kind, with a continued nuclear component, will be an essential feature of the relation-ships between the super-powers for the foreseeable future. Others of us, while accepting the necessity for deterrence, believe that we should divest ourselves of the nuclear element in a way that looks for, but is not dependent upon, a reciprocal response.' The General Synod found no difficulty in endorsing this comfortably agnostic conclusion, and has not returned to the subject since. (21)

This short resumé of the positions officially adopted in utterances of the major churches cannot begin to do jus-tice to the offerings of academic theologians, which amount to an enormous literature. Distinguished contri-butions have also been made, from an explicitly religious point of view, by a number of British civil servants who have worked or are working in the defence field. Notable among these are Sir Michael Quinlan (a Roman Catholic), Sir Arthur Hockaday (an Anglican), and David Fisher (who writes from a philosophical standpoint). And men-tion should also be made of a small self-selecting group with charitable status called the Council for Christian Approaches to Defence and Disarmament, inspired largely by the work of Sydney Bailey, which promotes thinking, debate and the production of books on this subject, all at a high intellectual level and reflecting a wide range of views on these issues. But it must be conceded that, in terms of forming public opinion or influencing political decisions, the impact of this activity has been small to vanishing. In this chapter, by concentrating on the officially expressed positions of the churches it has been possible to offer a general impression of the critique of British nuclear weapons policy obtainable from a specifically Christian standpoint. It is not in the least surprising to find how wide a spectrum of views is represented. Almost certainly, the majority of Christians are content to believe that the possession of nuclear weapons, as of all others, is lawful 'at the commandment of the magistrate' - in other words, on a matter of this importance the government knows best.

By way of summarising it may be useful to quote a short section from *Peacemaking in a Nuclear Age* which records a growing convergence, in the various reports and resolutions produced by the churches in Britain, around the following points: (22)

1. The conviction that Christians have a particular contribution to make in the process of reaching decisions which fundamentally affect the course of history,
2. A continued questioning as to whether the use of nuclear weapons or the threat of their use can be justified morally or theologically,
3. The conviction that the long-term peace of the world cannot be preserved by the present policy of deterrence, which is not a permanent basis for stable progress and genuine security,
4. The fear that the continuation of the arms race diverts resources from the more fundamental problems of world poverty and the need for a just international society,
5. A general opposition to the deployment of new weapons systems where these are seen as escalating and further destabilising a dangerous situation.
6. The conviction that the search for comprehensive disarmament and common security should be pursued with greater vigour and urgency in both East and West.

> ...[the] Christian debate must seek to arrive at principles and guidelines that will hold for very hard cases, not just for easier ones; and for the long term future, not just for the next few years. It will not do, I suggest, to claim

absolute moral authority for policies which Christians could prudently or responsibly follow only on (say) very left wing views of the world, or only on very right wing views, or only if all goes comfortably. We must be prepared to test our principles honestly against awkward scenarios. It is not a Christian approach to challenge God by assuming that He will never allow a nuclear armed Hitler to exist, any more than Christians of the time could assume that He would not allow an Attila or a Ghengis Khan, or Hitler himself. (23)

All-out nuclear war between the Soviet Union and the West would be immoral for two main reasons. First, it would be immoral destruction upon non-combatants. Direct attacks on non-combatants would be part of any all-out nuclear war between the superpowers and long term fall out, raining down upon the Earth for years after the holocaust, would bring agonising death to people throughout the world wholly innocent of involvement with the quarrels of the great powers. Second, the evil that all-out nuclear war would entail for all mankind would be out of all proportion to any good that might be secured. (24)

Conclusion

On a popular political level, the people and the churches intertwine and influence one another. But it is hard to show that religious opinion as such has had any real influence on policy making where nuclear weapons are concerned. At present the churches have put the issue of nuclear weapons on a back burner. There is no actual debate, and the churches do not regard it as highly relevant as there is no immediate threat. In fact, there has been no serious discussion of nuclear weapons since the end of the Cold War and nuclear weapons are no longer an important issue in public opinion. Yet on the assumption that the Labour government means what it says, and that it will join with other governments in gradually negotiating these weapons away, this is a time when the churches could make a difference. They could look at the structure of the arguments for retaining nuclear weapons and could criticise them. They could also give their backing to the various moves that are being made around the world towards nuclear disarmament. This would be a worthy and a manageable task.

References

(1) The Times 9 January 1998.

(2) *The Harvest of Justice is Sown in Peace*. A Reflection of the National Conference of Catholic Bishops on the tenth anniversary of the Challenge of Peace, November 17 1993.

(3) Interview with Canon Paul Oestreicher 5 August 1997.

(4) Michael Quinlan. Thinking About Nuclear Weapons, RUSI Whitehall Paper, 1997, p. 8.

(5) Michael Quinlan, 'Thinking about Nuclear Weapons' RUSI Journal December 1997 p. 1.

(6) David Fisher *Morality and the Bomb* Croom Helm, Beckenham, Kent, 1985 p. 90.

(7) Paul Abrechts and Ninan Koshy, (eds), '*Before it's too late, the challenge of nuclear disarmament*', Report of the Public Hearing, World Council of Churches, Geneva, 1983, p29.

(8) Sydney D Bailey, *Christian Perspectives on Nuclear Weapons*, Division of International Affairs, British Council of Churches, November 1984, p 43.

(9) Cardinal Hume, *The Universe*, 1 March 1992 p.1.

(10) Pope John XXIII, extract from the encyclical letter Pacem in Terris, 1963, ## 110-112.

(11) *The Challenge of Peace: God's Promise and Our Response*, Catholic Truth Society, London 1983, p.92. See also Philip J. Murnion, (ed) *Catholics and Nuclear War, A Commentary on The Challenge of Peace, The US Catholic Bishops' Pastoral Letter on War and Peace*, Geoffrey Chapman, London 1983.

(12) Pope John XXIII, 'Building peace: a pastoral reflection on the response to the challenge of peace', *Origins*, Volume 18, No 9, 21 July 1988 p.135

(13) Friedhelm Solms, Marc Reuver, *Churches as Peacemakers, An Analysis of Recent Church Statements on Peace, Disarmament and War*, IDOC International, Rome, 1985, p 57.

(14) 'The elimination of nuclear weapons', *CathNews*, 12

November 1997.

(15) *The Times* 17 November 1983.

(16) Archbishop Renato Martino, 'The new demands of global security', Text of a Speech given on 15 October 1997 to the United Nations General Assembly, by the permanent observer of the Holy See to the United Nations.

(17) Interview with Brian Wicker 29 July 1997.

(18) Interview with Pat Gaffney, General Secretary, British section, Pax Christi 18 August 1997.

(19) Baroness Symons, House of Lords Debate, 'Nuclear Weapons: Papal Policy', 17 December 1997, column 687.

(20) *The Church and the Bomb, Nuclear Weapons and the Christian Conscience*, The Report of a Working Party under the Chairmanship of the Bishop of Salisbury, Hodder and Stoughton, London CIO Publishing 1982. *The Church and the Bomb, The General Synod Debate*, CIO Publishing, February 1983, p. 67.

(21) *Peacemaking in a Nuclear Age* The Report of a Working Party of the Board of Social Responsibility of the General Synod of the Church of England. Church House Publishing, London, 1988, p. 132.

(22) *Peacemaking in a Nuclear Age*, p.167.

(23) Michael Quinlan, 'Nuclear Weapons, The Basic Issues', *The Ampleforth Journal*, Autumn 1996, Volume XCI Part II, pp 61-70.

(24) Barry Paskins 'Deep cuts are morally imperative' in Geoffrey Goodwin, (ed), *Ethics and Nuclear Deterrence*, The Council on Christian Approaches to Defence and Disarmament, Croom Helm, London, 1982, p. 94.

7. PSYCHOLOGICAL INSIGHTS

The aim of this chapter is to shed some light on the question why people have felt the need for nuclear weapons, using psychology rather than the theory of international relations. The dangers in this approach are obvious. Some will find the whole process repugnant, as though one were seeking to interpret the sober deliberations of highly intelligent and motivated people in terms more suitable to the psycho-analyst's clinic. We make no apologies. If some of the insights seem to make sense, it is worth exploring where they may lead us. We believe it is important to understand the use of psychology in understanding human motivations, some of which are hidden and very different from the rationales presented in public policies.

> The weapons have become such powerful talismans against fear that we cling to them like children in the dark, denying that such a way of seeking protection brings with it unprecedented dangers. For those who can face the reality of the dangers of nuclear weapons, however, only dismantling or destroying a nuclear weapon is an acceptable response to the risks. (1)

Ever since 1948, psychologists have been trying to understand the nature of nuclear confrontation, and there is considerable literature on the subject. Psychological approaches to the nuclear age fall into several categories. Some political scientists employ psychological theory as an analytical tool for exploring historical instances of nuclear deterrence and crisis diplomacy. Others have used psychological techniques to investigate the underpinnings of the nuclear arms race, and to prescribe ways to overcome it. A third approach examines the widespread psychological effects of nuclear terror. A fourth group follows the literature of political science and uses psychological theory descriptively rather than as a means to prescribe therapy for decision-making pathologies. It must be recognised, however, that psychology has not been very helpful as a way of looking at international relations in general, mainly because psychologists have been slow to move in this area, as though there were a self-imposed inhibition. Psychologists tend to emphasise the individual and neglect the collective; indeed this is feature of the general western approach to mental illness. Nor do psychologists have very good tools for understanding collective processes. Nevertheless, there is a psychological sub-plot which plays an important role in shaping international relations. Policy makers should not close their eyes to the insights offered by psychologists, psychiatrists, psychotherapists and others who are concerned with the inwardness of the nuclear phenomenon, and who want to promote new thinking in international relations.

> Unless we find better ways to educate ourselves as citizens, we run the risk of drifting unwittingly into a new kind of Dark Ages, a time when a small cadre of specialists will control knowledge and thus control the decision-making process ... (people) claiming to understand the complex issues and therefore able to tell us what we should believe and how we should act..(2)

The main bulk of work which has examined the reasons why Britain persists in keeping its own nuclear deterrent has been transacted in terms of military, political and socio-economic argument at what psychologists call a rational level. Psychologists argue, however, that people are also governed by irrational forces affecting their conscious attitudes, values and decisions. These unconscious forces operate at both the individual and the group level, on the so-called psycho-social dimension. On the whole, Britain's political, military and diplomatic planners have tended to ignore the existence of these forces, holding fast to conventional military logic. The lack of interest paid to this dimension is shown up clearly in the confusion surrounding whether or not violence, conflict, war and aggression are innate and inevitable.

> If you talked to the Dalai Lama, he would say that it is possible to have international relations based not on fear, but on trust and love. The Dalai Lama is not afraid to say things like that. Most international states-people would be, because the policy of realism in international politics has such enormous power. However, it is not the only political policy by a long way. The policy of realism is very effectively counterbalanced by the policy of transformation. (3)

Hans J. Morgenthau, the most famous realist thinker of the 20th century, wrote: 'Man's lust for power manifests itself as the desire to maintain the range of one's own person with regard to others, to increase it or demonstrate it. In whatever disguises it may appear, its ultimate essence and aim is one of particular reference of one person to others.' (4) Hence, prominent realist political thinkers, such as Henry Kissinger or George Kennan, view competitiveness as an innate dominant human trait. On the other hand, there are those who accept classical liberal assumptions about human nature, and accordingly share the belief that man is fundamentally good, and that mankind shares a harmony of interests. Much of Britain's culture is steeped in the philosophy of classical liberalism. There is no conclusive way of deciding between these different assumptions about human nature. What is it then that leads western decision makers in the 20th century to view the world through the eyes of Thomas Hobbes, a political philosopher and theorist of human behaviour, who was writing in the 17th century, and whose views were coloured by the long and bloody English Civil War?

Group thinking

> We must examine what forces produce flawed and dangerous thinking, what forces allow such thinking to be accepted unchallenged by the public, and how we, as agents of change, can treat these problems. (5)

Psychological approaches to decision making attempt to discover why people do not make rational choices. There appear to be two major sources of bias leading to irrational decisions. The first is cognitive bias, whereby human beings take short cuts in receiving and processing information about their environment. Cognitive psychologists have shown that these short cuts can severely distort reality. The second is motivated bias, which occurs when the fulfilment of emotional needs and desires dominates the decision-making process. Psychologists in the Freudian tradition argue that decision-makers often pay little attention to the outside environment, and instead chose alternatives which satisfy inner needs, such as avoiding guilt, shame or fear.

Dr. Anton Obholzer and Dr. Hannah Segal have explored the role of unconscious processes in individual and particularly group settings. (6) Dr. Segal describes how we need groups and the support of others for the positive and constructive part of our natures, but also to contain our maladaptive and more destructive parts. The groups we belong to help overcome individual anxieties, particularly extreme, primitive, psychotic type anxiety. But they also provide defence mechanisms that are not always realistic or advantageous. Indeed these group defences, if used by individuals, would be regarded as psychotic: self-idealisation, grandiosity, omnipotence, paranoia and freedom from conscious guilt (the latter because we merge our super-ego, or conscience, with the group, enabling soldiers, for example, to kill.) But Dr. Obholzer shows that we pay a heavy price for our feelings of security in a group and our loyalty to it. Individual doubts and questions are discouraged, and the group's denial of reality becomes our own.

Psychological processes in the individual, which lead to these maladaptive group-processes, are intensified by the nuclear threat under which we live. Dr Segal believes that the effect of the nuclear mentality is deep-rooted in the psychotic layers of our unconscious, because our worst nightmares can now come true, and the boundaries of reality are no longer clearly distinguishable. This terror leads to the use of psychotic defences. She explains that in a small group, its acknowledged 'work-task' can keep psychotic processes at bay, but this is more difficult in a large group, and even more so in a state or nation, where there is no single, clear work task to which the group's activity is directed. In states and nations, psychotic functions are delegated to subgroups: messianic and grandiose delusions to religious groups, omnipotent power to political groups, killing to the armed forces. She says that unthinkingly, we can adopt a mental posture that may be quite irrational and dangerous for our survival - for example, the present nuclear weapons policy. Here, denial is the main group defence mechanism employed, but other psychotic schizoid defence processes, such as projection and depersonalisation, are also involved. 'Our megalomania can also be aroused by thoughts of global warfare leading to feelings of terror and guilt, and the consequent projection of our own destructiveness outside which we can see it only in others, not ourselves. Thus, individual and group defence mechanisms often reinforce each other'.

Segal asks why, faced with the nuclear threat, we cannot use our sanity? She and Dr Obholzer suggest it is because 'sanity' ,too, can be projected onto leaders whom we then idealise (at the same time as denigrating the enemy). 'They'll keep us safe,' 'we say, just as children do of their parents, until they reach adolescence, when reality impinges and parental feet of clay become apparent. However, in some Western countries, reality does not seem to dawn in the case of nuclear coming of age: we seem stuck in collective childhood in relation to our leaders. Is this because we have thrown up governments and leaders who express our own defensive processes, so that we ourselves do not have to see the real danger, and are not forced to take personal responsibility for doing something about it? It is time that we *did* see the dangers and do take responsibility for our own aggression, as well as reclaiming our own capacity for concern and realistic thinking.'

Obviously, factors other than the psychological are often at work to produce irrational consequences. Organisational and political explanations cannot be ignored; bureaucratic interests influence what decision-makers do and say. The military provide clear evidence of the way in which an organisation can control the content of doctrine. It is obvious that the formation of nuclear policy, for example, is immediately linked to political and organisational interests which transcend the beliefs or emotional needs of individuals. Nevertheless, it is worth considering the psychologists' belief that there are deeper forces at work which cannot be ignored, and that we can attribute considerable significance to psychological motives.

The aftermath of war

> If mankind is to remain alive, then we are in need of a fundamentally new way of think-ing...men must radically transform both their attitude to one another and their concept of the future. (7)

A useful starting point is the European experience during the Second World War. This cannot be explained simply in political and economic terms, but needs to be understood also on a psychological level. There have been wars throughout history, and civilian populations have suffered appallingly. Territories have been overrun and families, villages and communities broken up. But until the 20th century, there was always the knowledge that families who fled their homes could regroup in new areas, and that the physical infrastructure could be rebuilt. Damage was done, but war was survivable. In a psychological sense, the belief in survivability had been seriously undermined by the end of the Second World War, and this created the framework from within which we have viewed all subsequent threats. In the early years of the War, Nazi Germany overran Norway and Denmark and, except for Switzerland, Spain and Portugal, the greater part of continental western Europe. The results were highly traumatic at the national level and for many different groups. Threats were not just military, to do with invasion and occupation of territory; there was the spectre of concentration camps and the ensuing Holocaust. The sense of security and safety had been assailed and subverted on a very personal level. Jews and gypsies were particular targets of Nazi racist slaughter, and among them, families were broken up and many were wiped out in the gas chambers. At the end of war there was a sense that an enemy could destroy one utterly. This applied not just in material or economic ways, not just destroying houses and cities, though certainly the mass indiscriminate bombings became lodged deeply in the collective mind. But beyond that, the sense of inner integrity and safety had been destroyed. In a comparison of the sense of threat in 1930 and 1950, the two would be very different. In 1950, any threat could be comprehensively and utterly destructive, and this deeply affected the popular sense of security. Ian Doucet says, 'Before, even after, great suffering, if one's self could not survive, at least one's children might or one's extended family. Individual suffering, however awful, happened within the context of an assured continuity of life in general. This sense of continuity was undermined.' (8)

Trauma of this kind has been recognised in psychological research done in the occupied countries of Europe, and people have described how this affected them in terms of the 'politics of memory'. Less work has been done on the way in which countries that were not invaded, have been affected. (9) Psychologists think it likely that attitudes to nuclear weapons and the perceived need for them were shaped by the different experiences of these countries at that time. A way of thinking arose, both in government and the military, based upon a fear of being caught unprepared, and of the huge cost if that were ever to happen again. And events that occurred within a few years after the end of the Second World War confirmed this fear, or were even called into being by this attitude of mind. They were external confirmation of something already felt. An example is the creation of the Iron Curtain. From one perspective, it can be argued that the Soviet Union was forced onto the defensive by British and American policies. However, having defeated the huge threat that Hitler's Germany presented, Britain and the US for their part seemed to feel the need for a new and equally powerful threat. Stalin and the Soviet Union filled the bill, and certainly did enough objectively to confirm this fear.

Projected evil

Although former enemies now ask for help and iron curtains have dropped, the psychosocial forces which fuelled that arms race for decades have not evaporated. They are evident, perhaps, in the minimum-change responses of Western politicians, the search for new enemies out of area, and in how little Western publics seem to be contributing to the new security order debate. (10)

Today, we are the product or children of the Cold War, and when we are in the middle of something, it is difficult to stand apart and view it. The way that we have survived with this awfulness, however, has been to split into two, a righteous self and a projected evil. Hence, we (the West) coped by making ourselves not only in the right, but also the place of complete virtue. This psychological dimension, seen in military threat assessment, is influenced by our desire to think well of ourselves and attribute the characteristics we dislike in ourselves to others. This phenomenon was clearly identified in January 1991 when over 200 mental health professionals met in London to identify the irrational processes that drove us towards the Gulf War. (11)

Psychologically what we fear is within ourselves as much as out there. However, it is convenient, and perhaps the only way we can sustain ourselves, to regard the awfulness as external rather than within. (12)

This process of large group formation, of mindlessness and of leadership that has, as

its unconscious task, the acting out of the
psychotic elements of the group, is not confined to any one side or any one conflict. It
happens on both sides of every divide. Put
into a world perspective, therefore, we have a
system in which nations act as defensive co-
operatives for their own citizens, and contract
as an unconscious group to deny personal
and national responsibility for themselves,
instead projecting all negatives into the other
side, in this instance the other nation. (13)

If we think in these terms, the Cold War was a classic
example of splitting between the righteous self (the West)
and a projected evil (the East). We made ourselves
absolutely self-righteous. We declared ourselves arbiters
of virtue in terms of decency and democratic political values. In hard fact, democracy in Britain and the West is
a partial business, but we made ourselves the repository
of all things good, of all civilised values. The Soviet Union
then became the place of evil, an idea which encom-
passed both its leaders and the people. There was justification for this, to the extent that anybody was able to
look at it objectively. What we made of it, however, exag-
gerated the reality and somehow locked it in. In the light
of that absolutist view, what was needed were absolute
weapons. Nuclear weapons measured up to this.

It is the case that the whole of what you call
realism in politics is based upon the projection
of evil intent out there; in other words, somewhere outside of our own nation. I mean the
other powers or governments who would wish
to threaten us, or might become a threat to us.
Therefore, we organise ourselves as best we
can to defend ourselves, and indeed we have
had experiences in the not too distant past
where we have been very seriously threatened
as an island nation and that has borne out our
fear. (14)

This approach throws some light on the origins of
nuclear weapons. The British and the Americans created
nuclear weapons and did so because they assumed that

the Nazis were doing the same. So, they invented something evil or capable of evil because they thought that something evil was being created by the 'other', by the 'out group'. In fact, we now know that Hitler's scientists never progressed very far with the development of the atom bomb. But because the Allies thought the Germans were about to explode a super-bomb over their heads, they created their own. There was an awful sense of responsibility about it, made only too real by the use of the atom bomb on Hiroshima and Nagasaki. This, in turn, led to a collective sense of wrong which made it hard to maintain the split between righteous selves and the evil 'other', even when that 'other' was not longer Nazi Germany, but had turned into Stalin's Russia. Having invented such a destructive weapon, some at least of the scientists began to feel guilt. (15)

Swords into ploughshares
One of the classic ways people have tried to come to terms with the horrors of war has been in the conversion of weapons to peaceful uses, turning swords into ploughshares. An excellent example of this has been the development of peaceful uses for atomic energy. In the 1950s, unrealistically high hopes were placed on the development of nuclear power. People spoke of electricity becoming too cheap to meter. It would be supplied to homes for a modest fee, like water. It would be clean too, unlike fossil fuels, and the disposal of waste was not seen as a problem. The promise made by the nuclear weapons states to share the benefits of nuclear power technology with developing countries was a crucial element in the bargain underlying the Nuclear Non-Proliferation Treaty. One of the driving forces behind all this was the determination, on the part of scientists and engineers, that some good had to come out of a technology with such fearsome power for evil. This was not a matter of conspiracy, or even of deliberate intent, but at the level of the 'collective psyche', it represented a way of rationalising what had happened. Having found that it was we ourselves who had created this great monster, not some evil 'other', good had to be made to come of it.

In fact, these hopes have been disappointed. The costs of nuclear power have remained obstinately high. The safety of some nuclear reactors has caused great concern. And no politically acceptable way to get rid of nuclear waste has yet been found. Nuclear power is certainly a practical way of producing electricity for advanced industrial countries that can handle the technology, and it is the main source of electricity in France. But the accident at Chernobyl showed that, if not properly managed, nuclear power generation can be disastrous. The construction of new plants has fallen sharply since its peak in 1980. With the need to shut down several reactors in the former Soviet Union for safety reasons and the political difficulties of building new plants in western democracies, nuclear power may well account for a diminishing share of the world's energy supply from now on. (16)

New enemies

> The possibility of implementing our infantile destructive megalomania induces both terror and guilt; guilt, because our own destructive impulses are stirred and we all feel implicated, and terror, because of the destruction released. Terror is also increased because the most primitive way of dealing with our destructiveness is to project it outside and create monsters. (17)

In the 1980s, US President Ronald Reagan famously described the Soviet Union as an 'evil empire'. He saw its true nature more clearly than most, and was almost the only person at that time to forecast its early demise. Indeed, according to one school of thought, he induced its collapse through an unyielding determination to build up American offensive and defensive strengths, thus spending the Soviets into the ground. On a more sober reading, the Soviet Union collapsed mainly as a result of its own inherent contradictions and weaknesses; most notably, the total unsuitability of a command economy to the information age. But our immediate concern is the way in which some commentators have sought to find another candidate for the mantle of 'evil empire'.

Some would say that militant fundamentalist Islam is now bidding for the part Communist Internationalism played after the emergence of the Soviet Union in 1923.

Certainly, a number of Islamic countries are hostile to the West. Some of them clearly have nuclear - not to say chemical and biological - weapons ambitions. A considerable number have ballistic missiles and, presumably, some ability to convert them for the delivery of weapons of mass destruction. It is also true that Muslim fundamentalists are a growing menace. Christian Arabs in Lebanon, Jordan, Iraq, Syria and Palestine have come under serious pressure, and hundreds of thousands have emigrated. Perhaps 500,000 Coptic Christians left Egypt in the last decade of the 20th century, and Islamic militants there have been bombing tourist attractions and buses, costing the state billions of dollars in lost revenue. The French are concerned about the network of clandestine terrorists in Paris, linked to Algeria's Armed Islamic Group. Four Palestinians, intent American government prosecutors charged, on punishing the US for supporting Israel, were convicted of bombing the World Trade Centre in New York in 1993; two further suspects were never caught. There is justified suspicion that an Islamic group, centred on the personality of Osama bin Laden, carried out the bombings of American embassies in Nairobi and Dar-es-Salaam in 1998. In that limited sense, there is an international conspiracy. But Arab and Muslim nations are notoriously bad at getting their act together. To paint their activities on anything like the canvas of former Soviet communism is the purest rent-a-threat, demonising for the sake of needing an enemy.

Much the same is true when it comes to personalities. Saddam Hussein of Iraq and, to a lesser degree, Colonel Ghaddafi of Libya have been turned into satanic figures, men with whom it is impossible to negotiate because there is no humanity in them. Admittedly, these men are unpredictable and prone to catastrophic errors of judgment. They are bent on acquiring weapons of mass destruction and the means of delivering them, cost what it will in the sufferings of their own people. Saddam Hussein has twice attacked largely innocent neighbours, waged long and bloody war to no advantage and proved infinitely duplicitous. The unstinting adulation he enjoys in Baghdad is driven to a large extent by fear, of Saddam himself. And support for him in other parts of the Arab world owes more to disillusionment with the policies of the US, mainly in regard to Israel, than to any qualities on his part, other than that of macho bully boy and strong man. But it appears beyond reason for the West to persist in maintaining sanctions, particularly against Iraq, despite their proven ineffectiveness in altering Saddam's behaviour and the all-too-evident penalties of impoverishment, disease and ill-nourishment being visited on the population. That Britain is at ease with this situation, and has backed the policy of air attack against the Iraqi regime, which is an even more irrational response, must owe something to the success which the image of an 'evil empire' has been projected. It is not wholly tendentious to point out - as Arab commentators habitually do - that Israel, too, is liable to engage in bloody frontier skirmishes, has long flouted resolutions of the Security Council mandating a political settlement with the Palestinians, and is in possession of weapons of mass destruction acquired clandestinely. Somehow, the Israelis are 'one of us' and not part of the 'evil other'. For instance, Israel is a democracy, the only one in its area. Secondly, a large part of Israel's population is, or was, of European origin. Thirdly there is a large Jewish population in the USA, and therefore a large Jewish vote. These factors ' ring bells' in the USA. Also relevant is the ongoing threat of Arab violence (including three full-scale wars) under which Israel has lived since 1948.

Guided by psychological insight it is plain that the world is more complex than it seems and within this complex world one can see that we - the British, or if you like the West - also are good and bad and shades of grey. Once we realise that there is good and bad in all and that all have to share responsibility, this produces a much more complicated and uncomfortable awareness to live out. Ian Doucet says of this phenomenon: 'People speak of uncertainty and a lack of clear moral values but it is good that we cannot divide the world into good and bad. Collectively we have matured beyond this, but we have matured into a less comfortable and less clear area: the complex world of the adult rather than the simple black and white world of the child.' (18)

Rivalry between friends

It is a commonplace that groups of all kinds, and not least governments are breeding grounds for rivalry. This can have a positive effect upon the work of the group, to the extent that individuals do their best under the spur of emulation. It can also be highly dysfunctional where internal disagreements hold up necessary progress, or degenerate into vendettas when hatred becomes the dominant motive. An interesting example, highly germane to the nuclear debate, is the relationship between Britain and its closest neighbour France. For 750 years after the Norman Conquest of 1066, the English saw the French as their archetypal enemy and, after the 17th century, their principal colonial rival. Until 1815, the British had good cause for their fears. However, with the defeat of Napoleon Bonaparte at the battle of Waterloo in that year, France ceased, in fact, to be a threat. Yet throughout the remainder of the 19th century, at the height of British imperial power and prestige, Britain remained obsessed with the fear of invasion by the French. The naval panic of the 1840s was driven by fear of French steam-driven warships. Expensive and entirely useless forts were built along the Medway and in the Solent. New classes of army reserves were created in response to clarion calls such as 'Riflemen Form!' from Alfred Lord Tennyson, the Poet Laureate. More absurdly, in the 1880s a plausible scheme for a Channel Tunnel was stopped in its tracks by the public warnings given by the Duke of Cambridge and Garnet Joseph, 1st Viscount Wolseley. These fears were not only entirely groundless, but were actually unreal. Yet they drove important aspects of British military and commercial policy. (19)

Since the threat of newly-united Germany arose after 1871, however, France and Britain have found themselves on the same side. The *Entente Cordiale* of 1904 was the political expression of this change. Subsequently, France and Britain have fought together in two world wars, and in numerous later campaigns, such as Suez (1956), in the Gulf (1990-1) and in Bosnia (1993-5). Yet the 750 years of enmity are not forgotten, and the British and French retain an instinctive and deep-seated wariness of each other that spills over into an undeclared but quite obvious rivalry. Nuclear weapons policy presents a fascinating instance. Consider, for example, the following classical statement of the case for Britain to maintain a strategic nuclear capability independent of the USA.

A Soviet leadership - perhaps much changed in character from today's, perhaps also operating amid the pressures of turbulent internal or external circumstances - might believe that it could impose its will upon Europe without becoming involved in strategic nuclear war with the United States. Modernised United States nuclear forces in Europe help to guard against any such misconception; but an independent capability fully under European control provides a key element of insurance. A nuclear decision would ,of course, be no less agonising for the Britain than for the United States. But it would be the decision of a separate and independent nuclear power, and a power whose survival in freedom would be directly and immediately threatened by aggression in Europe. (20)

While more than a generation old in its quoted form, this line of reasoning, referred to in short-hand as the 'second centre of decision' argument, is equally relevant to-day. It has been used quite explicitly to justify the presently planned size of the British Trident fleet. (21) As an argument, it is quite impressive. What is even more impressive, though, is that it contains a fatal flaw, never referred to, which is simply that the argument applies even more aptly to the French. The nub of the matter lies in what the Soviet Union (hereafter used as surrogate for any potential enemy) *might believe* would happen in certain dire circumstances: to wit, that the US would not be prepared to act, but the second centre of decision would. The three key elements would guide the 'Soviet Union' in its thinking on this point. These are the amount of independence that the second centre possessed, its technical ability to strike with assurance against key elements of 'Soviet' state power and the degree of political backing that it enjoyed in maintaining this ability. A moment's reflection shows that the French have the edge in all these respects.

Where independence is concerned, there is the obvious drawback for the British that their Trident fleet is beholden to the Americans for the supply of missiles, including their fire - control systems. The missile bodies rotate through the American base in Georgia for routine refurbishment, and rely on continual American help for repair, training, test-firing and technical support. The British also look to America for help with propulsion-reactor design and the supply of special materials as well as intelligence. The French, however, are dependent on America for none of these things. Admittedly, British dependency is long-term in nature, and need not in the last resort inhibit British prime ministers from ordering a nuclear strike on their own initiative. But the important question is that of carrying conviction *vis-à-vis* the Soviet Union. Which country, in their view, would be the more likely to act independently of the US? France is physically connected to the European mainland, yet has stood aloof from the military structure of NATO. It has no tradition of special relationship with the US as Britain has, but rather prides itself upon independence from the '*defi Americain*'. In the eyes of any potential adversary, therefore, France is far more like to act independently. (22)

As regards the ability to carry out assured destruction, again France has the advantage. Setting aside her Intercontinental Ballistic Missiles on the *Plateau d'Albion* and her long range strike force of *Mirage* bombers - Britain has no counterpart for either - the French ballistic missile submarine force alone exceeds the British in terms of deliverable warheads, and still more in gross megatonnage. No doubt, British submariners would claim that their boats are more survivable and their missiles both more accurate and more certain to defeat the defences of 'Moscow' than the French. But the point at issue is which force the Soviet Union would regard as the more destructive, and they are likely to rely on a simple count. On this basis, the French win hands down.

As regards solidity of political backing. the French position has always seemed fireproof. As Jean Lipkowsky has written: 'France has never wavered in her resolve to build and maintain an independent nuclear deterrent ... our national commitment to a continuing nuclear policy is absolute and clear cut'. (23) Few would dissent from that judgment. The same could be claimed for Britain, but in fact, the issue has not always been so cut and dried. In the 1987 election for example, even though the Labour party was heavily defeated on a non-nuclear platform, Labour and the Liberal - Democratic Alliance between them polled close on 60% of the vote. Both were in favour of cancelling the Trident programme and allowing Polaris to waste out without replacement. Many within the Conservative Party and in the armed forces would have agreed with them. An intelligent observer in the Soviet Union might well conclude that the political backing for an independent *force de dissuasion* had, historically, been better founded in France than across the Channel in Britain.

Not to labour the point so far as a European independent centre of nuclear decision is concerned, France since the mid 1960's, has filled the bill at least as well as Britain, and arguably better. In logic, the British deterrent should have been defended as, at best, an 'equal second' centre of decision, at worst a 'third' centre. Of this, however, no whisper has been heard. The reason is clear, and it is not rational. If the role of a second centre of decision were being carried out quite adequately by the French, at their expense, and with every prospect that they would continue to do so for as long as such a requirement made sense, then the reasonable thing for the British to do would be to let the French get on with it and save their own money for more useful things. Yet even to hint at this would be political suicide. Why? Because to allow France alone to enjoy the supposedly prestigious status of sole European nuclear weapon state would be to relegate Britain to the third division, well behind Germany in economic weight, and far behind France in terms of 'throw-weight'. Britain's position as a permanent member of the Security Council would arguably be placed in jeopardy. And without the *gravitas* conferred by the possession of nuclear weapons, the British might be more chary of punching above their weight in contests with rogue states and unhinged dictators. It would be fruitless to argue that realistically, a non-nuclear posture might be more practical and cost-effective, allowing the British to concentrate on what they do best. They excel, for instance, at low intensity operations of which the need is virtually unlimited. Suffice it to reply that in a matter of great political clout, Britain would be surrendering high ground to, of all people, the French. End of argument. Such is the psychological reality of our relationship with our closest neighbour, that in this era, no such discussion is worth a millilitre of any one's breath.

Why cling to Nuclear Weapons ?

> We must consider the implications of the fact
> that those people who have achieved the most
> dominant positions in our society, and are
> likely to be in control of nuclear weapons pol-
> icy, have typically succeeded through acquir-
> ing aggressively competitive values and hos-
> tility to co-operation. Such people could not
> be expected to respond to opportunities to co-
> operate for mutual advantage, nor to be com-
> petent in managing the co-operative process.
> Moreover, by perceiving the world exclusively
> in terms of confrontation, such people are
> much more likely to make the decision to
> launch nuclear weapons. (24)

Perhaps one reason why political and military leaders
have needed to cling to the possession of nuclear
weapons is because they dare not let them go, and are in
a form of psychological denial. Having lived with the
nuclear threat for so long, they find it hard to divorce
themselves from it. Nuclear weapons have become a part
of the background to everyday life, and all of us are products of the society that colludes in their possession. Scilla
Elworthy, leader of the Oxford Research Group, has
interviewed a number of British nuclear weapons decision-makers, ranging from weapons designers to military,
Ministry of Defence and Foreign Office officials. Her aim
has been to elucidate what the threat is, or was, and why
we needed these weapons. She started this work before
the end of the Cold War, and after it had ended, she
enquired further to see whether views had changed. In
general, she found that views had not changed at all.
This led her to conclude that our need for nuclear
weapons, or the need on the part of those who make decisions in our name, exists whether there is a perceptible
enemy or not. In other words, nuclear weapons are a
'given' for these people. They then have to find a threat
to justify them, and that is of key importance. She con-
cludes: 'British decision-makers make decisions to keep
nuclear weapons because they been socialised by a cul-

ture that is riven by fear, and they are trying to make the best decisions that they can from this perspective.' (25)

A Rational Debate

> A genuine solution to the problem of security presupposes a certain mutual trust between the parties involved, a trust that cannot be replaced by any system of mechanised regulation. (26)

One of the most interesting psychological issues arises here. It is extremely difficult to have a rational debate about nuclear weapons. Many people have tried, including the scientists who helped to create nuclear weapons and some other of the most brilliant 20th century intellects, such as Bertrand Russell and Albert Einstein. Of the people who invented nuclear technology, almost all have in the end come out against nuclear weapons. As noted in chapter 5; they have moved from an understandable scientific fascination with nuclear physics to a wider moral, human condemnation of the results. This represents a mature judgment on the part of well-balanced people, but until now has had little effect. Perhaps fifty years later we are arriving at the point of change. 'Paradigm shifts' come about as one generation loses influence and a new generation emerges which is more radical in its thinking. There in no rational argument against the psychological condition of needing absolute protection from an absolute threat to psychic survival. It can only be dismantled piece by piece. Most people simply lack the ability to stand back, look at matters from a rational point of view, and then discard their fears.

From this psychological viewpoint, the slow building-down of nuclear weapons is understandable. We are working from the basis of a hugely defended state of mind, and this has to be done gradually. We take a few courses of brickwork off the wall, and find that evil hordes do not come pouring over it. In a few years, it will be time to take another few bricks off. This is a frustrating process, but probably could not take place in any other way. It is testimony to the huge psychological trauma that we have lived in collectively since the end of the Second World War. Old and young alike have inherited this state of mind, and are governed it. Little by little, there comes a noticeable difference. But it is slow on the level of psychological recuperation. There is a long way to go.

Verification of arms control agreements is an obvious necessity but this also is influenced by a psychological dimension. There is a fear of being found out, as though we were children and feel guilty or inadequate. Secrecy and spying are also influenced by this dynamic. Arguably, a change in thinking is a necessary pre-condition for any departure from the dangerous politics of confrontation. And this change must be radical, otherwise any weapons scrapped by treaty will simply be replaced by others. Mutual trust is not secondary, and will not come tumbling into our laps simply as the result of so-called Confidence Building Measures, whether in the political or armament sphere. Trust is the primary concern and we must strive to strengthen it.

One can take some heart from the 'New Labour' government. At the election in 1997, the Labour Party were bound to support Trident because all the historical evidence showed that, had they not done so, they would have been defeated again. Because they have not been in power for 18 years, as the Conservatives were under Thatcher and Major, they are not as psychologically conditioned into a state of fear and threat as their predecessors. They are able to contemplate doing more, and can start in small safe ways. Psychologists argue that if a person has been doing bad things and wants to atone for them, the way he will set about this is by doing small good things. Banning anti-personnel landmines is a good example. Doing without them does not materially affect Britain's security. If the results are not threatening, and people feel better about themselves, they will continue to do better things. But progress will be slow, an indication of the psychological trauma that has been suffered. The Strategic Defence Review has resulted in greater openness about the Trident system, a reduction of one third in the potential explosive power deployed on a submarine, and a lower state of readiness. These are small but useful steps. Arguably, if this process continues, and the Labour Party wins a second term of office, when Trident needs replacing, they may decide against it. They will try to do this in a low-key way. People will then discover that they are no longer living in fear, and will begin to believe that they can survive in a less defended state, as most of the rest of the developed world has long since realised.

Leaders and the People

> The media does and our leaders tend to pander to our fearfulness and not our possibilities for joy. They are caught up in this fear as well, and impart this to the people. So what is the way out? It is by liberating ourselves from fear, gradually and methodically. (27)

It is an enduring feature of the British that decisions of the political leadership on questions of defence policy tend to be accepted by the electorate at large with a degree of disinterest bordering on apathy. Wars are a different matter and the British press and public follow them, at least at their climactic stages, with the interest and enthusiastic support for their own side that normally attaches only to great sporting contests. But decisions on defence policy in time of peace attract only perfunctory interest. A partial exception arises when the disbandment or amalgamation of famous army regiments are on the cards. Where large civilian job losses are at stake, some local interest can be aroused. But the British press and media carry little of the searching and continual analysis of defence issues found in the US, Germany and France. As current examples, one might note that the battle for survival of the European fighter aircraft has been dealt with in Britain only limply, largely in terms of its commercial implications. There was far more press interest in the Royal Yacht *Britannia*, until her decommissioning in 1997, than in the future of aircraft carriers. The pros and cons of the expansion of NATO have been debated in only the most perfunctory way. The issues involved in bombing Baghdad were feebly argued in Britain compared with the United States. And so it goes. Since 1945, British governments of whichever political colour have been solidly in favour of creating and then retaining a substantial independent strategic nuclear capability, and by an overwhelming majority, the British public has concurred. With rare exceptions, notably the Defence White Papers in which Sir Michael Quinlan had a hand, there has been a minimum of explanation.

Nuclear weapons represent, we are told, the bedrock of our security - and that suffices. The question is almost never raised as to why, if that is true for the British, it is any less true for other countries who certainly have the ability to produce their own nuclear weapons and are obviously open to much more immediate threats. On what possible basis of logic can one regard Israel, India and Pakistan as *proliferators*, let alone North Korea or Iran, when all these countries are under what they regard as mortal and immediate threat and not without reason. How is it that Finland and Turkey, who both shared frontiers with the Soviet Union, could rest comfortably without nuclear arsenals of their own? No nation guards its independence more zealously than the Swiss, and they do well enough without. The argument that nuclear weapons are essential to the security of our own unthreatened islands, if taken seriously by other countries, would guarantee the spread of these weapons to half the countries on earth. How in conscience can they be denied? Yet it is a matter of high policy to prevent the spread of weapons of mass destruction and the missiles to deliver them. This contradiction is ventilated only by small groups who interest themselves in peace matters. Nor have the efforts of organisations such as CND to publicise the perils of nuclear conflict carried much weight. (See Chapter 5) One interesting effect that has been noted by psychologists is that of switching off or numbing people to nuclear weapons. The unspoken reality may be that living with the fear of nuclear weapons is unbearable, and the general population saves itself from mental illness by a process of denial. The leaders are trusted to do all that is necessary.

> Our greatest fear is not that we are inadequate, it is that we are powerful beyond measure. When we liberate ourselves from our own fear we liberate other people too. (28)

Recently a number of senior politicians and military men, who were content to carry out their duties while in post within a defence framework totally geared to a nuclear concept, have chosen, on leaving office, to speak out against it. Some members of the Canberra Commission fall into this category. This is not to say that they were right or wrong in either case, nor that there is anything inherently amiss with a change of heart. But it suggests that even the brightest and best are able to see things differently and countenance change only after they have left an institution and its all-pervading mind-set. While in office, they were to some extent blinkered, perhaps in some cases silenced, and in large measure unconsciously. That was not the time or the place to rock the boat, and it may be one of the reasons why change in these matters comes so slowly.

Conclusion

> No agreement on arms reduction will be of any use if it not accompanied by psychological disarmament. (29)

Nuclear weapons were born of the urgent fears which drove the Allies during the Second World War, and were built up to the grotesquely inflated numbers seen in the 1970s and 1980s as a direct effect of the deeply split and antagonistic political climate of the Cold War. Those days are behind us now, and priorities have changed. The building-down of nuclear arsenals, and the fight against proliferation are more firmly on the agenda. But old fears have not been altogether laid to rest. In a way, we still live in fear, but it is much more generalised. Ian Doucet argues that the general level of fear and anxiety has not gone away, but has found another plausibly real and substantial basis in the environmental threat. (30) It has been brought home to us that what has happened is not simply a rational response to matters outside our control. To the extent that there is wrong in the world, some of it is of our own making. We need to take back in some sense the evil we have projected upon others. This is an uncomfortable, even perhaps a chaotic psychological state in which to be. Fear is unfocussed, and unfocussed anxiety needs time to fade away. Until this has happened, nothing much can be achieved because we will remain frozen in fear.

References
(1) Bradley Morris, 'Conflict dynamics and conflict reso-

lution, in Lynn Barnett and Ian Lee (eds), *The Nuclear Mentality, A Psychosocial Analysis of the Arms Race*, Pluto Press, 1989, p.54.

(2) Norman F. Dixon, *Our Own Worst Enemy*, Cape, London, 1987.

(3) Interview with Scilla Elworthy 14 March 1997.

(4) Hans J. Morgenthau, *Scientific Man versus Power Politics*, University of Chicago Press, Chicago, 1946, p.192.

(5) D.S. Goldman and W.M. Greenberg, 'Preparing for Nuclear War. The psychological effects', *American Journal of Psychiatry*, Volume 52, No 4, pp.580-1.

(6) Excerpted from Lynn Barnett's Introduction to Barnett: *The Nuclear Mentality*. In other chapters of the same book, Professor Norman Dixon adds real-life examples of how leaders mislead, and Air Commodore Alistair Mackie suggests that military training and ethos can be based upon paranoid assumptions.

(7) Einstein quoted in Horst-Eberhard Richter, 'The Threat of Nuclear War and the Responsibility of the Doctor", Stephen Farrow and Alex Chow (eds) *The Human Cost of Nuclear War*, Medical Campaign Against Nuclear Weapons, Cardiff, March 1983.

(8) Interview with Ian Doucet 28 February 1998.

(9) 'There is no comprehensive account and no research work into this phenomenon, and any mention of this is anecdotal or in passing in dealing with other subjects'. Interview with Ian Doucet 28 February 1998.

(10) *The Psychosocial Dimension*, The Medical Educational Trust, London, May 1991, p. 5-4.

(11) The group consisted of The Medical Campaign against Nuclear Weapons and Psychoanalysts for the Prevention of Nuclear War. Many eminent contributors attended. The group presented a document to the government claiming that the rush to war was largely driven by irrational psychological processes that must be recognised and addressed if sanity is to prevail. The document referred to:

a. an intergroup process which involves each side exaggerating its own virtues and the other's capacity for evil.

b. the denial of reality when it is felt to be too painful to face, e.g. the threatened devastation of war.

c. government obsession with secrecy which reduces an

individual's capacity to take r e s p o n s i b i l i t y through lack of information. Thus leaders who mislead attract further dependence on rather than being confronted.

d. individual leaders' needs for personal power and success may interfere with meeting the needs of their people and make it difficult for them to change previous misjudgments.

e. aggressive impulses may only be seen in other individuals or groups, not in one's own self or group.

f. the search for an enemy when there are difficult domestic realities to deal with, e.g.at the end of a war (such as the Cold War or the Iran/Iraq War), or during an economic crisis;

g. a tendency to replace feelings of fear, persecution and depression with those of worth, success and triumph even if the latter were based on a delusion, such as the possibility of `winning' a war;

h. unrecognised emotional factors which tend to replace reason when decisions are taken under extreme stress;

i. the great difficulty of bearing uncertainty, particularly over time, which leads to pressure to act impulsively and precipitately.

Self-evidently these points apply far more appropriately to Saddam Hussein than to the Allies. But it would be unwise, on these grounds, to disregard them totally.

(12) Interview with Ian Doucet 28 February 1998.

(13) Anton Obholzer, in Barnett: *The Nuclear Mentality*, p.36.

(14) Interview with Scilla Elworthy 14 March 1997.

(15) Freud popularised the notion of collective guilt as one of our most marked attributes. Guilt is an important process by which we can distinguish good from evil, right from wrong and truth from error. Our conscience enables us to discern absolute values and tells us to honour them. At the point where the conscience bids us feel guilty, we acknowledge error and promise ourselves and society to do better in the future.

(16) Hamish McRae, *The World in 2020: Power, Culture and Prosperity, a Vision of the Future*, Harper Collins, London 1994, p.128.

(17) Hannah Segal in Barnett: *The Nuclear Mentality*, pp.44-5.

(18) Interview with Ian Doucet, 28 February 1998.

(19) I.F.Clarke, *Voices Prophesying War: 1763-1984* Oxford University Press, London 1966 pp. 22- 24, 113.

(20) *Defence Open Government Document 80/23* issued by the then Defence Minister Francis Pym in July 1980.

(21) Sir Michael Quinlan, Lecture at the Royal Institute of Defence Studies, London, 15 October 1997, (from a note taken at the time by the authors).

(22) Peter Malone, *The British Nuclear Deterrent,* Croom Helm, London, 1984, p.128 quotes a German official as saying (in relation to the greater likelihood of French nuclear weapons being used independently of the Americans in extremis) 'and the Soviets know that'.

(23) Jean de Lipkowsky *The Times* 27 September 1996.

(24) Bradley Morris, in Barnett: *The Nuclear Mentality,* p.54.

(25) Interview with Scilla Elworthy, 14 March 1997.

(26) Albert Einstein, quoted by Horst-Eberhard Richter, 'The Threat of Nuclear War and the Responsibility of the Doctor', in Farrow: *The Human Cost of Nuclear War,*

(27) Interview with Scilla Elworthy, 14 March 1997.

(28) Nelson Mandela. Inaugural address as President of South Africa, 1994.

(29) Alfred Kastler, (French Nobel Prize Winner) quoted by Horst-Eberhard Richter, 'The Threat of Nuclear War and the Responsibility of the Doctor', in Farrow: *The Human Cost of Nuclear War.*

(30) Interview with Ian Doucet 28 February 1998.

Other sources

Interview with Colin Fraser 15 May 1997

Ian Fenton (ed.) *The Psychology of Nuclear Conflict* Conveture Ltd, London 1986.

Erik Yesson, 'Strategic make believe and strategic reality, psychology and the implications of the nuclear revolution', *International Security,* Volume 14, Number 3, Winter 1989/1990.

James Thompson, *Psychological Aspects of Nuclear War,* The British Psychological Society, John Wiley and Sons Ltd, Chichester, 1985.

8. BRITAIN AND DISARMAMENT

> It is a great pity that a politician has not been brave enough to see the enormous possibilities there are at this moment for Britain in taking the lead towards a nuclear weapon-free world. It does not have to endanger our official policy of multilateral negotiations at all. Everything is there, there is a public which is ill-disposed to radioactivity and radioactive materials. There is a huge potential advantage in taking this wonderful opportunity, of leading the world into a non-nuclear future. (1)

It is clear that one of the major dangers facing the world today is posed by the large number of nuclear weapons that still exist: tens of thousands in the hands of the US and Russia; hundreds in the hands of Britain, France, China and (in all probability) Israel; small but unknown numbers in India and Pakistan, and some possibly in quite unknown and unauthorised hands. While most of these weapons are under strict control, they still present a hazard. So long as the nations possessing nuclear weapons remain as separate sovereign states, the possibility always exists of war between them which could lead to a nuclear exchange, whether by malice or miscalculation, most probably on a regional basis (the Middle East,

South Asia, Korea). There is the possibility of ill-judged confrontations of the kind that produced a situation of such peril at the time of the Cuban missile crisis in 1962. And quite apart from authorised use in war, there are the chances, however remote, of mechanical malfunction, possibly triggered by unintended launch of a missile or an accident to a warhead in transit. There is also the dire possibility that warheads in the hands of criminals or terrorists could be used to further their wholly irresponsible ends. Apart from these obvious dangers, nuclear weapons, by their very existence, create the risk of nuclear proliferation. They also present the problems of dismantling surplus warheads and the disposal of surplus material. These facts are unwelcome and tend to be swept under the carpet, but they have been obvious enough ever since nuclear weapons first existed. The issue of nuclear disarmament has been on the agenda since the earliest days of the nuclear era. The first resolution ever passed by the United Nations General Assembly, on 24 January 1946, recommended that atomic weapons and all other weapons adaptable to mass destruction be eliminated from national armaments.

Nuclear Disarmament

Nuclear weapons are a useless luxury. (2)

I believe history will show that the insistence on a UK nuclear capability was fundamentally misguided, a total waste of time of resources and a significant factor in our relative economic decline. (3)

Until very recently, the basic concept of nuclear deterrence has not been questioned by mainstream strategic thinkers, and nuclear disarmament has been seriously promoted only by protest groups (see Chapter 5). In Britain, these groups have never managed to capture the public imagination or persuade the general public of the dangers associated with nuclear weapons. One obvious reason is that the main prescription offered by these groups has been unilateral nuclear disarmament by Britain. Not surprisingly, this is unappealing to the vast majority of the British public. Bruce Kent has conceded:

'The greatest failure has been to convince the majority of the people in this country that British nuclear weapons are not independent, and they are not weapons; they are useless and they are very expensive. We have not managed to convince people. The newspapers tell us that nuclear weapons are necessary and add to our security. This is a perception that remains even in these post-Cold War days.' (4)

The commonly held belief in Britain up to now has been that nuclear weapons were a necessary evil to deter our enemies, and disarmament was an issue that could not realistically be entertained. While this opinion is still prevalent, a different view is now beginning to emerge. People from various points on the defence spectrum are beginning to think that the time may now be ripe for involving Britain in the process of nuclear disarmament. The role of British nuclear weapons is being questioned now that their Cold War rationale has disappeared. The idea of a nuclear weapons-free world, first mooted by Mikhail Gorbachev in 1986, is taking root. But as David Fischer has said: 'If Britain is to reduce or eliminate its nuclear arsenal, it will do so because of compelling political factors which have made it conclude that nuclear disarmament serves the national interest. These would include the end of the Cold War, the end of *apartheid* and political isolation in South Africa the advent of civilian democratic governments in Argentina and Brazil and the end of rivalry between military juntas. While there is still immense uncertainty as to the future, the prospects for stopping proliferation and eliminating nuclear arsenals seem better in 1997 than at any time since the first atomic weapons were dropped on Hiroshima and Nagasaki in 1945'. (5)

At present, the British government does not wish to grapple head-on with this issue. Trident, we are told, 'still has an important contribution to make in insuring against the re-emergence of major strategic threats, in preventing nuclear coercion and in preserving peace and stability in Europe'. (6) But the ranks of the nuclear dissenters are widening, and the arguments which British governments have deployed in the past against non-nuclear strategies are beginning to lose their political weight. Members of the Labour government and progressive thinkers within the Ministry of Defence are well aware of this trend. In the near future, the government will have to face difficult choices about what is to happen to British nuclear weapons. If some form of reduction is decided upon what choices are open? Will Britain go it alone or will she disarm in conjunction with other nations?

Unilateral disarmament revisited

> These things are now more realistic possibilities than they were a few years ago. They can be discussed sensibly now...I can see no reason why the British public should not be persuaded of the merits of disarmament, cuts, reductions, and the removal of nuclear weapons entirely.... In the future, if the plans for a nuclear weapons-free world take off, and politicians can sell the ideas at the right time, it could result in international agreements and discussion. (7)

There are still advocates of unilateral British nuclear disarmament. A Pugwash Study Group has argued that such a policy would have several advantages. Obviously it would reduce the numbers of nations physically capable of using nuclear weapons and thus starting a nuclear war. It would signal the determination of Britain to maintain peace by non-nuclear means, and it would be a step towards demilitarisation of international relations. They argue that if Britain were to disarm independently, this would be a move of great significance, because this country has been involved with nuclear weapons from the very beginning. (8) No country with the standing of an official Nuclear Weapons State within the NPT has ever renounced this status and become a Non-Nuclear Weapons State. The study group says: 'Given that the possession of nuclear weapons will not bring any benefit to Britain for the foreseeable future, and since the costs of possession are substantial, then it is an obvious conclusion that, regardless of what other nations may do, Britain should dispense with its nuclear arsenal. This would be a simple (although not easy) decision to take. To provide for continuity in Britain's collective security independent disarmament should consist of a sequence of steps spread over a number of years, each step being useful on its own.' (9)

The biggest problem with the notion of unilateral disarmament is that the general public does not want it. The majority of the British public, when questioned, does not support unilateral nuclear disarmament and, as has been noted earlier, it was this policy (amongst others) which barred the Labour Party from power for many years. Opinion polls show that the majority of the British public believe in *multilateral* disarmament. A prime concern of the government is not to forfeit public esteem, particularly by reneging on matters clearly set out in its election manifesto. It is therefore highly unlikely to revert to its earlier vote-losing policy. A second problem is that unilateral disarmament could not be a truly independent action, because an essential first step would be to secure the agreement of NATO. Collective security could be much impaired if independent action by Britain on a matter if such importance upset the Alliance, alienated the US or even led Germany to revoke its non-nuclear weapons status. (10) A third point is that a programme of disarmament undertaken unilaterally would in any case be much less satisfactory than an action taken in co-operation with others and subject to a strict verification regime.

Partial disarmament

The Labour government has promised more openness in the Ministry of Defence, and has undertaken to look at some controversial defence issues from a more liberal standpoint. (11) In recent statements, the government has expressed its support for the ultimate goal of eliminating nuclear weapons. It will work for progress in multi-lateral disarmament negotiations and will bring British weapons into this process when reductions on the part of other nuclear weapons states make this appropriate. Britain's arsenal will meanwhile be kept at a minimal effective level. (12) The need for cuts in the defence budget may focus minds upon the fact that nuclear weapons are costly, and are arguably detracting from Britain's overall war fighting capability. But the total decommissioning of Trident on grounds of economy seems extremely unlikely from a political point of view within the foreseeable future.

Successive governments have been at pains to argue

that the Trident force as at present planned is as small as it could be. In support of this. it is argued - purely for purposes of sizing the force - that Russia must remain the notional target to serve as a benchmark. It is only realistic for purposes of nuclear deterrence, where supreme national interests are assumed to be at stake, that Britain, in the last resort, must be prepared to act alone. Moreover, now that air-delivered nuclear weapons have been removed, the Trident system has to cover the whole operational spectrum. These were the arguments supporting the thesis that Trident, as planned by the previous, Conservative, government represented an irreducible minimal deterrent.

Four Trident submarines are being built but it is generally acknowledged that only enough operational strategic warheads need be provided to equip three boats at one time, thus allowing for one boat in long refit. (13) It is known that each submarine will be fitted to take 16 missiles and that each missile *can* be equipped with six warheads which can be independently targeted. These figures would imply a maximum of 96 operational warheads for each boat. In 1993, the Conservative government confirmed that the boats would carry no more than this, and might indeed carry fewer.

Since well before the 1997 election, it had been the stated policy of the Labour Party that Trident would carry no more warheads than *Polaris*, (14) but it was unclear what this meant. The original *Polaris A3* missile deployed in the late 1960s carried three warheads. This was replaced in the period 1982-96 with the *A3TK Chevaline*, which carried two warheads only, leaving more room for decoys. Thus, the number of warheads carried by each boat was originally 48, but after the introduction of *Chevaline* the number became 32. It has now been announced, following the Strategic Defence Review, that the number of warheads carried by each Trident submarine will be 48, the same as *Polaris* when first introduced. It is pointed out that these 48 warheads will cover both strategic and sub-strategic needs and will have an explosive power one third less than the 32 *Chevaline* warheads. Allowing for spares to cater for refurbishment, and some flexibility, the number of operationally available warheads to be provided will be 'fewer than 200 a reduction of one third from the previous government's plans'. (15) The question is whether a minimum effective level could be set at any lower figure.

In practical terms reduction would clearly present no difficulty. For example, the number of missiles on each boat could be reduced to 12 and the redundant tubes made inoperable or removed. Half the remaining missiles could be fitted with three warheads each, the remainder with single warheads. On this notional basis, the number of warheads in each boat could be reduced to 24, with an overall total of perhaps no more than 100. For purposes of bargaining in an arms control context, this could be represented as a reduction of 50% on previously announced totals. It is pointless to pursue the numbers game exercise any further, since its basis is speculative, but the underlying possibilities are quite clear. In terms of deterrent capability the ability of a single submarine to deliver 24 warheads, each of 100 kilotons, on separate targets, with high accuracy, would be enough to knock the heart out of any developed country. And if this were in doubt (say China was the notional adversary) a second boat, once mobilised, could deliver an utterly convincing *coup-de-grace*.

This suggestion raises a number of interesting issues. The first is a fundamental one. It could be argued that if Britain were intending to inflict unacceptable damage upon a country the size of Russia, and had only two dozen nuclear warheads immediately available for this purpose, it would have to direct them upon targets of high value where their political impact would be greatest. This, almost by definition, implies city-busting, and thus the deliberate attack upon large populations. But this is morally abhorrent. Ethical considerations clearly require that only targets of high military importance be selected and that collateral damage to the innocent be kept to a minimum. This is only possible, it is argued, if the number of warheads is substantial, because military targets are widely dispersed and individually not of great significance. This reasoning has great force where operational planning is concerned. But as an argument in favour of retaining larger numbers of warheads, it has a flavour of perversity about it - as though inflicting more pain could in fact cause less damage. A serious question mark must also be raised over the assumption that Britain must be ready to act alone in circumstances where the US was positively not prepared to do so. If this is true for Britain, and France, why should it not apply to every other NATO member, not least Germany?

A second issue concerns the possibility that a putative target state might in future equip itself with an effective anti-strategic missile defence of its territory, thus rendering attacks by small numbers of missiles ineffective. Under the terms of the Anti-Ballistic Missile (ABM) Treaty, the US and Russia have categorically undertaken to do no such thing. There have been lengthy discussions between these two countries concerning the permissible limits of testing anti-ballistic missiles for tactical or theatre use, and agreement appears to have been reached on a framework that does not prejudice the ABM Treaty. But there is an enduring lobby in America determined to resurrect the plans for a strategic missile defence of the whole US proposed by the Reagan administration in its Strategic Defence Initiative (the Star Wars programme). The mandate presently given to the US Ballistic Missile Defence Organisation includes the development of nation-wide protection against limited or rogue missile attacks, capable of evolving to counter future threats. (16) This has to be very carefully watched. If any plan for the general defence of the US went ahead, it would risk blowing apart not only the ABM Treaty, but the entire process of strategic arms reduction presently under way between the US and Russia. Politically, this seems all but inconceivable at present. At worst, if the US were to break out from the ABM Treaty and Russia, however reluctantly, tried to follow suit, this might force Britain to reverse any curtailments of the Trident system. Trident was in the first instance sized to cope with the predicted Soviet ABM defences that might have been deployed early in the 21st century. Over a period of years, if the US was willing, the Trident force could presumably be rebuilt to the size originally planned. For purposes of present policy, this is no more than a remote theoretical consideration.

A third issue concerns the stage at which any British reductions in the strategic missile force might be brought into play. START II was signed by the US and Russia in January 1993. When this treaty is fully implemented the US will be allowed some 3,500 deployed warheads and Russia about 3000. The US ratified START II in 1996 but the Russian Duma has yet to do so. At Helsinki on 20-21

March 1997, Presidents Yeltsin and Clinton agreed the outline terms for START III under which both countries would reduce their warheads to 2,500 and to 2,000 by 2007. The US is not prepared to begin negotiating on this basis until the Russian Duma has ratified START II. However there are solid budgetary reasons why the Duma should do so, and it is possible that negotiations for START III might begin in 1999.

When President Yeltsin signed the START II Treaty, he called upon Britain, France and China to promise cuts or limits on their nuclear weapons programmes, and he has often repeated this. Officials in these three countries have indicated that the appropriate stage for their countries to join the START process would be when the U.S. and Russia have reduced to a level of about 1000 deployed warheads. (17) Since this level would be a logical goal for a START IV Treaty, it would follow that only in START V would Britain begin to play. British officials no doubt hope that this stage lies at least a decade ahead. Douglas Hurd, then Foreign Secretary, said at the Non-proliferation Treaty Extension Conference in April 1995 that the UK would join the reduction process only when the Russian and American stockpiles were in the hundreds. This point must lie still further in the future. The Strategic Defence Review adds further confusion on this point. It says, in paragraph 61, that 'Britain's deterrence requirement 'does not depend on the size of other nations' arsenals'. But in paragraph 70, it reverts to the familiar theme that 'considerable further reductions' in the arsenals of the major nuclear powers would be necessary before more British reductions could become feasible. (18)

Another question concerns what the UK might hope to gain by taking part in the reduction process. Britain has little leverage *vis-à-vis* the other acknowledged Nuclear Weapons States. She is unlikely to accelerate the START process by taking part in it, although by refusing to do so at some future stage, she might impede it. But once negotiations become multi-lateral, they may well slow down in any case. China, for example, is likely to insist both on comparability between all five NWS and on assurances about observance of the ABM Treaty. She might well add political conditions such as insisting on the other NWS joining in the Chinese no-first-use commitment, and perhaps seeking new undertakings over Taiwan. Nor is a commitment to reduce the British strategic capability likely to influence India, Pakistan or Israel in any positive way, let alone other would-be nuclear powers. So long as Britain keeps any strategic nuclear capability of her own, she will no doubt continue to insist that this remains a crucial guarantee of her own security. Every other state on Earth can then claim as much. So any British initiative other than abolition is likely to have little exemplary force. This means that the British government is unlikely to obtain a quid pro quo for reducing its nuclear inventory in the shape of concessions by any other country. The notion of occupying moral high ground might have some appeal to a Labour Government, but the most solid motive would be to save money.

One way of doing this would be to reduce the Trident fleet to a force of three boats. (19) With a force of that size, it would normally be possible to keep one boat on patrol at all times. If, however, when one of them was on extended refit, an accident happened to another, continuous patrolling would no longer be possible. In the new context, this might be an acceptable risk if the cash saving were substantial. Though the fourth boat will not come into service until early in the 21st century, very little of its acquisition cost remains uncommitted and the only financial saving from a three-boat fleet would be on maintenance costs, together with some further reduction in numbers of missile bodies and warheads. The cash involved in such reductions could only be modest in the context of an annual defence programme well above £20 billion but might not be negligible as the purse strings are drawn ever tighter.

Multilateral disarmament
Britain is party to a number of arms control treaties relating to nuclear weapons, of which the most important is the Nuclear Non-Proliferation Treaty (NPT) of 1968. Under this treaty, all parties except the existing five declared Nuclear Weapons States - US, Russia, China, Britain and France - have permanently renounced possession of nuclear weapons. Britain was a foundation member of this treaty. Almost all the countries in the world are now parties but not, unfortunately, India, Pakistan and Israel. At a Review and Extension Confere-

nce in May 1995, it was agreed to extend that Treaty indefinitely. A condition for this agreement was the adoption of a document dealing with Principles and Objectives for Nuclear Non-Proliferation and Disarmament. Specific objectives included a Comprehensive Test Ban Treaty (CTBT), to be concluded no later than 1996 and early conclusion of a ban on the production of fissile materials for nuclear weapons purposes. Most relevantly, the document mandated 'the determined pursuit by the Nuclear Weapons States of systematic and progressive efforts to reduce nuclear weapons globally, with the ultimate goal of eliminating those weapons and by all states of general and complete disarmament under strict and effective international control'.

The CTBT was duly adopted by the General Assembly of the United Nations and opened for signature in September 1996. This was a great achievement so far as it went, and more than 130 countries have now signed up. But a question mark still hangs over the issue of how and when the Treaty will come into force. This was fully discussed in Chapter 3. Some concern also remains about possible ways in which the aims of the treaty might be effectively subverted by one or more of the nuclear powers. In May 1997, the US, for example, launched a very expensive ($4bn. a year) programme of nuclear weapons systems sustainment. (20) In respect of the nuclear warheads for submarine-launched strategic missiles, the Department of Energy and the US Navy are instructed to maintain the capability to develop replacement warheads, should new warheads be needed in the future. It is explained that this programme is driven not by any new weapons requirement, but by the need to improve sensitivity to aging, better design margins and ability for surveillance by above-ground testing. These aims are benign enough, and it is also made clear that any resulting designs will have to be certified without any underground nuclear testing. A very extensive range of test facilities, simulators and so forth is being provided for this purpose. The British government has similarly instructed the Atomic Warfare Establishment to provide the same level of assurance of the safety and reliability of British nuclear warheads as hitherto, and to retain the capability to develop new warheads. (21) In both cases, the term 'new warheads' is used with the clear implication that 'new physics packages' could be involved. The danger is that such developments might be viewed by other parties as breaching the intention of the CTBT thus making the problems of entry into force still more intractable.

So far as fissile material is concerned, the US and Russia have such excessive stocks of weapons grade uranium and plutonium that they do not know what to do with them. In March 1995, the Conference on Disarmament (CD) agreed on a negotiating mandate for a convention banning all such production in future. (22) As we explained in Chapter 3, the way now seems open for further progress. This brings us to the third item in the programme of 'Principles and Objectives', namely systematic and progressive efforts to reduce nuclear weapons globally, with the ultimate goal of eliminating these weapons. It seems that the Weapons States, possibly excluding China, take the position that this cannot be negotiated multilaterally, in the CD or anywhere else, only among the nuclear powers themselves. But no negotiation among the five is being contemplated at present. Indeed, it seems that for the immediate future, the negotiation of any multilateral global agreement or treaty leading to actual nuclear disarmament is not on the cards. While this deadlock persists, the nuclear weapon states remain in breach of their obligations, not only to undertake systematic and progressive reductions, but even to negotiate in good faith to that end, as the original NPT (in Article VI) clearly requires. The British Ministry of Defence may, however, be content with this situation. Not only is it keen to preserve its own freedom of action over warhead numbers but is no doubt concerned about other implications of a Nuclear Weapons Convention. These would include not only declaration of existing stocks of fissile materials, but also strict verification measures, intrusive surveillance of all nuclear installations and control of the dissemination of any form of technology related to nuclear weapons. It would involve giving authority to an international body and maintaining an enforcement agency with powers to expose cheating that are stronger than those of the existing International Atomic Energy Authority. The British government deserves some credit for progress in this area. In the Strategic Defence Review, it has gone further than other governments in announcing its total stocks of fissile material, and in placing some of them under safeguards. But the disclosure is incomplete, and defence nuclear facilities will remain outside international supervision. Britain is plainly not ready as yet for the 'full Monty'. (23)

A change in nuclear doctrine

Since nuclear disarmament, other than in the context of the START process between the US and Russia, is not a promising avenue at present, there is need to examine other ways of reducing the part played by nuclear weapons in the dealings between nations. One area well worth re-visiting is the question of 'first use 'of nuclear weapons. For the past 20 years or so, it has been the common position of the Nuclear Weapons Powers that they would not use or threaten to use nuclear weapons against any state which had forsworn nuclear weapons under the NPT. This so-called 'negative security assurance' was given by way of declaration, and lacks the force of treaty obligation. It now applies to virtually all countries of the world except the five official Nuclear Powers and India, Pakistan and Israel. But there is an important exception. The negative assurance does not apply to any country that carries out an attack (e.g. on the UK or its allies) *in association with* a Nuclear Weapons State. This has allowed NATO to maintain its declared policy of using nuclear weapons in response to any large-scale conventional attack in Europe by a Nuclear Weapons State or its allies, if there were no other way of defeating it. That policy was devised early in the history of the Alliance as a means of providing a defence in the face of what was then regarded as the overwhelming conventional superiority of the Warsaw Pact forces. In 1982, the Soviet Union, no doubt partly for propaganda purposes, declared that it would never be the first to use nuclear weapons, a position which had been held by China for some time. Since the demise of both the Warsaw Pact and the Soviet Union, the correlation of conventional forces in Europe has been reversed, with the West now enjoying a large numerical superiority over Russia. It is therefore not surprising that in the early 1990s, the US was seriously considering a 'no-first-use' (NFU) declaration. But in October 1993, Russia withdrew its declaration, and the idea was dropped. It would be well worth picking it up again.

The core concept of nuclear deterrence is to deter any use of nuclear weapons by threatening the destruction of the would-be user through an assured retaliatory 'second strike' carried out by the power under threat. Adoption of a policy of NFU would in no way contravene that concept; rather, by making it the only nuclear policy, it would clarify and strengthen it. This could be given effect in the first instance by a NFU pledge given severally by the nuclear powers, but would be greatly strengthened if this were coupled with an undertaking to negotiate a treaty or other legally binding instrument for that purpose. The theoretical benefit of NFU is self-evident. If it were adhered to, then logically, no nuclear war could ever break out. In practice, there will always be the possibility that when supreme national interests were threatened, a nation would fail to honour its NFU undertaking, even if this had the force of law behind it. But this objection loses much of its force when balanced against the many practical benefits of a NFU policy. We examine these under the headings of NATO doctrine and force posture, implications for the future of Europe and Russia and the future of arms control, and finally, the prospects for global non-proliferation.

So far as NATO is concerned it seems clear that the balance of conventional forces as between the Allies and any future hostile coalition, even if led by a recidivist Russia, would be weighted heavily in favour of the West. NATO officials, led by the US, continue to argue that sustaining doubts in the mind of any adversary about NATO's willingness to escalate to the nuclear level is an important psychological tool; the more so that Russia still keeps tens of thousands of nuclear weapons on alert status. But there is little logic in this. The new German government of Gerhard Schröder is strongly committed to a NFU policy, as is Canada. It is difficult to conceive of any attack upon one or more of the member states of NATO in Europe or North America, (the triggering event under Article V of the North Atlantic Treaty), which the Alliance could not cope with acting in concert (the response mandated by that article) *without* the need to use nuclear weapons. The only arguable instance to the contrary is the need to deter use of Chemical and Biological Weapons (CBW) by an adversary who might not find the threat of conventional retaliation either plausible or persuasive.

During the Kuwait crisis of 1990-91, when there was great anxiety that Iraq might use its ample stocks of CBW against the Allies, US Secretary of State James Addison Baker III warned his Iraqi counterpart, Tariq Aziz, that any such use would be met by retaliation that would be overwhelming and devastating. Tariq Aziz is reported as having said subsequently that he understood Baker to be threatening a nuclear strike, and that this threat had been believed. It was for this reason, he said, that Iraq did not make use of the chemical shells and bombs that were being held well forward for that purpose. (24) The truth of this will probably never be known. It is not difficult to think of other reasons why the Iraqi CBW arsenal was not used - fear that the Allies would follow through to Baghdad, for example. And the official American line continues to emphasise that the negative security assurances given in connection with the indefinite extension of the NPT Treaty remain watertight.

The strongest argument against harnessing nuclear deterrence to the task of keeping 'rogue states' in order is that the rulers of nations it is intended to deter may not act in ways consistent with the pattern of US-Soviet deterrence during the Cold War. The stakes of the aggressor and defender may be quite different - survival in the one instance and more limited concerns in the other - and the former may be willing to hazard much more than the latter to secure his interests. For want of strategic understanding, the state against which deterrence is being exercised may fail to comprehend the linkages implicit in a deterrent threat or may not operate on the same basis of rationality as has been assumed. Being subjected to overwhelming and devastating retaliation may be a quicker way to Heaven, and therefore a fate to be courted rather than feared. These arguments undermine the concept of nuclear deterrence as normally understood. It is widely argued, not least in the US, that given adequate conventional forces and the highly discriminate firepower they now command, the option of nuclear first use can be surrendered. To do so need not affect the likelihood of major war, or the ability to cope with regional conflicts where vital interests are at stake. And it is important to recognise that the negative security assurances already described allow for no exceptions in respect of CBW. In international law, there is admittedly a doctrine of belligerent reprisal to justify a military response that violates a treaty if the enemy has already broken another treaty, e.g. the Geneva Convention banning first use of CW. But it is hard for the US, for example, to argue that it needs recourse to nuclear reprisal against being gassed whereas other likely target countries, like Iran, are allowed no such capability. Nor is it clear that a nuclear response to a chemical attack could be conducted in a proportionate manner. It would be more logical, and in many ways safer, to restrict the threat of nuclear reprisal to its core function of deterring a nuclear attack.

During the Cold War, it was an integral feature of NATO's force posture that there were many thousands of tactical or battlefield nuclear weapons, those with a range under 500 km., stockpiled on mainland Europe or on ships at sea. Of these, the vast majority were American, although a considerable proportion were to be delivered by European guns, rockets and aircraft subject to dual-key release procedures. NATO no longer possesses nuclear artillery, surface-to-surface or surface-to-air missiles, and since 1991, all such weapons have been withdrawn from ships at sea. It is, however, a little known but well-attested fact that the US still maintains a small stockpile of nuclear bombs, perhaps fewer than 100 all told, for use by Allied strike aircraft deployed in a number of European countries including Britain. (25) Their purpose is supposed to be political rather than military. Up to now, the host nations in Europe have resisted any suggestion of withdrawing these weapons, apparently valuing the linkage with American strategic nuclear capability that they supposedly represent. The Turks in particular seem wedded to this view. But in fact these weapons serve no useful purpose. The adoption of an NFU strategy would allow, indeed effectively require, their removal back to the US. The situation would then be that no possessor of nuclear weapons was stationing them on foreign territory, and this could rapidly be made a matter of international agreement.

An immediate corollary could be the negotiation of a nuclear weapons-free zone (NWFW) for the whole of the European mainland, including Turkey but of course excluding Russia and France, similar in intention to the four formally constituted Nuclear Weapon Free Zones in other parts of the world. One obvious purpose would be to reassure the Russians. They have a sense, however unjustified, that there has been some reneging on the tacit understandings made at the time of the unification of Germany in 1990, principally by the enlargement of NATO. In December 1996, the North Atlantic Council declared that NATO nations had no intention, no plan and no reason for stationing nuclear weapons forward in central Europe when NATO was enlarged, but they have so far declined to rule out doing so a priori. This is a serious misjudgment. The Russian Duma has now voted to ratify the Chemical Weapons Convention. The next step is to seek their approval of START II. This is proving a slow and politically difficult process. Permanent removal of American nuclear weapons from European territory would remove any sense of a double-cross on this issue, would make the enlargement of NATO easier to stomach, and would thus ease the path of ratification for START II. It would also cast a helpful light over the negotiation of revised force levels under the Conventional Forces in Europe (CFE) Treaty now in progress.

A final advantage of this package would arise in the multilateral context. For a long time, it has been a grievance of the Non-Nuclear Weapons States (NNWS) that their adherence to the NPT has never been rewarded by unconditional negative security guarantees. An NFU Treaty, formally adopted by the five nuclear powers, would provide exactly the result that the NNWS desire. It would leave India, Pakistan and Israel exposed as the only hold-outs, and would put the nuclear powers in a stronger position *vis-à-vis* future NPT review conferences. This might in turn help to unlock the whole nuclear logjam discussed earlier in this chapter. There is, of course, no reason why repatriation of the American nuclear bombs need await the adoption of an NFU strategy. Indeed that act alone might induce a virtuous spiral, making Russian acceptance of NFU more palatable. It is a simple measure, but high stakes are riding on it.

Nor would it be difficult to devise a sequential programme embracing all these ideas. The first step would be the formal, albeit low-key, abandonment by NATO of its existing flexible response strategy accompanied by the final removal of all American nuclear warheads back to the US. This could be followed by the adoption of a policy in NATO whereby the use of nuclear weapons would be confined to retaliation in response to use of nuclear weapons against any member of the alliance. Russia could then be invited to revert to its own previous NFU strategy. Since this is already the declared position of China, the way would be open for a mutual pledge of NFU among the five nuclear powers, together with an undertaking to follow this up with a legally binding treaty. The next step would be a move towards negotiating a NWFZ for Europe, perhaps in the setting of the NPT review machinery or under the aegis of the OSCE or the UN. The point to emphasise is that this would in no way prejudice the security of any NATO member, nor compromise the core concept of deterrence for the nuclear powers. The resulting improved atmosphere *vis-à-vis* the Russians could pay dividends not only in the arms control arena (START II, CFE), but also in making the expansion of NATO more palpably innocuous, giving more substance to the 'Partnership for Peace' and the 'Founding Act' between Russia and NATO. This would be good for the future stability of Europe. And progress along these lines would play well in such arenas as the NPT review process, perhaps making progress possible towards a fissile material cut-off, ratification by India and Pakistan of the CTBT and the beginning of moves towards five-power *ad hoc* negotiations for multilateral nuclear disarmament. There is no reason whatever why Britain should not give the lead. (26)

De-alerting, De-targeting and De-mounting

Deterrence is obviously unstable in a situation where either side can hope to knock out most or all of the enemy's retaliatory force in a surprise attack. Such a posture invites pre-emption. During the Cold War, both sides accordingly strove to acquire an invulnerable second-strike capability, meaning that enough of their weapons would remain effective even if the other side struck first. The best method was to place them on submarines whose construction and operating patterns ensured that their position was never discoverable by the other side. Fixed land-based systems were hardened to the extent possible, by placing them in underground silos, but remained vulnerable to a direct hit. To avoid being disabled by a surprise attack, the concept was developed of launch-on-warning. This was full of perils. On 25 January 1995, President Yeltsin's nuclear suitcase sounded an alert in response to a meteorological rocket fired from Norway. He had four minutes to decide if it was an American attempt to disable Russia's defences. Many people have concluded that in the immediate future it is less important to reduce the size of forces than to lessen the risk of their being launched by accident or miscalculation. This can be done in various ways. De-alerting means increasing the response time of nuclear weapons by taking them off 'hair-trigger' alert. It applies primarily, but not exclusively, to systems liable to destruction in a disabling first strike, such as land-based fixed missile systems. De-targeting of strategic missiles means increasing their reaction times by re-directing them towards neutral points in the ocean. This is largely a cosmetic gesture, since most missile systems have a default targeting capability that permits reversion to pre-stored targets in a matter of minutes. De-mounting refers to the physical removal of nuclear warheads from their delivery systems. Physical separation will obviously reduce reaction times and induce confidence that nuclear arsenals are not on hair-trigger alert.

Proposals along these lines are now gaining international support. In December 1996, the then US Secretary of State Warren Christopher said that no NATO nuclear weapons were presently on alert. (27) The Americans, Russians and British say that they have now de-targeted their strategic nuclear forces. (28) The question of de-mounting is more problematic. In the case of land-based missiles, there is no difficulty in principle over removing warheads and placing them in separated storage. Admiral Stansfield Turner, one-time Commander in Chief of NATO's Southern Command, and later Director of the Central Intelligence Agency in the US, has proposed the notion of 'strategic escrow'. (29) As an example, some 1000 American strategic warheads could be detached from their missiles and placed in secure storage some distance away under observation by Russian monitors, and vice versa. The numbers of warheads in escrow could then, by mutual agreement, be gradually increased. The storage sites need not even be in the warhead owner's home territory. Admiral Turner speculates on the use of Scandinavia, Greenland, a south Pacific atoll or ships anchored in remote sea areas. But it is less clear how these ideas might apply to Britain. British submarine-launched ballistic missiles are not in any case on a hair trigger alert. (30) It is obviously difficult, if not impossible, to de-mount or remount their warheads when at sea. One suggestion is that the guidance systems could be held separately but this would presumably result in only a relatively short delay.

Once again the British Government has taken on board some of these ideas. In the Strategic Defence Review, it is explained that a while a deterrent submarine patrol will still be maintained at all times, this is to consist of only one submarine and at a reduced readiness. In particular this means that the 'notice to fire' will be measured in days rather than the few minutes' notice which applied during the Cold War. Submarines on patrol will be available for secondary tasks such as exercises with other vessels, equipment trials and hydrographic data collection, without compromise to their security. The double crews provided for each submarine will be reduced over time to single crews, reflecting reduced operational tempo.

Other possible steps like taking submarines off deterrent patrol altogether, or storing their missiles ashore were rejected as potentially destabilising. (31) Sailing a submarine in a time of rising tension could in itself exacerbate a crisis. Either measure could force a government into earlier and hastier decision-taking and undermine the stabilising role that British nuclear forces would otherwise play in a crisis. (32) These arguments have some force. If a submarine-based deterrent force is to be retained at all, it would be paradoxical to forgo its most basic advantages - being both available and invulnerable at all times.

Transparency

There remain a number of measures under the general rubric of transparency which could have a useful effect. (33) For example, the reductions in warheads already carried out unilaterally by Britain and France could be internationally entrenched, the remaining inventories declared in detail and made subject to the same sorts of verification as Russia and America are prepared to apply mutually under the START Treaties. At a later stage, Chinese holdings could also be brought into account.

Information and best practice could be exchanged much more freely on such matters as safety of storage, handling, management and possibly even design of nuclear warheads. And there would be merit in adopting more widely the various techniques for verifying and implementing existing arms control arrangements which have been pioneered by the UN Inspectorate in Iraq following the Gulf War. These would cover such matters as information gathering, collation and analysis, the handling of materiel and disposal or destruction of unwanted systems. Once again, Britain could take the lead. A final suggestion is that Britain could work still more closely with France. There is scope for a degree of co-operation in integrated patrolling schedules and refit schedules. These were examined by the Defence Select Committee in 1997, and it seems that they might save the country a substantial amount of money. (See Chapter 4)

References
(1) Interview with Dr Scilla Elworthy 14 March 1997.
(2) Interview with Professor Robert O'Neill 17 March 1997.
(3) Sir Michael Atiyah, 'Royal Society Anniversary Address', 30 November 1995.
(4) Interview with Bruce Kent 8 February 1997.
(5) Correspondence with David Fischer, International Atomic Energy Agency April 1997.
(6) *The Strategic Defence Review*, Cm. 3999, The Stationery Office, July 1998, p. 5-1.
(7) Interview with Professor John Simpson, 21 February 1997.
(8) Christopher R. Hill, R. Sebastian Pease, Rudolph E. Peierls, Joseph Rotblat, *Does Britain Need Nuclear Weapons*, A Report from the British Pugwash Group, 1995, p.55.
(9) Hill: *Does Britain need Nuclear Weapons?* p.54.
(10) Hill: *Does Britain need Nuclear Weapons?* p.56.
(11) The government is examining the defence diversification issue: the role of women in the armed forces; homosexuals in the armed forces; the issue of export licensing for military equipment and, in certain circumstances, are looking favourably at the issue of market testing .

(12) George Robertson, Lecture at the RUSI on 18 September 1997, *RUSI Journal*, October 1997,p.4.

(13) Malcolm Chalmers. Nuclear Weapons Policy and the New British Government *International Security Information Service* May 1997.

(14) *A Fresh Start for Britain: Labour's Strategy for Britain in the Modern World*, Labour Party 1995.

(15) *The Strategic Defence Review*, Cm. 3999, The Stationery Office, July 1988, Supporting Essay Number Five, p. 5-2.

(16) Dr. J. David Martin,' The Current Situation in Ballistic Missile Defence: The View from Washington' *RUSI Journal* October 1997 p.64.

(17) The Atlantic Council, Nuclear Weapons and European Security, *Bulletin*, Vol. VI, No 13, 31 October 1995.

(18) Strategic Defence Review, Cm. 3999, The Stationery Office, July 1998, pp. 17, 19.

(19) Chalmers: 'Nuclear weapons policy'.

(20) *Nuclear Weapons Systems Sustainment Programs*, Office of the Secretary of Defense, May 1997.

(21) Hill: *Does Britain need nuclear weapons?* p.26

(22) William Epstein, 'Preparations for the next NPT Review Conference. Nuclear Weapons: Immediate Steps'. Paper prepared for the Pugwash Conference, Lillehammer, 1-7 August 1997.

(23) 'The full Monty' is 'everything that is necessary or appropriate'. (Oxford Dictionary of New Words, 1997). Britain has declared some 15,000 tonnes of uranium, of which 7.6 tonnes is highly enriched, and 7.6 tonnes of plutonium, but has not said how much of the latter is weapons-grade. Over half of the plutonium and non-highly enriched uranium is being placed under international supervision, but only 0.3 tonnes of weapons-grade plutonium and none of the HEU. All future reprocessing and enrichment in Britain will take place under international safeguards, but with a let-out until a Fissile Material Cut-Off Treaty is in place. An initial report on defence fissile material production since the 1940s is promised, but not until spring 2000. *(The Strategic Defence Review*, Cm. 3999, The Stationery Office, July 1998, Supporting Essay Five, p. 5-10).

(24) Dr. Lawrence Scheinman 'Responses to Use of Chemical or Biological Weapons', paper prepared for

Conference on Human Security and Global Governance. Taplow Court, 26-28 September 1997.

(25) Otfried Nassauer, Oliver Meier, Nicola Butler, Stephen Young *U.S.Nuclear NATO Arsenals 1996-7*, BASIC, London, February 1997.

(26) The ideas in this section have been fully discussed in two recent Adelphi Papers. See; David.S.Yost, *The USA and Nuclear Deterrence in Europe*, Adelphi Paper 326, Oxford University Press, Oxford, 1999 and Bruno Tertrais, *Nuclear Policies in Europe*, Adelphi Paper 327, Oxford University Press, Oxford 1999. Although both these studies, for the most part, adhere faithfully to existing policy the latter is prepared to counternance some of the ideas discuss here.

(27) Cited in DFAX: *Disarmament Diplomacy*, December 1996, p.37.

(28) Statement on the Defence Estimates,H.M.Stationery Office, May1996, p17.

(29) Stansfield Turner, *Caging the Nuclear Genie*, Westview Press, Oxford, 1997 pp 65-73. He borrowed the term 'strategic escrow' from Alton Frye.

(30) When Britain was looking for a nuclear delivery system in the late 1950s. she specifically sought a system that would be invulnerable to pre-emption, so that British strategic nuclear forces would not need to be launched on a warning which could subsequently prove to be false. This requirement resulted in the procurement of *Polaris* in 1962. The Royal Navy has always claimed that none of the submarines on deterrent patrol was ever detected and located by the Soviet Union. Nevertheless throughout the Cold War, they were sustained at Quick Reaction Alert, measured in a few minutes notice to fire. (*The Strategic Defence Review*, Cm. 3999, The Stationery Office, July 1998, Supporting Essay Five, p. 5-2.).

(31) As was the case with *Polaris* missiles, Trident missiles when not deployed on patrol are stored away from their submarines, and the warheads are removed from the missiles. On coming back from the patrol *Trident* submarines dock first at the Royal Navy's facility at Coulport where the missiles are removed from their launch tubes, and stored in the special facilities constructed for the Polaris missiles. The warheads are then removed from the missiles and stored in another special-

ly constructed facility. Next, the Trident submarine moves on to the Royal Navy base at Faslane, where it undergoes maintenance or re-fit prior to its next patrol. Consequently, unlike Russian practice, British Trident missiles are not kept ready for re-firing, let alone on hair trigger alert, when they are not on patrol.

(32) *The Strategic Defence Review*, Cm. 3999, The Stationery Office, July 1998, Supporting Essay Five pp. 5-2, 5-5.

(33) Michael Quinlan, *Thinking about Nuclear Weapons*, RUSI Whitehall Paper Series 1997, pp. 68-72.

9. FUTURE POLICY ON NUCLEAR WEAPONS

> As I have already made clear to the noble
> Lords on a number of occasions, we intend to
> use our position to work for the global elimi-
> nation of nuclear weapons. To achieve that,
> we will press for multilateral negotiations
> towards mutual, balanced and verifiable
> reductions. Once satisfied with verified
> progress towards our goal, we will ensure that
> British nuclear weapons are included in the
> multilateral negotiations. (1)

This statement, made in the House of Lords by a minister on behalf of the Labour government in December
1997, seems perfectly clear as far as it goes. It could
come, one would have thought, only from a government
which had decided, in principle, that the world as a
whole, and Britain in particular, would be safer once
nuclear weapons had been banished. And there are
excellent reasons why a British government should so
decide. But first we will examine the counter-arguments.
Some five future roles for nuclear weapons have been
proposed by Sir Michael Quinlan, the most articulate
advocate for their retention. (2)

The first proposed function for nuclear weapons is to
deter the possessors of 'residual or emerging' nuclear
arsenals. Plainly, the British are not concerned to deter

the Americans or the French in this way, nor has it ever-been suggested that our nuclear weapons serve to keep the Chinese in line. It follows that the states intended to be deterred can only be Russia, India, Pakistan, Israel and, if their arsenals were to 'emerge', then likewise North Korea, Iraq, Iran or whomsoever. But Russia is now no longer regarded as a military threat to the Western nations and since the break-up of the Soviet Union, has become linked to them by a plethora of multilateral ties. These include the Council of Europe, the Euro-Atlantic Partnership Council and the Organisation for Security and Co-operation in Europe; not to mention the Founding Act signed with NATO in May 1997 and its accompanying Permanent Joint Council. Of course, Russia retains a formidable nuclear arsenal, and no one can say with any certainty that that she will not one day revert to hostile mode. The fuse of resentment lit by weakness and humiliation can burn slowly, as it did in the Germany of the 1920s and 1930s. But this creates all the more urgency to prosecute the multilateral build-down of nuclear weapons that the British government says it wants, rather than acting as an excuse for drag-ging the feet. And in the last resort, if a Russia were to turn sour and brandish nuclear weapons by way of threat or blackmail, it is not the single British Trident submarine always on station or, for that matter, any French equivalent, but the nuclear strength of the US that will keep her in check. The notion of a 'second cen-tre of decision' made sense against the threat of an over-whelming conventional attack in Europe, but this no longer exists so far as Russia is concerned. The dangers inherent in the India-Pakistan-China triangular nuclear relationship are obvious enough, as are those bedevilling relations between Israel and (say) Iran or Iraq. But no mechanism has ever been suggested whereby British nuclear missiles could usefully be brought into these equations. Indeed, a well-publicised ministerial utterance by the previous, Conservative, government gave good rea-sons why they could not. (3) It was argued that in the absence of an established deterrent relationship, such as that between East and West in the Cold War, it was unclear that an intended deterrent would work as intend-ed, and possible that it could have unpredicted and even counter - productive results. The notion of a war - fight-

ing role by way of 'surgical strike' was expressly repudi-
ated. If these arguments are accepted, and on the face of
it they are compelling, then the case for keeping Trident
to deter 'residual or emerging' nuclear arsenals loses all
force.

The second role proposed is to deter major conventional wars, thereby preventing war once more becoming a
normal method of settling disputes (the reductio ad
absurdum argument). Presumably the wars referred to
here would be those involving one or more states possessing nuclear weapons. (Wars between non-possessors
have been raging throughout the nuclear era e.g. between
Iran and Iraq in 1980-88). Even so, this proposition raises a number of questions. First, has deterrence worked in
this way in the past? It is often said that the mutual balance of terror prevented a major East-West war in Europe
between 1945 to 1991. But it is far from clear that the
Soviet Union, at the political level, had any real intention
of attacking western Europe in the first place. (4) In any
case, the most important reason why she did not do so
must have been the resolution with which America and
western European countries, acting together, defeated
the blockade of Berlin in 1948-9 and then coalesced as a
treaty-bound alliance in 1949. They set up an integrated military structure, mainly in what was then West
Germany, with large American forces and their families
permanently stationed on the front line. In other words.
it was forces in being and the political cohesion of NATO
that gave the Soviets pause.   The existence of nuclear
weapons did not deter, though it may have helped to
abort, the Anglo-French invasion of Suez in 1956. It did
not deter the invasion of the Falkland Islands by
Argentina in 1982, nor the annexation of Kuwait by Iraq
in 1990. And in a similar vein, nuclear weapons were of
no assistance when America was defeated in Vietnam in
1973, and the Russians in Afghanistan in 1989. In short,
this form of deterrence, however plausible, is ill-support-
ed by the record. Can it be expected to work better in
future? An obvious test-bed may be provided by Kashmir.
India and Pakistan fought over this territory twice
between 1947 and 1972. For the next 25 years they kept
peace of a kind, though India has retained a strong military presence in Kashmir and exchanges of shell-fire
along the border are as common as ranstorms. Since the

two countries 'came out' as nuclear weapons states byvirtue of their successful testing in May 1998, the military on both sides have said that this has made a full-scale war over Kashmir unthinkable. (5) But given the instability of the Indian government and the overwhelming influence of the military in Pakistan, one cannot be too confident. Are there safer means of ensuring that war will not once more become a normal way of settling disputes? Almost certainly there are. For example, it is widely believed that war between fellow-members of the European Union is now inconceivable. This falls as a special case within the wider thesis that war no longer happens between advanced democracies. If this is true, and it seems much more persuasive than the nuclear thesis, then what matters is the spread of democracy, the rule of law, free markets, human rights and civil society. None of this is easy to bring about though, given the chance, nations show a remarkable aptitude for getting the hang of it. Nuclear weapons do not help and, to the extent that they absorb scarce economic resources, they can actively hinder.

The third role is to prevent the risks associated with a possible 'break-out' from a nuclear free world. If the five existing officially recognised nuclear weapons powers ran their arsenals down to very low numbers or zero, then any state that cheated would put the whole system in great hazard, or so it is said. Nuclear weapons are needed as an insurance against this possibility. Another way of putting the point is to say that final reductions of nuclear arsenals towards zero could be countenanced only when the degree of trust and transparency between nations has been put on an altogether more confident footing, in a world very different to the one we know. The danger of break-out is real and obvious. As the former Prime Minister of India, I.K. Gujral has pointed out: 'Money is very difficult to make, a bomb is not'. (6) But there are several points to be made in response. First, the fact that difficulty is foreseen further down the line is no reason for not starting; all the more so because successive steps can be expected to bring about the very growth in confidence the later steps require. Secondly, this argument has little immediate application to the British. It is a problem to be addressed only when the arsenals of Russia and America have come down to much lower levels. Then, all the states party to a putative nuclear weapons convention will have to confront the problem of break-out collectively. There is no reason to suppose that, given the will and a patient approach, solutions will be impossible to find.

Fourthly, nuclear weapons are said to be of value in deterring the possession or use of other weapons of mass destruction, such as biological or chemical weapons (BCW). This argument is weak on a number of grounds. First Britain, like other nuclear weapons states, has categorically undertaken not to use nuclear weapons against any non-nuclear-weapon state party to the non-proliferation treaty. Possession or use of gas or germs does not annul this undertaking. It follows that nuclear deterrence of BCW by Britain could realistically apply only against Russia, China, India, Pakistan, Israel or any country attacking us in alliance or association with one of these. (7) So this justification is pretty thin. Moreover, as the difficulties over the inspection of Iraq and the confusion surrounding the attack by the US on a chemical factory in the Sudan in 1998 have shown, it can be hard to obtain evidence of manufacture or possession of BCW to a level of assurance that could remotely justify pre-emptive nuclear assault upon factories or stockpiles. In the past, even the use of CW has proved has difficult to establish with any certainty, and in the case of BW is likely to prove elusive in the extreme. The only rational way to outlaw possession and use of BCW lies in the combination of internationally accepted norms with the backing of a reasonably rigorous inspection regime and, above all, determined attempts to defuse the underlying regional tensions that make BCW an attractive option in the first place. Prudent states will reinforce these with sensible anti-BCW defensive precautions and the means to retaliate conventionally against any indisputable infringements. A policy of 'counter-proliferation' using nuclear weapons against BCW threats bears the hallmark of disproportion, not to say despair.

The final justification for nuclear weapons is to provide a low-key element of insurance in support of world order. Exactly what this means is far from clear. It has been suggested from time to time that a world in which one single authority (the UN or, more plausibly, the US) possessed a nuclear monopoly 'in trust' would be a safer one than a nuclear weapon-free-world. But Britain can hardly be a candidate for this exacting role. In any case, the reasoning is problematic. An examination of existing flash-points does not suggest any obvious instances where nuclear weapons would be likely to help in finding a solution. The great majority of conflicts are internal ones, where the use of nuclear weapons is almost literally inconceivable. As to war between nations, how could such use by an outsider help to bring wars between Eritrea and Ethiopia or between India and Pakistan to an end, any more than it served to moderate the long-drawn-out and bloody conflict between Iran and Iraq? If Greece and Turkey come to blows over the Aegean, Cyprus or the Balkans; if the Russians choose to annex Estonia; if China tries to coerce Taiwan by force; if Iraq and Israel bombard each other's cities, what good will nuclear weapons in the hands of a third party do? Who will the intervening power threaten to attack with nuclear weapons; how will they select their targets and how will they obtain sufficient agreement from the international community to proceed? In bad times, there may be some primitive comfort in the thought that if the worst comes to the worst 'our' side can always 'nuke' 'them'. But can we? Is not the very thought itself a false counsellor, serving only to dull the proper responses to real dangers? Is not the concept of a low salience nuclear world inherently unstable? And what part, in any case, could British nuclear weapons play in any such concept? The hows and whys accumulate endlessly.

Why Trident?

If the arguments just discussed are the best that can be said for retaining a nuclear deterrent system, why do the British doggedly hang on to it? In response to a question from a Labour MP, about the military threats that nuclear warheads on Trident submarines were designed to combat, Dr. John Reid, Under Secretary of State for the Armed Forces replied: 'Our nuclear deterrent forces ensure that the United Kingdom is safe from any threat of nuclear coercion and contribute to the Alliance's policy of war prevention'. (8) This is notably evasive, as answers to this question have always been in recent years. In a House of Lords debate, Baroness Symons, Parliamentary Under Secretary of State at the Foreign and Commonwealth Office, was much more reductionist: 'The United Kingdom's nuclear deterrent policy remains entirely defensive: we would only ever consider the use of nuclear weapons in extreme circumstances of self-defence, which includes the defence of our NATO allies'. (9) This answer is interesting on at least three counts. First it is so worded as to follow closely the ruling handed down by the International Court of Justice on 8 July 1996. (10) The Court found itself unable to conclude definitively whether the threat or use of nuclear weapons would be lawful or unlawful 'in an extreme circumstance of self-defence, in which the very survival of a state would be at stake'. Baroness Symons added that the use of nuclear weapons would always be subject to those requirements of international law applicable in armed conflict. In this respect, her answer was admirable. Secondly, coping with an 'extreme circumstance of self-defence' is very much more of a last-ditch matter than the previously quoted task of insulating the UK from any threat of nuclear coercion or contributing to a NATO policy of war prevention. It is a far cry from providing a 'low-key element of insurance in support of world order' and sits rather uneasily with the other four roles for nuclear weapons discussed in the previous section. Thirdly, in mentioning our NATO allies, this answer shows admirable loyalty to the principles of the North Atlantic Treaty. Members undertake to treat an attack upon any one of them in Europe as an attack upon all. But the British public deserves a rather fuller explanation of what the announced policy might involve.

We are asked to assume that a member country of NATO (take, for example Hungary) is being attacked. The assailant must be a nuclear weapon state (e.g. Russia) or acting in association with a nuclear weapon state, otherwise it is protected from nuclear attack by Britain under the Negative Security Assurance given to all non-nuclear states party to the NPT. Under the present NATO doctrine, we are required to imagine that our ally is subjected to a conventional assault so massive that it could not be fended off by conventional defence alone. It must also be a part of the picture (under the 'second centre of decision' scenario) that the US is not prepared to respond with nuclear weapons. If she were so prepared, then any British nuclear response would be an unimportant

adjunct. So we have to believe that in these dire circumstances, rather than see our ally overrun, the British
would go it alone and mount a nuclear attack in order to
force the aggressor to desist and come to the negotiating
table. The question then arises whether our nuclear
strike should be targeted on the attacking forces in
Hungary (for which the Hungarians might not thank us)
or perhaps on the nuclear backer of the assailant (i.e.
Russia). In either case, a likely result would be that
Britain, having broken the taboo on nuclear use, would
herself be subject to massive nuclear retaliation. Putting
Birmingham, Manchester and London at hazard in
defence of Budapest is a contingency that few Britons
would accept if it were spelled out to them. How realistic
is such a scenario anyway? A rationale of this kind may
have had some plausibility at the height of the Cold War.
Today, it is flimsy to the point of absurdity. The real reason for bringing NATO into the picture at this point is,
quite evidently, to keep Washington in play. This, in itself,
is a worthy aim. But the question must be faced whether,
on such minimal grounds, British Trident is worth keeping at all. Robert O'Neill has argued cogently that: 'Given
Britain's close links with NATO and the United States,
British nuclear weapons play virtually no role in increasing Britain's security at present'. (11) This position might
be acceptable if Trident could be kept on at virtually no
cost, but this, as we shall see, is not the case.

The down side

> The most likely initiators of nuclear threats
> will not be large, well staffed and well-advised
> governments who understand and worry
> deeply about the losses entailed in a nuclear
> conflict: rather they will be desperate, hate-
> driven, small to medium-sized powers or sub-
> national groups who see resort to nuclear
> force as their only option to break an inter-
> national system which disfavours them, or to
> take revenge on a more powerful force which
> is subverting their power bases. (12)

If the British stick to their current line that nuclear
weapons, at least ad interim, are desirable in themselves

and in some sense are the ultimate guarantee of national security, they run the risk of making matters worse both for themselves and for the world as a whole. The reason is that they could be encouraging others to develop nuclear weapons and to threaten their use. This can be clearly seen in the case of India. It would be unrealistic to claim that the Indians, presumably with nostalgic regard for the long-gone British Raj, pay special attention to the nuclear posture of Britain, and can be influenced, one way or the other, by what the British say or do. The fact is that Britain's arguments have influence only in proportion to her weight. But clearly, by stressing the ultimate importance of nuclear weapons to a small, wealthy and relatively secure country like Britain, we contribute to a way of thinking in which power, status and, in the last resort, survival are all seen as enhanced by membership of the nuclear club. The government of India, when newly elected and insecure, saw every advantage in playing the nationalist card. Having promised to induct the nuclear option, it should not have been in the least surprising that they chose to put in play their long-rehearsed plans for nuclear tests. Having now claimed on this basis to be a nuclear-weapons-capable state, they say, perhaps surprisingly, that they do not intend to build a large nuclear arsenal or create the elaborate command and control infrastructures other nuclear powers use to manage their systems. This sits oddly with reports that India is within months of beginning construction of nuclear-powered submarine capable of carrying nuclear warheads. (13) The Indians claim that they carried out the tests, at least in part, to prod the five established nuclear weapons states into disarming. (14) These statements are not particularly convincing. The paramount reason for testing was the thirst for status. In the words of a well-known Indian newspaper editor 'It was clear that China had run ahead of us and they were being incorporated as the world's No. 2 power and that we were being told to stay in a small box while the US gave Asia to China'. (15) In these ways, India exactly conforms to the model described above, of a power which sees overt possession of nuclear force 'as their only option to break an international system which disfavours them, or to take revenge on a more powerful force which is subverting their power bases'. Once India had tested, Pakistan felt compelled to follow suit and so the mischief spread. Few of those who argue in favour of nuclear weapons as a stabilising influence - in the right hands, of course - regard the situation in south Asia as being safer in consequence. And Robert O'Neill has pointed out the way in which a small and single-minded state can obtain disproportionate leverage by skirting the edges of proliferation. North Korea has been promised a new nuclear power generation system costing $4 billion, free fuel oil meanwhile, emergency food supplies and a huge uplift in its diplomatic status. (16) All this continues to call forth a vast political effort on behalf of the Clinton administration to keep the cash and the food supplies flowing.

It is an obvious fact, but always played down by the defenders of nuclear deterrence, that the very existence of these weapons creates a risk of detonation by mistake. Though this risk may be very small, and arguably grows smaller as the degree of technical sophistication invested in these weapons increases, nevertheless mishaps whose statistical chance is tiny are actually happening day by day, whether in aircraft fuel tanks, train wheels or 'near misses' in the air. No doubt some degree of human error would be involved, as occurred among the technicians in charge of the reactors at Chernobyl. Some incidents have recently been reported involving serious internal damage to live nuclear weapons. None of these have been officially denied, although the point is made, no doubt correctly, that these mishaps have never involved a release of nuclear material into the environment. (17) We may not always be so lucky. It is rational to conclude that the fewer nuclear weapons there are in the world, and in the fewer hands, the less likely such a mishaps become.

The risk of an inadvertent nuclear discharge is compounded many times over by the possibilities of political misjudgment. The disclosure on 22 October 1962 that the Soviets had stationed nuclear missiles and bombers on Cuba precipitated a crisis which is generally held to be the point at which the world came closest to a nuclear show-down. It is now known that the Soviets had stationed on Cuba not only missiles but warheads, including some for short-range weapons to be used tactically against an invasion. Had Khrushchev not backed down, an invasion by the US would have been all but certain. In Robert McNamara's words: 'We came so close - both

Kennedy and Khrushchev felt events were slipping outside their control'. (18) The story is also well known of the
rocket launched somewhere off Norway on 25 January
1995 which was spotted by radar stations in northern
Russia. Given the possibility that a single missile fired by
an American submarine in those waters could dispense
multiple warheads over Moscow within 15 minutes of
launch, President Yeltsin was instantly informed, and his
'nuclear briefcase' made ready for emergency use. After
about eight minutes, it became clear that the rocket was
headed far out to sea and the alert was stood down. The
rocket was indeed American, but had been launched for
purely scientific purposes to investigate the Aurora
Borealis. The Norwegians had warned the Russian
authorities some weeks earlier, but the notice had in
some way been mislaid. (19) On 7 March 1996, the
American cruiser Bunker Hill monitored three M-9 ballistic missiles fired by the Chinese nuclear rocket force
from the Hunan mountains towards Taiwan. They
splashed down in the shipping lanes close to Taiwan's
two main seaports. One of the missiles had passed over
Taipei before landing 19 miles off the coast. (20) The risks
inherent in this sort of behaviour need no underlining.
And it was disquieting to learn that the Soviet-era KGB
had been equipped with suitcase-sized nuclear devices
for use by special military intelligence units in border
regions. General Aleksandr Lebed, President Yeltsin's
national security adviser, told CBS television that some of
these were unaccounted for. Shortly afterwards, in 1997,
the environmental campaigner Aleksei Yablokov wrote to
Novaya Gazeta confirming what the general had said. (21)
All these examples serve to underline the dangers inherent in the very existence of nuclear weapons.

Quite apart from these intangible risks, there is a significant price-tag attached to a nuclear weapons programme. The British government says that over 90% of
the £12.5 billion estimated procurement cost of the
Trident programme has already been spent, and that the
average running cost of Trident submarines, missiles and
nuclear warheads over a 30-year service life has been
estimated at around £700 million a year, forming little
more than 3% of the defence budget. (22) This is a far
from negligible sum. In no other area of military expense
would the Treasury countenance provision for a capabil-

ity justified only under the rubric of general assurance against the unforeseen.

Steps already taken

It is to their credit that the British government has recently taken tangible steps towards nuclear disarmament. The free-fall nuclear bombs (WE-177) were withdrawn from British service in March 1998, leaving the country with Trident as its single nuclear deterrent system. Britain has joined some 130 states, including the four other official nuclear weapons states, in signing the Comprehensive Test Ban Treaty. It has ratified the treaty and promised to support the international monitoring system being set up under it and to work for its universal adoption. The government remains committed to a fissile material cut-off treaty and will 'work hard' to bring about the start of negotiations in the Conference on Disarmament. The UK has been supportive of the treaties creating nuclear weapons-free zones in Latin America, the Pacific, South Africa and South East Asia, having signed three of these and acceded to two of them. And Britain has reaffirmed its commitment never to use nuclear weapons against the non-nuclear-weapons states party to these zones (as to the Nuclear Non-Proliferation Treaty), unless they attack Britain in alliance or association with a nuclear weapon state. These are solid achievements. Equally welcome are the measures taken under the Strategic Defence Review to reduce the number of warheads and missiles to be deployed on Trident submarines, to reduce their alert status and to inform the public about these matters. (23) So far so good.

What next?

Sir Michael Quinlan has laid out a substantial prospectus for international action to reduce still further the number of nuclear weapons world-wide, to lower their salience, diminish what safety risks they pose and the likelihood of their further spread. These are admirable in intention, if not always wholly transparent in detail. He invites us to consider the following list:

1. Reducing further, under the existing START process

between the US and Russia, the number of delivery vehicles and warheads, and perhaps bringing warheads themselves under direct limitation and verification;

2. Relaxing, wherever they still remain, tense and costly, high-alert operational deployments.

3. Reducing the spread of weapons deployments.

4. Exchanging information more freely and openly about remaining nuclear armouries, in particular about best practice in the safety of storage, handling, management and perhaps design, if possible bringing China into a dialogue;

5. Entrenching still more durably, for political reassurance of non-nuclear nations, the norm against nuclear testing;

6. Further constraining the production of weapons materials;

7. Bringing under more assured account and control the nuclear matériel and expertise of the former Soviet Union;

8. Developing further, where possible on an international basis, the tools of information collection, analysis and verification, and of safe weapon and matériel disposal;

9. Strengthening the various instruments of constraint or incentive which work together to prevent or impede further proliferation;

10. Consolidating and perhaps extending nuclear weapons-free zones;

11. Developing and presenting more clearly non-confrontational doctrines;

12. Easing any political friction by emphasising that remaining armouries are not directed against particular adversaries.

This is an excellent list, providing a blueprint that will keep arms controllers busy well into the next millennium. Quinlan offers these steps in substitution for, and as a way of avoiding, the distractions of an out-and-out abolitionist agenda. (24) However, in our opinion, he shies away from the two measures which could best further the ends he has in view. The first of these would be to promote a Nuclear Weapons Convention. The parties to this convention would be the existing nuclear weapons powers in the first instance, but it would be the aim to draw in also India, Pakistan and Israel. The declared objectives of the Convention would no doubt include eventual abolition. But this would be no novelty, since wording to that effect is entrenched in the Non-Proliferation Treaty itself, and in the principles governing its indefinite extension, and have already been explicitly accepted by the British Government. It would be important not to set this objective in the context of 'general and complete disarmament'. To do so would be to render the whole exercise utopian. The substance of the convention should be exactly what the Labour government professes to intend; namely, 'mutual, balanced and verifiable reductions' laid out in phases, perhaps in the form of equally proportionate steps for all. It would be important not to press for a pre-set and rigid timetable for the whole process at the outset, since at best this would be unrealistic and at worst, counter-productive. But Britain, France and China would have to commit themselves to the process, presumably in the phase after START-III, and when that time came, a deadline could be set for the next phase. The inclusion of limits on warheads would be of the essence, as would a verification regime by extension of the START-II model. There appears to be no reason whatever why Britain should not take the lead. Indeed there might well be a direct political advantage in so doing. Baroness Symons has said that the government 'pays close attention' to the findings of an opinion poll in October 1997. in which 87% of those questioned supported negotiations to prohibit nuclear weapons. (25)

The ground would have to be prepared with great care. A right-wing knee-jerk reaction would have to be absorbed and argued down. A great deal of institutional inertia would have to be overcome - a task at which Prime Minister Tony Blair excels. The historical view that opposition to nuclear weapons is a certain vote loser will have to be handled with care, pointing out that this applies only to unilateral nuclear disarmament, which is not the present issue. By far the most powerful and insidious political reaction would derive from considerations not of security, but of status. The cases of India and Pakistan are particularly instructive on this point. Both countries went ahead with their tests in May 1998 knowing full well that they would incur not only universal condemnation from abroad, but serious economic penalties. They went ahead in pursuit of national prestige, the status of a nuclear weapons state, the honour that would glorify their scientific standing and the hope of being taken more seriously elsewhere in the world - above all by China, Russia and the USA. Kudos was the all-important consideration.

The results of an extraordinary survey on national pride have recently been published in the United States.(26) Based on a poll of 28,000 people in 23 nations, the National Opinion Research Centre at the University of Chicago has found that where pride in the general sense of regard for country was concerned, Britain scored very moderately, behind such nations as the USA, Austria, Ireland, Japan, Spain, Norway and Bulgaria. But the survey showed that the British rank their military above all else, including democracy, politics, science, history, sport and the arts. It is far from clear how much weight should be given to such findings. To the extent that the reported effect is real, the British military can take great credit. But it seems overwhelmingly likely that this is due to the campaigns the British military have actually fought, taking casualties in action every year since the Second World War except 1968, as well as their generally high standards of conduct and their ceremonial prowess. Nuclear capability can play little part in creating this glow of esteem for the military. The question was not raised. To be sure, the British have drawn some strength from the equation of nuclear weapon capability with permanent membership of the UN Security Council and therefore first-class nationhood. They will have to be weaned off this frame of mind. To repose a major element of national self-esteem in a weapons system is militaristic and totally out of key with reality. There is no reason why the British people should not accept these facts if the full weight of the government's formidable powers of persuasion were brought to bear. It would be essential to bring the French along pari-passu; one thing the British could barely endure would be to see France occupying the locus of 'only nuclear weapon state in Western Europe'.

This brings us to the other area in which the British could usefully take a lead. The case has been argued in Chapter 8 for a new posture in NATO. The first step would be the formal, albeit low-key, abandonment by NATO of its existing flexible response strategy. The first use of nuclear weapons by NATO, in response to a massive conventional attack that could not be contained by other means, is now quite obsolete. It should be replaced in NATO by a policy whereby the use of nuclear weapons by any member of the alliance would be countenanced only in retaliation for use of nuclear weapons against any member of the alliance. Russia could then be invited to revert to its own previous No First Use (NFU) strategy. Since this is already the declared position of China, the way would be open for a mutual pledge of NFU among the five nuclear powers, together with an undertaking to follow this up with a legally binding treaty. The logical corollary would be the final removal of all American nuclear warheads back to the US. This would open the way to negotiating a nuclear weapons-free zone for Europe, (27) perhaps in the setting of the Non-Proliferation Treaty (NPT) review machinery or under the aegis of the UN. The point to repeat is that this would not in any way prejudice the security of any NATO member nor compromise the core concept of deterrence for the nuclear powers. The resulting improved atmosphere vis-à-vis the Russians could pay dividends not only in the arms control arena (START), but also in making the expansion of NATO more palpably innocuous, giving more substance to the Partnership for Peace and the Founding Act between Russia and NATO. This would be good for the future stability of Europe. And progress along these lines would play well in such areas as the NPT review process, perhaps making progress possible towards a fissile material cut-off, ratification by India and Pakistan of the CTBT and the beginning of moves towards five-power negotiations for multilateral nuclear disarmament. A pioneering role for Britain in these moves would be highly appropriate.

Vested interests
There remains one serious vested interest to be confronted, and that is the British nuclear weapons Establishment. By far the largest part of this Establishment, numerically, is the firm called British Nuclear Fuels limited (BNFL). This is a government-owned company, employing around 15,000 people, with a turnover of about £1 bn. a year. Its main business is providing and reprocessing nuclear fuel for electricity gener-

ating plants but it has a division devoted to the defence sector, which accounts for about 10% of its turnover. BNFL owns eight Magnox reactors, running on natural uranium, with the capacity to produce over 200 kg. of weapons-grade plutonium a year without interrupting electricity supplies. The British inventory of weapons grade plutonium stands at about 3 tonnes. This would be enough for some 500 warheads, more than sufficient for the Trident programme. It is understood that no more is being produced at present. The same reactors also have the capacity to produce 10-100 gm. of tritium a year, enough to maintain a stockpile of about 1-2 kg. Tritium can also be bought on the open market from Canada and France. Under the terms of the 1958 agreement with the USA, Britain has traded plutonium for HEU and also purchased HEU. The UK has 21.9 tonnes of HEU available for military use, enough for the lifetime of Trident and for naval propulsion. Material from obsolete warheads will also be recycled. The then British Foreign Secretary, Douglas Hurd, agreed at the NPT Review and Extension conference in 1995 that the UK would not produce any more fissile material for weapons purposes, thus signalling that there is sufficient material in the stockpiles. The major part of BNFL's current military turnover is presumably accounted for by providing services for submarine reactors. There are also charges for dealing with plutonium from warheads being serviced or retired. The cost of producing tritium is only about £1m. a year. (28) It follows that BNFL's interest in the weapons programme is not of major consequence to the firm.

The same is certainly not true of the Atomic Warfare Establishment (AWE) at Aldermaston. This is owned by the Ministry of Defence and operated by a consortium called Hunting BRAE, with a budget of some £300 m. a year. Its mission is to provide, maintain and certify the UK's nuclear deterrent and to decommission redundant weapons, all in a safe and cost-effective manner. The establishment is at present completing the manufacture of Trident warheads, a task planned to finish by the year 2000. By then, the work force will have reduced to about 4000 people and Hunting BRAE's present management contract will run out. From then, on Aldermaston will be responsible for a stewardship programme, refurbishing warheads at the same rate as they have been manufac-

tured over recent years, and seeking a better understanding of the basic physics of the Trident warhead.
Stewardship involves a number of subsidiary tasks
including:

1. Developing a science-based understanding of the warhead ageing process,
2. Assuring the safety and reliability of the warhead,
3. Supporting the repair or re-manufacturing of warhead
components as necessary, perhaps using materials different from the original,
4. Decommissioning a few hundred redundant warheads
from WE-177 and *Chevaline* which entails removing the
high explosive, storing or recycling the fissile core of the
weapon and scrapping the rest,
5. Maintaining exchanges with the USA and developing
collaboration with France,
6. Developing computer models and upgrading laser facilities,
7. Maintaining a theoretical capability to develop a new
warhead.

Clearly, Aldermaston will be needed, in roughly its
present form, for as long as the UK has nuclear weapons,
and no doubt for many years thereafter to oversee the
decommissioning of redundant warheads. But it is open
to question whether the stewardship programme of itself
be enough of itself to sustain a national laboratory with
the necessary levels of skill and motivation. Apart from
the last and somewhat controversial task listed above,
the scientific work is on the humdrum side and the salary
levels are uncompetitive with those in the private sector.
This makes it difficult to recruit and retain first-rate people. And it will be difficult in any case to justify the level
of public funding needed. The answer seems to lie in
some form of diversification. (29) This would help in two
ways. It would bring new work, and with it much needed
revenue to Aldermaston. And by making the establishment more open, it could make it a more attractive place
in which to work. A working party under the aegis of
Pugwash has argued persuasively for extending AWRE's
mission to include technical research in the areas of
nuclear arms control, non-proliferation and disarmament (30) Work of this kind would match well with the

resources and expertise available at Aldermaston, and would support the establishment's raison d'être in the post-Cold War world. It forms a substantial part of the work of the nuclear weapons laboratories in the United States, and to a lesser degree in France.

For the last 40 years, Aldermaston has maintained a small group of about 15 staff engaged in seismological monitoring of nuclear test explosions round the world. This group works, on an unclassified basis, at Blacknest just outside the AWE perimeter. The Blacknest staff have become world experts in estimating the yield of underground nuclear explosions and of distinguishing explosions from earthquakes, a field known as forensic seismology. This work has provided crucial underpinning to the emerging test ban regime, most recently by demonstrating that the ambiguous seismic disturbance near Novaya Zemlya in August 1997 was an earthquake rather than, as some suspected, a Russian nuclear explosion in defiance of the Comprehensive Test Ban Treaty. A formal Anglo-American Test Monitoring Joint Working Group has been in existence since the 1960s. Scientists in the USA openly acknowledge their debt to Blacknest and the excellence and independence of its work. Paradoxically, its future is now in doubt. Responsibility for running a National Data Centre in support of the CTBT has been contracted to the British Geological Survey in Edinburgh, mainly as a cost-saving measure. This has undermined morale at Blacknest, where there is now a critical shortage of staff. For a minimal cash saving of £2-3m. a year Britain risks losing its position in forensic seismology and the chance to lead in the areas of nuclear arms control and non-proliferation. The Pugwash Group has proposed that teams be set up in the AWE, perhaps 100 strong all told and with a budget of £10-20m. a year, to work in the following areas, collaborating to the greatest feasible extent with the US:

1. Verifying the dismantlement of nuclear warheads without revealing classified design details,
2. Collaborating with countries of the former Soviet Union on protection, control and accounting for nuclear materials,
3. Developing technologies for detection of small-scale

nuclear activities and for international monitoring by organisations such as the International Atomic Energy Authority in support of their extended safeguards regime,
4. Accounting and verification work in support of a fissile materials cut-off convention,
5. Strategies for disposal of surplus fissile material,
6. International monitoring of nuclear weapons and fissile material stockpiles which could include production facilities, storage vaults, matériel in transit, container monitoring, dismantlement and all matters concerning openness, transparency and confidence building.

Activities of these kinds would be of value whatever the future shape of Britain's nuclear weapons programme. The British Government has made a useful start in announcing the formation of a small verification team at AWE looking forward, it is hoped, to Britain's participation in the START process early in the next century.

The fact must be faced, however, that this task will not of itself suffice to maintain nuclear weapons expertise, or attract scientists of the highest quality. For this reason, Aldermaston is certain to press the case for Britain remaining in the nuclear weapons game indefinitely. It will need a clear and public political decision to persuade the British nuclear weapons Establishment to throw its full force behind the implementation of a Nuclear Weapons Convention. And if that is true of Aldermaston, it applies a fortiori to the technical mandarinate in Whitehall. We are talking here of people, many of high ability, whose mind-set has been formed by the Cold War, and who believe with complete sincerity in the need for nuclear weapons to keep the peace. Some are scientists; most, if not all, are career civil servants. They operate behind the veil of atomic secrecy. The mystique surrounding this closed kingdom is daunting to outsiders of any rank, whether politicians, military men or uninitiated civil servants. These experts pursue their projects outside the normal committee structure of Whitehall. As was explained in Chapter 3, they answer to a tiny group of ministers for policy direction and to Parliament scarcely at all. They work in the close association with Aldermaston and the weapons laboratories in the USA. Discussing the arguments preventing a comprehensive nuclear test ban in the late 1970s, Lord Owen says of the

British and American nuclear weapons experts that: '(they) worked in cahoots, sensing that their job security and scientific satisfaction were threatened. They lobbied hard inside the military and political Establishment. They were even prepared to undermine the politically agreed negotiating stance of their governments. In the UK, the insubordination reached such a serious level that one official had to be disciplined.' (31) It would be foolish not to recognise that people of this ilk may still exist in ministries and   constitute probably the most powerful and most insidious brake on the development of policy in ways that seem inimical to their interests. Here, above all, it is necessary to ensure that the tail does not wag the dog.

References
(1) Baroness Symons of Vernham Dean, Parliamentary Under Secretary of State, Foreign and Commonwealth Office, speaking in the House of Lords Debate, 'Nuclear Weapons: Papal Policy', 17 December 1977, Hansard Column 685.
(2) Sir Michael Quinlan, 'The Future of Nuclear Weapons: Policy for Western Possessors", *International Affairs*, Vol 69, No.3, 1993, p. 486-488.
(3) Malcolm Rifkind, 'UK defence strategy: a continuing role for nuclear weapons?' Speech to the Centre for Defence Studies, London, 16 November 1993
(4) Raymond L. Garthoff, *Soviet Military Policy: A Historical Analysis*, Frederick A. Prager, New York, 1966, chapters 1,4,10 and 12.
(5) Colonel Mehta and General Pal quoted in John F. Burns, 'In Brinkmanship's Wake, All Quiet on Kashmir's Front' *International Herald Tribune*, 16 June 1998, p. 2
(6) Quoted in Thomas L. Friedman, 'India asks why America ignores it and courts China". *International Herald Tribune*, 22 June 1998
(7) We discount, for this purpose, France or the US as potential enemies. Iran, Iraq and North Korea are non-nuclear-weapon states party to the NPT.
(8) Dr. John Reid, Under Secretary of State for the Armed Forces, *Hansard*, London, 16 June 1997, col. 81.
(9) Baroness Symons of Vernham Dean. As in note 1. Col. 687.

(10). Legality of the Threat or Use of Nuclear Weapons, International Court of Justice, The Hague, 8 July 1996, #105F.

(11) Robert O'Neill, 'Britain and the Future of Nuclear Weapons'. *International Affairs*, 71, 4 (1995) p. 760

(12) O' Neill: 'Britain and the Future', p. 748.

(13) Keith Sullivan, 'With Russian aid, India moves closer to building a nuclear submarine', *International Herald Tribune*, 29 June 1998, p. 6.

(14) Prime Minister Atal Bihari Vajpayee quoted in Kenneth J. Cooper 'India eschews big nuclear arsenal', International Herald Tribune 18 June 1998, p. 4.

(15) Raj Mohan, strategic editor of The Hindu, quoted in Gerald Segal, 'Overrating China is a bad American habit', *International Herald Tribune*, 22 June 1998, p.8.

(16) O'Neill: 'Britain and the Future', p. 750

(17) Britain reportedly hid nuclear mishaps. Reuters Report in International Herald Tribune, 20 June 1999

(18) Robert McNamara from a CNN "Worldview" interview on 16 June 1998, quoted in *International Herald Tribune* 19 June 1998.

(19) Bruce G. Blair, Harold A. Fieveson, and Frank N. von Hippel, 'Taking nuclear weapons off hair trigger alert', *Scientific American*, November 1997, p. 75.

(20) Barton Gellman, 'Face-off over Taiwan led to a U.S.-China Strategic Partnership', *International Herald Tribune* 22 June 1998, p. 2.

(21) *International Herald Tribune* 15 September 1997, p. 5, *The Times*, 23 September 1997, p. 13.

(22) *The Strategic Defence Review*, Cm. 3999, H.M. Stationery Office, London, July 1998, p. 20.

(23) *The Strategic Defence Review*, Supporting Essay Five, p. 5-11.

(24) Sir Michael Quinlan, 'Thinking about Nuclear Weapons' *RUSI Journal*, December 1997, p.2.

(25) Baroness Symons. As in Note 1, column 684

(26) Tom Rhodes, 'British value military above all else', The Times, 26 June 1998,p. 19.

(27) It is of course extremely unhelpful that the US Administration, in exchange for Senator Helm's support for NATO expansion on 27 April 1998, accepted a number of conditions laid down by the Senator. One of these 'explicitly rejects Russian efforts to establish a 'nuclear weapons-free zone' in central Europe'. See Tassos Kokki-

nides and Alistair Miller, *Senator Helms drags NATO back towards its Cold War mission*, BASIC Papers No. 27, May 1998, p. 6.

(28) Christopher R.Hill, R. Sebastian Pease, Rudolph E. Peierls, Joseph Rotblat, *Does Britain Need Nuclear Weapons*, British Pugwash Group, 1995.

(29) *Progress of the Trident Programme*, Second Report of the Defence Committee, 1993-4, p. xxiv.

(30) Tom Milne and Henrietta Wilson, *Verifying Nuclear Disarmament: A Role for AWE Aldermaston*, A Report from the British Pugwash Group, 63A Great Russell Street, Lodon WC1B 3BJ UK, 1999.

(31) In a speech given in the University of California at Berkeley, published in ADIU Report, Vol.7, No.2, (Mar-Apr 1985) See Scilla McLean (ed), *How Nuclear Weapons Decisions are Made*, Macmillan 1986, p. 118.

Envoi

In this book we have tried to examine the issue of British nuclear weapons from a wide variety of points of view. We have told the history of deterrence, both strategically and on the battlefield, as straightforwardly as we could. But neither of us is a historian by training and no doubt we have committed errors of fact and judgement. For these we take full responsibility and apologise. In much of what followed we have discussed technical matters and issue s of policy with the aim of giving fair weight to all reasonable points of view. This will annoy some people. We shall be accused by some of treasonously giving undue credence to people opposed to the West in general or to the nuclear project in particular. We may be derided for dallying too much with psycho-social jargon. Perhaps we can be accused of taking too favourable a view of the prospects for the human race in terms of reason, prosperity and peace. Certainly our predisposition is optimistic rather than gloomy. And there is no doubt that in places our own preferences show through. For this we make no apologies. We believe that fewer nuclear weapons are better than many and that none would be best of all.

The British government, in one of its voices, says much the same thing. 'The Government wishes to see a safer world in which there is no place for nuclear weapons'. (The Strategic Defence Review, paragraph 60). But its other voice echoes the prayer of Saint Augustine 'Lord make me virtuous, but not yet'. Thus the next sentence to that just quoted, says 'Nevertheless, while large nuclear arsenals and risk of proliferation remain, our minimum deterrent remains a necessary element of our security'. So while they have made important changes in nuclear weapons policy the fundamentals remain unchanged.

Of course it would be foolish to suggest that one could simply remove nuclear weapons and leave the old psychology and inadequate structures standing. Something else must be put in place to fulfil peoples' need for security. The important thing is that British policy makers should become fully aware of the possibilities that the end of the Cold War has brought, should take the opportunities offered to start engaging in serious discussion on these matters and should begin to prepare public opinion accordingly. There are two areas where British policy could begin to make a more forceful contribution. The first is arms control where Britain could dare to take a much more positive attitude. This could be translated into a change in style without necessarily much immediate change in substance, because the size of the presently planned British nuclear arsenal is not unduly lavish in any case. The second and related issue is that the end of the Cold War has provided an opportunity for Britain's defence establishment to take seriously the question of global nuclear disarmament as a long-term goal.

'...I do not think there has ever been a case for British nuclear weapons, and I do not think there is a case for one now. We created one in order to assert comparable status with the United States... they are purely instruments of prestige with virtually no military utility.'

(Quotation from interview with Sir Michael Howard, 6 March 1997).

ACRONYMS

A-Bomb - Atomic Bomb

ABM - Anti-Ballistic Missile

ACDA -Arms Control and Disarmament Agency in the US

ADM - Atomic Demolition Munition

AEA - Atomic Energy Agency

AEC - Atomic Energy Commission

ANF - Atlantic Nuclear Force

APC - Armoured Personnel Carrier

AWE - Atomic Weapons Establishment

AWRE - Atomic Weapons Research Establishment

BAOR - British Army of the Rhine

BNFL - British Nuclear Fuels Limited

BPC - British Peace Committee

C 100 - The Committee of 100

CAC - Council for Arms Control

CANWT - Committee for the Abolition of Nuclear Weapon tests

CBW - Chemical and Biological Weapons

CD - Conference on Disarmament (in Geneva)

CDNWT - Conference on the Discontinuance of Nuclear Weapon
Tests.

CDP - Chief of Defence Procurement (for the UK)

CFE - Conventional Forces Europe (arms control treaty)

CFSP -Common Foreign and Security Policy (within the European
Union)

CIA - Central Intelligence Agency (in the US)

CIS - Commonwealth of Independent States (most countries of the former Soviet Union)

CND - Campaign for Nuclear Disarmament (in the UK)

COE - Conference of Experts

COS - Chiefs of Staff

CTBT - Comprehensive Test Ban Treaty (for nuclear weapons)

D5 -   A version of the Trident Missile

EEC -   European Economic Community

END - European Campaign for Nuclear Disarmament

ENDC - Eighteen-Nation Disarmament Conference

ENDS - Enhanced Nuclear Detonation Safety

ESDI - European Security and Defence Identity

EU - European Union

FOE - Friends of the Earth

FCO - Foreign and Commonwealth Office (UK)

FR - Flexible Response

FRP - Fire Resistant Pits

FSU - Former Soviet Union

GCHQ - Government Communication Headquarters (British interception service)

GLCM - Ground Launched Cruise Missile

GSP - Global Strategy Paper

H-Bomb - Hydrogen Bomb

HEU - Highly Enriched Uranium

HQ - Headquarters

IAEA - International Atomic Energy Agency

ICBM - Intercontinental Ballistic Missile

ICJ - International Court of Justice

IHE - Insensitive High Explosive

IISS - International Institute for Strategic Studies (in London)

IMS - International Monitoring System

INF - Intermediate-range Nuclear Force

IRBM - Intermediate Range Ballistic Missiles

KGB - Komitet gosudarstvennoi besopasnosti = "Committee of State Security' the State Security police (1954-91) of the former Soviet Union.

Kt. - Kilotonne (=1000 tonnes)

LEU - Low Enriched Uranium

MAD - Mutually Assured Destruction

MIRV - Multiple Independently-targetable Re-Entry Vehicle

MOD - Ministry of Defence

MOX Mixed Oxide Fuel (uranium and plutonium oxides mixed)

MR - Massive Retaliation

MRC - Medical Research Council (in the UK)

Mt. - Megatonne (= 1,000,000 tonnes)

MTCR - Missile Technology Control Regime

NATO - North Atlantic Treaty Organisation

NBC - Nuclear Biological and Chemical (sc. Weapons)

NCANWT - National Committee Against Nuclear Weapon Tests

NDRC - National Defence Research Council

NFU - No First Use

NGO - Non-Governmental Organisation

NPC - National Peace Council

NPG - Nuclear Planning Group (in NATO).

NPT - Non-proliferation Treaty

NRPB - National Radiological Protection Board

NWFW - Nuclear Weapon Free World

NWFZ - Nuclear Weapon Free Zone

NWS - Nuclear Weapon States (as defined in the NPT)

NNWS - Non Nuclear Weapon States

OPCS - Office of Population Censuses and Surveys (in the UK)

ORG - Oxford Research Group

OSCE - Organisation for Security and Co-operation in Europe

OSI - On-Site Inspections

PPNN - Programme for Promoting Nuclear Non-proliferation

PTBT - Partial Test Ban Treaty

PUS - Permanent Under Secretary (sc. of State)

RAF - Royal Air Force

RN - Royal Navy

RUSI - Royal United Services Institute

SAC - Strategic Air Command (in US)

SAS - Special Air Service (in the UK)

SALT - Strategic Arms Limitation Treaty

SCUD - A short range surface to surface missile of Soviet origin.

SDI - Strategic Defence Initiative (in the US)

SDP - Social Democratic Party (in Germany)

SIOP - Single Integrated Operations Plan (US)

SLBM - Submarine Launched Ballistic Missile

START - Strategic Arms Reduction Treaty

TASM - Tactical Air to Surface Missile

TGWU - Transport and General Workers Union (in the UK)

TTBT - Threshold Test Ban Treaty (also known as the Partial Test Ban Treaty)

UN - United Nations

UNA - United Nations Association

UNDC - United Nations Disarmament Commission

UNESCO - United Nations Educational, Scientific and Cultural Organisation

UNGA - United Nations General Assembly

UNSC - United Nations Security Council

UNSCEAR - United Nations Standing Committee on Atomic Radiations

US - United States

USSR - Union of Soviet Socialist Republics

UK - United Kingdom

WDC - World Disarmament Campaign

WE-177 A free fall Nuclear Bomb (British)

WTO - Warsaw Treaty Organisation

WEU - Western European Union

WHO - World Health Organisation

WMD - Weapons of Mass Destruction (i.e. nuclear , biological and chemical)

Acknowledgments

The authors warmly acknowledge the help and support they have received from many sources during the writing of this book. In particular they would like to thank the following who have given time, either to be interviewed or to comment on the text, or in other ways:

Lorna Arnold has collaborated on two major volumes about Britain's A-bomb programme and has also written many articles on the subject.

Sir Michael Atiyah was President of the Royal Society 1990-1995 and Master of Churchill College Cambridge 1990-1997.

Rt. Revd. John Austin Baker was bishop of Salisbury 1982-1993. He chaired a working party on Defence Theology in 1980-1982.

Professor Frank Barnaby was a physicist at the Atomic Weapons Research Establishment 1951-1957 and Director of the Stockholm International Peace Research Institute 1971-1981.

Lynn Barnett is a social scientist and child psychotherapist.

Professor Ian Bellany has been the professor of Politics at the University of Lancaster since 1979.

Rt. Hon. Tony Benn was Postmaster General 1964-1966, Minister of Technology 1966-1970, Secretary of State for Industry 1974-1975 and for Energy 1975-1979.

Professor Hugh Berrington was head of the Department of Politics at the University of Newcastle 1965-1994.

Frank Blackaby - is a former Director of the Stockholm International Peace Research Institute .

Alan Brooke Turner was a member of the UK Delegation to the Nuclear Tests Conference, Geneva 1962.

Professor Christoph Bluth is Professor of European and International Studies at the University of Reading.

Dr. Ben Cole is a former member of the Arms Control and Disarmament Research Unit at the Foreign and Commonwealth Office.

Lord Callaghan of Cardiff was Chancellor of the Exchequer 1964-1967, Home Secretary 1967-1970, Foreign Secretary 1974-1976, and Prime Minister 1976-1979.

Menzies Campbell has been Chief Spokesman for the Liberal Democrat on Foreign Affairs, Defence and Europe since 1997.

Dr. Terence Carr was a radiobiologist at the Medical Research Council at Harwell 1953-1986.

Lord Carrington held office as First Lord of the Admiralty 1959-1963, Defence Secretary 1970-1974 and Foreign Secretary 1979-1982. He was Secretary-General of NATO 1984-1988.

Field Marshal Lord Carver was Chief of Defence Staff 1973-1976.

Frank Cook is a Labour MP and a member of the Defence Select Committee.

Rt. Hon. Sir Frank Cooper was permanent secretary at the Northern Ireland Office 1973-1976 and at the Ministry of Defence 1976-1982.

Professor Norman Dixon was professor of psychology at University College London.

Ian Doucet is a writer, editor and psychotherapist.

John Edmonds was head of Arms Control and Disarmament at the Foreign Office 1974-1977 and British Ambassador to the Comprehensive Test Ban Treaty negotiations 1978-1981.

Dr. Scilla Elworthy is Director of the Oxford Research Group, which she founded in 1982.

Dennis Fakeley served in the Royal Naval Scientific Service 1944-1963 and Ministry of Defence 1963-1984.

David Fisher is deputy head, Defence and Overseas Secretariat at the Cabinet Office.

David Fischer was assistant director general for external relations at the International Atomic Energy Agency 1975-1981.

Brigadier General Eckart Fischer was the defence and military attaché at the German Embassy in London 1996-1998.

Rt. Hon. Michael Foot was Secretary of State for Employment 1974-1976, leader of the House of Commons 1976-1979, leader of the Labour Party in opposition 1980-1983.

Dr. Colin Fraser is fellow in Social Psychology and senior tutor of Churchill College, Cambridge.

Professor Lawrence Freedman has been Professor of War Studies at King's College London since 1982.

Pat Gaffney is the General Secretary of the British section of Pax Christi.

Bruce George MP is chairman of the House of Commons select committee on defence.

Lord Gilbert of Dudley, was financial secretary to the Treasury 1974-1974, Minister of Transport 1975-1976, Minister of State, Ministry of Defence 1976-1979, and since 1997 - 1999.

Dr. Eric Grove is at the Centre for Security Studies, Department of Politics, University of Hull.

Lord Hailsham of Saint Marylebone was First Lord of the Admiralty 1956-1957, Minister of Education 1957, Minister for Science and Technology 1959-1964, and Lord Chancellor 1970-1974 and 1979-1987.

Rt. Rev. Richard Harries has been Bishop of Oxford, since 1987.

Michael Herman was Secretary of the Joint Intelligence Committee 1972-1975.

Rear Admiral John Hill was flag officer, Admiralty interview board 1981-1983.

Professor Robert Hinde was master of St. John's College Cambridge 1989-1994.

Sir Arthur Hockaday was second permanent under secretary at the Ministry of Defence 1976-1982.

Sir Michael Howard was Regius professor of Modern History Oxford 1980-1989.

Dr. Daryl Howlett is a senior research fellow and lecturer at the University of Southampton.

Rt. Hon. Sir Geoffrey Johnson Smith was parliamentary under secretary of state for the Army 1971-1972, and chairman of the military committee of the North Atlantic Assembly 1985-1989.

Peter Jones was director of the Atomic Weapons Research Establishment 1982-1987.

Lady Kennet (Elizabeth Young) has written extensively on arms control and disarmament topics for the British and the American press.

Lord Kennet (Wayland Young) was SDP spokesman in the House of Lords on Foreign Affairs and Defence 1981-1990.

Bruce Kent was general secretary of the Campaign for Nuclear Disarmament 1980-1985, vice chairman 1985-1987, chairman 1987-1990.

David Knight has been the Chair of the Campaign for Nuclear Disarmament since 1996.

Lady Olga Maitland has been president of the Defence and Security Forum since 1992.

Professor Michael McGwire was a senior fellow at the Brookings Institute, Washington 1979-1990 and a visiting professor in global security studies at Cambridge 1990-1993

278 ACKNOWLEDGMENTS

Tom Milne is the Research Assistant at the British Pugwash Group.

Norman Moss is a journalist and writer.

Martin O'Neill was an Opposition spokesman on defence 1984-1992, and is currently chairman of the select committee on trade and industry.

Professor Robert O'Neill was director of the International Institute for Strategic Studies 1982-1987, and has since then been Chichele Professor of the History of War at Oxford.

Canon Paul Oestreicher was chairman of the British section of Amnesty International 1974-1979 and vice Chair of the Campaign for Nuclear Disarmament 1981-1982.

Lord Owen of Plymouth (David Owen) was Secretary of State for Foreign Affairs 1977-1979, a co-founder of the Social Democrat Party in 1981 and its leader 1983-1987.

Dr. Sebastian Pease was director of the UK Atomic Energy Agency Culham laboratory 1968-1981.

Mr William Peden is a former campaigner for Greenpeace.

Clive Ponting was a senior civil servant in the Ministry of Defence.

Lord Pym of Sandy (Francis Pym) was Secretary of State for Defence 1979-1981, leader of the House of Commons 1981-1982 and Secretary of State for Foreign Affairs 1982-1983.

Sir Michael Quinlan was permanent under secretary at the Department of Employment 1983-1988 and at the Ministry of Defence 1988-1992.

Dr. John Reid was a Minister of State at the Ministry of Defence since 1997 - 1999.

Christopher Rootes is Director of the Centre for the Study of Social and Political Movements.

Professor Sir Joseph Rotblat was secretary general of Pugwash 1957-1973 and has been its president since 1988. Winner of the Nobel Peace Prize 1995.

Lord Shore of Stepney (Peter Shore) was secretary of state for Economic Affairs 1967-1969, for Trade 1974-1976, for the Environment 1976-1979.

Professor John Simpson is Director of the Mountbatten Centre for International Studies and co-director of the programme for promoting nuclear non-proliferation (PPNN) at Southampton University.

Dr Anthony Sivers was the research officer at the Council for Arms Control 1985-1989.

Robert Worcester has been chairman of Market and Opinion Research International (MORI) since 1973.

Brian Wicker is a vice president of Pax Christi and Chairman of the Council on Christian Approaches to Defence and Disarmament.

Dr Roger Williamson is policy and campaigns director of Christian Aid.

C W Wright was a deputy under secretary in the Ministry of Defence 1968-1971.

TECHNICAL ASSISTANCE

Thanks to Mr Ernest Bow for preparing the typescript for reproduction. He currently works as a freelance script-writer.